ROYAL WARRIORS

FOR KATHERINE

ROYAL WARRIORS

A MILITARY HISTORY OF THE BRITISH MONARCHY

CHARLES CARLTON

Harlow, England • London • New York • Boston • San Francisco • Toronto
Sydney • Singapore • Hong Kong • Tokyo • Seoul • Taipei • New Delhi
Cape Town • Madrid • Mexico City • Amsterdam • Munich • Paris • Milan

PEARSON EDUCATION LIMITED

Head Office:
Edinburgh Gate
Harlow CM20 2JE
Tel: +44 (0)1279 623623
Fax: +44 (0)1279 431059
Website: www.pearsoned.co.uk

First published in Great Britain in 2003

ISBN 0 582 47265 2

British Library Cataloguing in Publication Data
A CIP catalogue record for this book can be obtained from the British Library

Library of Congress Cataloging in Publication Data
A CIP catalog record for this book can be obtained from the Library of Congress

10 9 8 7 6 5 4 3 2 1

Typeset in 10.5/13pt Galliard by Graphicraft Limited, Hong Kong
Printed and bound in China
GCC/01

The Publishers' policy is to use paper manufactured from sustainable forests.

CONTENTS

Acknowledgements		vi
chapter one	THE TRADE OF KINGS	1
chapter two	A FATAL DAY TO ENGLAND	18
chapter three	WITH GRACE AND MIGHT OF CHIVALRY	46
chapter four	NO OTHER AIM OR THOUGHT THAN WAR	72
chapter five	TO THREATEN BOLD PRESUMPTUOUS KINGS WITH WAR	106
chapter six	AND HE MARCHED THEM DOWN AGAIN	125
chapter seven	LOOKING THEM IN THE FACE	150
Index		177

ACKNOWLEDGEMENTS

I am grateful to the History Department of the Australian Defence Forces Academy, Canberra, for awarding me a visiting fellowship that enabled me to write the last third of this book, and for many stimulating discussions about monarchy and war. John Reeve helped me think about navies, while Peter Dennis provided insights on George V's role in the First World War. John Coates, Robin Prior and Jeff Grey taught me much about Australia's armed forces and its equally superb red wines. I was able to try out some of my ideas on monarchy and war at seminars at the Defence Forces Academy, the Australian National University and at Flinders University, Adelaide, where I received many useful and, at times, passionate comments. I am grateful to Dick Kohn of the University of North Carolina at Chapel Hill, who, without realising it, first gave me the idea for this book. I am sure that his forthcoming monograph on the military role of US presidents will be an invaluable comparative study. Since the conception of this book Heather McCallum has been all that a good editor should be: encouraging in her praise, constructive in her criticisms. Editors such as she make not only writing, but revising, a pleasure. To my old friend and comrade – if not in arms, at least in the Intelligence Corps – Tony Clayton, I owe an immense debt. He has not only been a constant source of inspiration and stimulating ideas, but has read the manuscript with his usual diligence. As a visiting professor at Duke University I have been able to test my thoughts on war with my students, as I have with the members of the Triangle Institute for Security Studies. Friends at Wolfson College, Cambridge, provided a congenial environment for research, while the staffs of the Cambridge University Library and the D. H. Hill Library, North Carolina State University, have been unfailingly helpful. I would like to thank Peter Boyden of the Army Historical Museum for answering questions, John Morrill from Cambridge for wisdom and encouragement so freely given, and Joe Hobbs, friend and colleague for over three decades, for numerous discussions about military history. Joe Caddell and William Leuchtenburg answered questions on naval history and the US presidency. Finally to my wife Caroline, my greatest debt is due.

Raleigh, NC
1 April 2003

chapter 1

THE TRADE OF KINGS

'War is the Trade of Kings'. John Dryden, King Arthur, II (1691)

Every year on the second Saturday in June the sovereign takes the salute as her Guards troop her colour on the Horse Guards Parade at Whitehall. The custom of showing the standard before all of the regiment goes back to the seventeenth century, if not before, when the colours were a rallying point in battle [Plate 1.1]. Soldiers not only had to be able to recognise them in the smoke and chaos of combat, but on campaign had to gather around the colours every morning in case of sudden attack or, more often, to assemble on parade in their ranks to march off as a unit. While the first record of trooping the colour can be found in the order books of the Coldstream and Grenadier Guards for 1749, the modern practice dates from 1805 when the ceremonial was carried out to celebrate George III's birthday. During Queen Victoria's reign it was held on 24 May, her actual birthday, while today it is held in June to mark Queen Elizabeth's official birthday.[1]

For the tens of thousands who watch the trooping in person, and for the millions more who see it on television, the rousing music, the precise marching, colourful ceremonial, and martial discipline of this ritual are part of the pomp and circumstance which the British rightly claim to do so well. It is a reassuring link with a safe past, a constant custom in a changing world with an uncertain future. Yet the excellence with which the Queen and her soldiers perform this ritual hides three important points about the relationship between the monarch, her people and war.

'Whether we like it or not,' the journalist Gwynne Dyer observed, 'War is a central institution in human civilization.'[2] The cliché that wars settle nothing is absurd. Men fight because they believe doing so will solve their problems. The Second World War, for instance, solved the problem of Hitler and Japanese militarism, although it did produce the

Plate 1.1   Trooping the colours © Tim Graham/Corbis

new problems of the cold war and nuclear annihilation. Societies spend huge resources in men, material and money on wars, not only because they perceive there to be advantages in winning, but because the costs of losing may be horrendous. The vanquished may be killed, their property destroyed, their children abused, their women raped and consigned to concubinage. The Russian treatment of Germans in 1945 showed that the fate of the defeated has changed little over the centuries.

Gwynne Dyer also noted that war 'has had a history practically as long as civilization'.[3] Thus it is not surprising that the origins of kingship, the first form of hierarchical leadership, lie in war. Ancient societies chose as their chief the man best able to lead the tribe into battle.[4] The earliest Anglo-Saxon kings had to be good at waging war because they spent much of their time fighting: nearly as many of them died in combat as did in their beds.[5] Thus until she was sixty, the Queen would ride on a fine horse, the symbol of knightly courage, to lead her guards out onto Horse Guards Parade. 'The characteristic of the English monarchy,' observed William Bagehot, the Victorian historian who did more than anyone else to define the modern constitutional monarchy, 'is that it retains the feeling by which the heroic kings governed in their rude age.'[6]

To make their age less rude later Anglo-Saxon monarchs added a patina of Christianity, which, as John Cannon has observed, 'transformed the very nature of kingship' by giving it a sacradotal quality.[7] Thus the Queen not only stands at the head of her armed forces as the colours are trooped past, but in doing so reconsecrates the flags as sacred icons. The regimental colours are more than a convenient rallying point: they are symbols treated with more reverence than the union jack. The monarch – or members of her family – present each exquisitely embroidered colour, after priests of the church of which she is head have blessed it, making it sacred like the bread and wine of Holy Communion. This totem represents the spirit of the regiment – past, present and even future. The carefully stitched colour, bearing the names of battle honours the regiment has won over the centuries, links those who have died in the sovereign's service to those who currently serve Her Majesty.

Second, soldiers serve the sovereign, not the democratically elected government of the day. Like airmen and marines (although not sailors), on enlisting they must take an oath of allegiance to the Queen and to her heirs and successors. While the government may pay them, and pass the legislation that compels their obedience, the sovereign is the focus of their loyalty. When at the end of the ceremony, riding in her coach, Elizabeth II leads her soldiers back into barracks, she is making the point that as titular commander-in-chief of the armed forces her job is to make sure politicians (as did Oliver Cromwell) never again use them

Plate 1.2   Prince Harry in a light tank © PA Photos

to take over the legally elected government. The Royal Navy does not take a personal oath of allegiance to the monarch, not because – as they would have us believe – sailors are especially loyal to the crown. Mutiny has been as common on water as on land. Being confined to the sea or coastal depots, sailors cannot readily take over landlocked seats of government.

That the Royal Navy is an exception is in many ways ironic because the personal links between the senior service and the monarchy are extremely close. As members of the Royal Family stand in their various military uniforms to salute the colour as it is trooped past, they make a third point about the relationship between the monarchy and war. The Windsors are a military family. The Queen's husband, her two eldest sons, father, grandfather and great-grandfather were active naval officers. She served as an army officer in the Second World War. The first official duty of her eight-year-old grandson, Prince Harry, was to ride in a Scimitar tank, proudly watched by his mother and hordes of journalists and cameramen[8] [Plate 1.2].

It is, of course, easy to confuse the public relations aspect of soldiering with the reality. War is about courage, duty and honour, all values which the royal family would like to symbolise, even though they have (except for Prince Andrew in the Falklands), of late failed spectacularly to do so. For centuries the sovereign was expected to be a heroic leader.

'The English will never love or honour their sovereign unless he be successful and a lover of arms,' observed Jean Froissart, the French historian, nearly seven hundred years ago.[9] In 1745, two years after the king stopped leading his troops personally into battle, the national anthem asked God to 'send him victorious, happy and glorious'. The sovereign is still the fount of honour: she recognises bravery, the highest martial virtue, with the award of the crosses named after Queen Victoria and King George VI. She, or a member of her family, personally confer them, as they do other medals for courage.

Yet during such investitures, usually held in the gilded throne room of Buckingham Palace, as a band plays selections from Gilbert and Sullivan, the reality of war seems as far away as it does on a fine June day, after the colour has been trooped and the crowds head for home. Some will follow the sound of marching bands up the Mall to Buckingham Palace, to glimpse once more the symbols of power. Others may stroll down Whitehall past 10 Downing Street, where executive power resides, and then on to Houses of Parliament, the locus of constitutional sovereignty. If they look across the road, they can see on the Embankment along the Thames the statue of Boadicea, the first of Britain's great royal warriors [Plate 1.3].

Cassius Dio, the third-century Roman historian, described Boadicea as 'a woman of the royal family, possessed of greater intelligence than often belongs to women.'[10] She was married to Prasutagus, the king of the Iceni, a tribe that occupied modern Norfolk and Suffolk. When he died in 60 AD, he left half his property to his two children, and the other half to the emperor Nero in order to appease the Romans who had just conquered Britain. Catus Decianus, the Roman procurator, however, decided to seize the lot, sending a gang of thugs to Boadicea's palace near Norwich. When she protested they flogged her, and gang-raped her fourteen- and sixteen-year-old daughters.

The atrocity drove the Iceni and the neighbouring Trinovantes into revolt. A huge army assembled near Caistor St Edmund, Norfolk, where Boadicea addressed them. According to Dio:[11]

> She was huge of frame, terrifying of aspect, and with a harsh voice. A mass of bright red hair fell to her knees, she had a great twisted golden necklace, and a tunic of many colours, over which was a thick mantle fastened by a broach. Now she grasped a spear to strike fear into all who watched her.

She reminded her audience how the Romans (whom they greatly out-numbered) had reduced the British to slavery, thus shaming them before their ancestors. Then she released a hare that she had secreted in the

Plate 1.3 Boadicea and her daughters © Boadicea by Thomas Thorneycroft (1815–85), Victoria Embankment, London, UK/Bridgeman Art Library

folds of her dress, to run free in full view of the Celtic warriors. The omen convinced the host to march on Colchester.

Colchester, or to use its Latin name Camulodunum, was a colonia, a settlement of Roman army veterans. Not content with the land they had been given for their military service, they had stolen all they could from the native Britons, whom, the Roman historian Tacitus observed, they treated no better than 'prisoners and slaves'. In doing so they had neglected to complete the city's defences, leaving it wide open for Boadicea's forces. In a desperate attempt to save the city Petilius Cerialis set out from near Peterborough with three thousand men from the Ninth Legion. He was ambushed near Godmanchester, losing most of his infantry; only his cavalry escaped.

Inspired by this victory the British took Colchester within two days. The sack of the city was as brutal as it was thorough. No one was spared: many were tortured to death; their looted homes were burnt to the ground.

The news of the disaster persuaded Catus Decianus to flee to the continent, leaving his military counterpart, Paulinus Suetonius, to clean up the mess. Suetonius was a distinguished Roman general, who had earned a reputation in the Alps as a mountain fighter. When the revolt broke out he was in Anglesey dealing with the Druids, who had risen against the Roman occupation. His initial reaction was to gather his cavalry and march south east down Watling Street to London, telling the rest of the Fourteenth and elements of the Twentieth Legions to follow as soon as they could. He also ordered the Second Legion based in Exeter to join him in London.

The relief forces arrived too late. So Suetonius had to withdraw leaving London, the largest and most prosperous city in the province, to its fate. The destruction of Londinium, a metropolis of perhaps 30 acres with a population of 90,000, was complete and merciless. Boadicea's troops burned, slashed, crucified, hung and disembowelled all they could find. Women had their breasts cut off and sewn into their mouths; others were impaled on stakes. So thorough was the destruction that archaeologists have discovered a 15-inch red layer of burned debris 13 feet below the ground: so intense was the fire storm that temperatures reached 1,000°C, as extreme as those experienced in the blitz.[12] While Tacitus' estimate that 70,000 people, Romans and Romanised Britons, perished may be an exaggeration, the loss of life was truly appalling. It grew even greater a few days later when the Britons took and sacked St Albans, 30 miles to the north.

The atrocities strengthened the Romans' resolve while diverting British attention away from preparing for the inevitable denouement. The two sides eventually met, most modern authorities agree, at Mancetter, just off Watling Street, about ten miles north of Coventry.[13] Suetonius drew his forces up before a forest to protect his rear, with his legionnaires in the centre, auxiliaries on either side and cavalry on the flanks. The British arrayed in an uncoordinated horde of foot soldiers, interspersed with charioteers. Behind them in a half moon were the British wagons, piled high with wives and children, who surely cheered as their menfolk advanced upon the Romans. Just before they reached his lines Suetonius ordered his men to throw two volleys of javelins, and charge. The hail of 12–14,000 javelins decimated the British horde. In the mêlée the short Roman swords jabbed and cut, wreaking a terrible revenge among the British who, jam-packed together in a milling crowd, had no room to use their longer weapons. As the Roman cavalry charged, Boadicea's forces broke, but their baggage wagons prevented most from escaping. Trapped, the Romans cut them down with as little quarter as they gave the women and children who had come to watch what they were sure was going to be a great British victory.

Tacitus estimated that 80,000 Britons perished that day, as compared to only 400 Romans. Boadicea was one of the few to escape with her life. Soon afterwards she committed suicide. The site of her burial place has been the subject of considerable speculation. Some have suggested Norwich, others London, one even underneath Platform Eight at King's Cross Station![14] Her followers were wise to keep her final resting place secret, for the Romans would have surely dug up and desecrated her remains. As it was Suetonius took so horrendous a revenge on the British that he was recalled home in disgrace.

The British queen and the Roman general remained largely forgotten for over twelve centuries, until Bocaccio rediscovered Tacitus' manuscripts in Monte Cassino Monastery. Boadicea's appeal to the Elizabethans was obvious: both she and Gloriana were Amazons who had defied the foreign foe. For the next two hundred years her reputation declined; in his *History of Britain* (1670), John Milton called Boadicea's followers 'right barbarians'.[15]

Boadicea did not become a warrior heroine of mythical proportions until the latter part of the nineteenth century, when another woman ruled the British Empire. In a way this is ironic, since the event which most closely resembled Boadicea's revolt was the Indian Mutiny of 1857 in which the British played the part of Romans, while Bai Jhansi, the Rani of Jhansi, was a Boadicea who led a brave yet futile revolt against the foreign invaders. In 1900, just before the death of Queen Victoria (whom many wanted to associate with Boadicea), Peter Thorneycroft's statue of the royal warrior was unveiled on the Embankment, anointing Boadicea almost as the epitome of imperial grandeur. In 1937 one biographer rhapsodised:[16]

> In Boadicea's noble and patriotic effort I think we behold the first example of that love of liberty which has ever distinguished this island of ours and which has developed in the course of the centuries the most enlightened, the most just and the most humane system of government and administration known to mankind.

All this is, of course, utter nonsense. In truth Boadicea was a wronged woman, who in her outrage led a revolt against the Roman invaders, the ferocity of which was akin to, say, the resistance of Native Americans or Maoris to white encroachment. But she was history's first British hero, or rather heroine, for in a male-dominated society women are not supposed to lead men into battle. They may follow their men into combat, as she-soldiers, disguised in male clothing, but until very recently women did not become warriors. As current debates about women in combat have shown, men feel uneasy about this role, often resorting to stereotypes. Many a chauvinist has commented 'typical woman driver', on seeing the statue of Boadicea holding her hand out to signal she is turning one way as her chariot is in fact turning the other. As a widow, however, Boadicea has greater authority, since she no longer has a husband to whom she should defer. She is avenging the honour of her violated daughters, the lioness defending her cubs. In doing so she shames men, who are supposed to be able to protect their womenfolk. Since shame, or the fear of being shamed and thus losing honour, is a major motivating drive in making men fight, Boadicea becomes a potent symbol as a royal warrior.

She is not just a hero, but a British one. As an island nation the British have had to resist invasion, be it from Philip II, Napoleon or Hitler. Even though Boadicea failed (and the British have always loved gallant failures), she provided an example to encourage posterity. She was not, however, the last royal warrior whom posterity metamorphosed into a symbol of patriotic and chivalrous virtues.

So little is known about the real King Arthur that some have doubted whether he actually existed. He could well have been one of the leaders of the Romano-British resistance to the Anglo-Saxons whose raids started in 367 AD, becoming far more intense after the Legions evacuated Britain in 410. Recent scholarship, however, tends to support the view that 'Arthur was a genuine historical figure, not a mere figment of myth and romance'.[17]

Arthur may have been born about 475, the son of a noble Celtic family with Roman links. As a young man he hunted and trained as a soldier, his outstanding leadership abilities attracting a number of followers, whom legend later transformed into the Knights of the Round Table. Apart from a passing reference to him eighty years after his death, the first record of Arthur comes in 'The Annals of Wales', written in the late eighth century, which says he fought at the Battle of Mount Badon in 518, and was killed at Camlann nineteen years later. The ninth-century Welsh historian Nennius elaborates on this, asserting that Arthur fought the Anglo-Saxons in eleven battles. It is likely that Arthur and his men fought as mounted infantry, gaining an advantage over the Anglo-Saxons who battled on foot.

Arthur's historical legacy is hard to ascertain. At most he may be credited for delaying the full impact of the Anglo-Saxon invaders for over a hundred years. While it took the Franks a generation to conquer Gaul, the Anglo-Saxon invasions lasted a century and a half. This meant that by the time they dominated Britain the Anglo-Saxons were no longer so savage, and their impact on the country was not as calamitous as it might have been. Had Arthur not delayed their conquest Wales could well have fallen under Anglo-Saxon influence, and not remained a separate culture and nation.[18]

Nonetheless, the only justification for describing the two centuries after the fall of the Roman Empire as 'the Age of Arthur' is that these years were so dark a period for the British Isles that there is no one else after whom they may be called. To argue, as does John Morris, that 'the Age of Arthur is the foundation of British history' is an exaggeration.[19]

While the reality of Arthur is debatable, and his importance has been inflated, there can be no doubt about the significance of the legends associated with the king. 'For over a thousand years,' writes Rodney Castledan, 'the story of Arthur's life and death has been the principal myth of the island of Britain.'[20]

The Arthurian legend really began in about 1135 when the Welsh cleric, Geoffrey of Monmouth, wrote his *History of the Kings of Britain*. He asserted that Arthur was born in Tintagel, Cornwall, and as a young man was given a magical sword, with which he conquered Scotland, Ireland and Western Europe. After being mortally wounded at the Battle of Camlann he returned to the Isle of Avalon to die. In the middle of the twelfth century Chrétien de Troyes, a French poet, elaborated on the legend, adding the themes of chivalry and courtly love. In 1190 Robert de Boron, a Burgundian poet, included the search for the holy grail that possessed miraculous healing powers. A decade later Layamon, the English poet, turned Arthur into a messianic figure who did not really die, but would some day rise from his sleep to rescue his people in their hour of need.

Because it was one the first books William Caxton printed in 1485, Sir Thomas Malory's *Le Morte D'Arthur* brought the legend to a wider readership. It also filled in most of the details – the Round Table, Guinevere's affair with Sir Lancelot, the Sword in the Stone, the Lady of the Lake, and Arthur's transportation to Avalon. All these themes can be found in the Arthurian poems by Edmund Spenser, Thomas Gray, Algernon Swinburne, Alfred Lord Tennyson, John Masefield and C. S. Lewis, as well as the musical *Camelot* and the Disney film *The Sword in the Stone*.

Over the centuries the British monarchy linked itself to the legend of this warrior king. Henry II, who after coming to the throne in 1135, brought stability following the civil wars between Stephen and Matilda, named his grandson Arthur, influenced by Geoffrey of Monmouth's *History*. Sir Thomas Malory's *Le Morte D'Arthur* likewise persuaded Henry VII – who became king in 1485 (the same year as the book was printed), and brought order after the Wars of the Roses – to name his eldest son Arthur [Plate 1.4]. During Queen Victoria's reign the revival of the Arthurian legend (which Prince Albert encouraged) by poets such as Tennyson, and artists such as Sir Edward Burne-Jones, William Morris, Gustav Doré, J. Waterhouse and Dante Gabriel Rossetti, did much to rehabilitate the royal family after the hiatus of George IV and William IV.

Yet the popularity of the Arthurian legends went well beyond enhancing Queen Victoria's reputation. Arthur was, as A. L. Rowse put it, 'the hero of the losing side'.[21] As the king of lost causes, he (like Boadicea), became a symbol of noble defeat against overwhelming odds. But his image went further than the pagan warrior queen's. As the seeker of the holy grail, Arthur embodied the monarch's magical ability to heal, as demonstrated by touching to cure scrofula, the king's evil. Most important of all, the legendary King Arthur combined the two foundations from which monarchy developed – its priestly and military roles. He was the tribal leader in war, who adopted the code of chivalry and behaved like a perfect knight to defend the weak and right the wrong. As Christianity took hold in England, it tried to mitigate the effects of war, not only through the concept of a just war, but with the ideal of a just warrior. And thus Arthur perfectly merged the royal warrior with the Christian gentleman.

This combination of warrior and gentleman can be seen in the reign of King Alfred (871–99), a monarch about whom much more is known, yet who is most famous for the legend of burning the cakes.

Every schoolchild knows how when on the run from the Danes Alfred took refuge in a swineherd's hut in the Athelney Marches, in Somerset.

Plate 1.4   MS 6 f.66v, Battle between King Arthur and Mordred, English with Flemish illuminations, St Alban's chronicle, Lambeth Palace Library/Bridgeman Art Library

Not recognising the king, the swineherd's wife told him to watch the cakes she was baking, and when he failed to notice they were burning she scolded him, 'Yet you are quite happy to eat them when they come from the oven!'[22] Although the story is completely apocryphal (being an eleventh-century invention), it has lasted for nearly a thousand years because it encapsulates both Alfred's achievements as a warrior as well as his virtues as a Christian gentleman, both of which enabled him to be the only English king to earn the title of 'Great'. He was contrite – perhaps a little distracted – in defeat, accepting the good wife's reprimands. Like Shakespeare's Henry V, he passed incognito amongst humble folk before rising to achieve victory. Over the next few months he beat the Danes in a series of battles so decisive that, according to Christopher Brook, his reign 'proved not to be the end of England's history, but, in a way, its beginning'.[23]

The Viking invasions were part of a movement of people migrating from Scandinavia as far west as North America, east as Russia, and south as Sicily. The Vikings loved fighting. 'It was to me a pleasure equal to holding a girl,' boasted one of their leaders. They terrified all they violated. 'From the Fury of the Northmen, Good Lord, Deliver us,' ran an Anglo-Saxon prayer, while Alcuin, the eighth-century monk and historian from Northumberland, recorded, 'Never before has such terror appeared in Britain.'[24] About two generations later, in 865, the pressure of Viking attacks on England significantly increased, largely because Count Odo of Paris had stalled their French offensive. After one of their leaders, Ragnar Leather-Breeches, was captured in Northumberland, and executed by being thrown alive into a snake pit, his sons Ubba, Healfden and Ivan the Boneless (born, it was said, without a skeleton) invaded Northumbria in 867. They captured York and installed Egbert as their puppet king. The following year they took control of the Anglo-Saxon kingdom of Mercia, and in 869 conquered East Anglia, murdering its king Edmund by tying him to a tree for their bowmen to use for target practice.

Alfred, who had been born in Wantage in 849, had grown up in the shadow of the Danish invasions, and the atrocities committed by both sides. He was the fourth son of King Ethelwulf of Wessex, and as a boy had twice visited Rome as a pilgrim. Bishop Asser, his friend, chaplain and first biographer, suggested that he owed much of his military prowess to being 'a keen huntsman, who was without equal in his skill and good fortune'.[25] In 868, the year he married Elswitha, a Mercian noblewoman, he first saw action in Mercia fighting the Danes with his brother, King Ethelred.

The conflict became far more intense the following year when the Danes invaded Wessex, capturing Reading. The only Anglo-Saxon success, the Battle of Ashdown, was due to Alfred's courage. When King Ethelred was delayed at mass, declaring he would not 'leave Divine service for the service of men', Alfred immediately attacked, 'like a wild boar,' recorded Bishop Asser, and 'moved his army without delay against the enemy', whom he routed.[26] Four months later, in April 871, Ethelred died, most likely from wounds sustained fighting the Danes, leaving Alfred king of

Wessex. Soon afterwards at Wilton the Danes beat his forces by pretending to run, tricking the Anglo-Saxons into breaking ranks so they could be more readily slaughtered.

So in 872 Alfred made peace with the Danes, paying them a huge indemnity that he hoped might buy him time, which he used to build up his navy, and which the Danes employed to consolidate their hold on Mercia and Northumbria. After the Danes staged an abortive amphibious attack in 877, that quite literally floundered off Swanage (where their fleet ran aground on a hidden reef and sank losing four thousand men), the main Viking assault came early the next year.

Soon after Twelfth Night 878 the Danes, led by King Guthrum of East Anglia, attacked Alfred's palace at Chippenham forcing him to flee into the Marshes around Athelney (the scene of the story of the burning cakes). Here on a thirty-acre island, in the dead of winter, surrounded by waist-deep water meadows, Alfred prepared for his last stand. His situation seemed hopeless. 'He had nothing to live on except what he could seize,' wrote Asser. His mental state was just as bad. He 'passed a restless time in much anxiety,' Asser adds. Guthrum sent a fleet of shallow draft Viking ships to attack Athelney, but the Anglo-Saxons ambushed them, killing Ubba, their leader.

It was the turning point. With his base secure, Alfred assembled levies from Somerset, Wiltshire and Hampshire, and in the summer of 878 routed the Danes at Edington. So decisive was the victory that Guthrum had to sue for peace: he promised to leave Wessex alone, surrender hostages, and become a Christian.

Far from resting on his laurels, Alfred used his victory to prepare Wessex's defences. He first built up the navy, constructing sixty oared vessels which were far larger than the ones the Vikings used. He strengthened coastal fortifications, and greatly expanded the system of burghs, fortified bulwarks, where folk could take refuge from marauding Danes. In order to maintain a standing army, Alfred divided the *fyrd*, or militia, into two, rotating the halves between active duty and cultivating the land.

The strengths and weaknesses of these policies were demonstrated in 892, when two hundred and fifty Danish boats landed on the south coast at Lympe, and a further eighty commanded by Haesten sailed up the Thames to build a base at Milton, near Gravesend. To counter this threat Alfred made a peace treaty with the Danes who lived in Northumbria and East Anglia. He attacked the enemy encamped at Lympe, whom his son Edward defeated near Farnham. Yet he had failed to neutralise the main Danish threat, Chief Haesten's forces concentrated at the mouth of the Thames. The following year, taking advantage of Haesten's absence on a raid, Alfred managed to capture the main Danish camp at Benfleet, taking Haesten's wife and sons prisoners. In an extraordinarily magnanimous gesture Alfred released them on the grounds that they were recently baptised Christians. In 894 Alfred moved west to deal with a Danish attack on Exeter. This allowed the Danes to break out of their new base at Shoeburyness, and march along the Thames, across the Cotswolds and up the Severn Valley where the Anglo-Saxons ambushed and routed them at Buttington. The surviving Danes escaped to Chester and then North Wales: a few made it back to Mersea. After spending the summer of 894 here, they rowed up the Thames to Lea, some twenty miles past London, where Alfred built a dam and forts blocking their return to their main base. So they broke out once more and marched to Bridgenorth on the Severn, remaining there until the summer of 896, when they broke up into small groups to sneak back to East Anglia.

'The raiding army, by the Grace of God,' exulted *The Anglo-Saxon Chronicle* with uncharacteristic understatement, 'had not altogether crushed the English race.'[27] The burghs that Alfred had built severely limited the ability of the marauding Danes to collect loot or live off the land, which meant that they had to continue moving, as Anglo-Saxon forces shadowed them and finally trapped them so they could retreat no further.

Alfred defeated the Danes so thoroughly that, apart from minor pirate raids, the last three years of his reign passed peacefully. With the help of Mercia, his son, Edward the Elder (899–924), continued to push back the Danes, as did his grandson Athelston (924–59), who regained much of Northumbria. It was not until the reign of Ethelred (978–1016), later nicknamed 'The Unready', that the Danes were able to overrun Wessex. Ethelred neglected the navy, chose poor leaders as his generals, tried to buy off the Danes with excessive amounts of Danegeld, and then on St Brice's Day 1002 ordered all Danes found in Anglo-Saxon territory to be massacred. Sweyn Forkbeard, the Danish king, was incensed, his sister Gunnhild being one of the victims. So his forces exacted a terrible revenge, roaming the land, murdering, raping and plundering at will, even killing the Archbishop of Canterbury. In 1016, having utterly failed to deal with the Viking invasions, Ethelred fled to Normandy, unwittingly laying the foundations for the last invasion of the British Isles.

Ethelred lacked all the soldierly virtues that made Alfred so superb a royal warrior. Alfred was brave and energetic. Within six months he recovered from his nadir at Athelney to triumph at Edington. Then he built up the kingdom's defences using the navy, burghs and *fyrd* to ruthlessly counter-attack the Danes. Alfred had all the martial virtues that the Anglo-Saxons celebrated in such poems as *Beowulf*. Like Beowulf, the epic's protagonist, Alfred added a Christian devotion to his pagan warrior base. Perhaps Bishop Asser, the king's friend and biographer, exaggerated his sanctity. For instance, he asserted that for the whole of his life Alfred was in constant pain, the nature of which he is vague, except to record that one bout, which lasted for a quarter century, started on his wedding night. Since contemporaries attributed the mortification of the flesh, even to the point of seeking illness, particularly when associated with the joys of the flesh, as a sign of holiness, Asser could well have attributed such suffering to Alfred to bolster his reputation as a sanctified warrior king. Yet it is hard to believe that a man so crippled by anguish and physical weakness could have fought for so long, so hard, and so well.[28]

But this does not mean that Alfred lacked piety. He pushed back the Danes and brought peace for the church, which because of its wealth was a prime target for their pillaging. He looked after the church, encouraged learning and education, oversaw the writing of *The Anglo-Saxon Chronicle* (which gratefully recorded all of his achievements in fulsome detail), and even personally translated such devotional works as Pope Gregory's *Pastoral Care* into English. Alfred drafted England's first legal code, based largely on Old Testament principles. Most importantly he saw everything he did to defend all of his kingdom as part of a whole. A king, he wrote, 'must have praying men, fighting men and working men'. He must have 'weapons, food, ale, clothing and whatsoever is necessary for each of the three classes'.[29] By recognising defence as part of an integrated system which produced victory, Alfred was able to expand the power of the monarchy.

By combining the two strands from which kingship derived – military prowess and Christian virtues – he became an example for well over eleven hundred years. Oxford University twice fraudulently claimed Alfred the Scholar as their founder – as did the preparatory and night school movements. In 1740 the song 'Rule Britannia' was composed as a masque honouring his achievements, amongst which the Victorians included founding the British Empire. Soon afterwards Lord Rosebury used Alfred, the Father of the Royal Navy, to justify spending millions on the Dreadnought battleship building programme and arms race with Kaiser Wilhelm's Germany.[30] Indeed there seemed to be no limit to the greatness of Alfred the Great, which, as Professor Henry Loyn has rightly concluded, was due to the fact that he was 'the thoughtful warrior king'.[31]

Notes

1. A. Duncan, *The Reality of Monarchy* (London: Heinemann, 1970), 263–64.
2. Gwynne Dyer, *War* (London: Guild, 1986), xi.
3. Ibid., xi.

 4. J. Keegan, *War and our World: the Reith Lectures* (London: Pimlico, 1998), 28–30.
 5. G. R. Elton, *The English* (Oxford: Blackwells, 1992), 6. R. Bendix, *Kings or People: Power and the Mandate to Rule* (Berkeley: University of California Press, 1978), 27.
 6. W. Bagehot, *The English Constitution* (London: H. S. King, 1872), 92.
 7. J. Cannon, *The Oxford Illustrated History of the British Monarchy* (Oxford: Oxford University Press, 1988), 19–20.
 8. Anthony Barnett (ed.), *Power and the Throne: the Monarchy Debate* (London: Vintage, 1994), 20.
 9. Quoted by R. Perry, *Edward the Second Suddenly at Berkeley* (Wotton-under-Edge: Ivy House, 1988), 14.
10. Quoted by L. Spence, *Boadicea: Warrior Queen of the Britons* (London: Routledge and Keegan Paul, 1937), 29.
11. Quoted by D. Dudley and G. Webster, *The Legend of Boudicca* (New York: Barnes and Noble, 1962), 54.
12. P. Marsden, *Roman London* (London: Thames and Hudson, 1980), 33.
13. G. Webster, *Boudicea: the British Revolt against Rome, AD 60* (London: Batsford, 1978), 111–13.
14. A. Fraser, *The Warrior Queens* (New York: Knopf, 1990), 100.
15. Dudley and Webster, *op. cit.*, 123–4.
16. Spence, *op. cit.*, 269.
17. L. Alcock, *Arthur's Britain: History and Archaeology, AD 367–634* (Harmondsworth: Penguin, 1971), xvi.
18. M. Holmes, *King Arthur: a Military History* (London: Cassell, 1996), 155–7.
19. J. Morris, *The Age of Arthur: a History of the British Isles, 350–650* (London: Weidenfeld and Nicolson, 1973), 506, 510.
20. R. Castledan, *King Arthur: the Truth behind the Legend* (London: Routledge, 2000), 1.
21. Quoted by E. Jenkins, *The Mystery of King Arthur* (London: O'Mara, 1990), 214.
22. A. P. Smyth, *King Alfred the Great* (Oxford: Oxford University Press, 1995), 325–6.
23. C. Brook, *From Alfred to Henry III* (New York: Norton, 1966), 32.
24. H. R. Loyn, *Alfred the Great* (London: Oxford University Press, 1967), 10.
25. Ibid., 203.
26. Ibid., 187.
27. M. J. Swanton (ed.), *The Anglo-Saxon Chronicle* (London: Dent, 1996), 89.
28. Smyth, *op. cit.*, 199–200.
29. B. Yorke, *Kings and Kingdoms of Early Anglo-Saxon England* (London: Seaby, 1990), 160–4.
30. Smyth, *op. cit.*, xix, 153.
31. Loyn, *op. cit.*, 56.

chapter 2

A FATAL DAY TO ENGLAND

'This was a fatal day to England, and melancholy havoc wrought in our dear country during the change of its lord. For in the first years of their arrival they were barbarians in their look and manner, warlike in their usages.' William of Malmesbury, monk and historian (c.1080–1143), on the Battle of Hastings[1]

They had been fighting for nearly two hours, since about nine that morning of 14 October 1066, and both sides were desperately tired. The invaders had been on stand-to all night, sleeping as best they could, dressed in full armour beside their weapons, to fend off a surprise attack. They had risen long before dawn to march the seven miles north along the London road to the place now known as Battle. The defenders were equally exhausted: they had arrived piecemeal the previous evening and in the early hours of the morning, some having force-marched the two hundred miles from Yorkshire, to snatch a brief troubled sleep atop the ridge.

Both sides were roughly of equal size, of some 7,000 men. The invaders had more archers and cavalry, although they were drawn up in an inferior position below a 60-foot high ridge. A lone hoar-apple tree was the most prominent feature of the 600-yard long ridge, on top of which the Anglo-Saxon infantry stood. Some were local levies, the *fyrd*, reasonable enough troops, ready to fight the invaders. In front of them and concentrated in the centre around the king, were the housecarls, an élite force of mounted infantry, the pride of King Harold's army. Arguably the best soldiers in Europe, they were flushed with confidence from a recent victory in the north. But now the housecarls were too tired from their march south to dig defences, or hammer sharpened stakes in the ground. Instead they relied on the kite-shaped shields that they linked in a phalanx to make a virtually impenetrable wall.

The battle started at about nine in the morning. The sound of trumpets ordered the invaders to attack. 'You fight not merely for victory but also for survival,' their general told them, 'there is no road for retreat.'[2] The infantry was in the van, with cavalry behind. French from the area around Paris held the right flank, Bretons the left, and Normans the centre. Steadfastly the invaders moved forward. Before and beside them auxiliaries hurled javelins, and archers fired arrows, the whole host being led into battle by a minstrel called Taillefer, who sang as he juggled.

Such levity did not survive the initial contact. (Neither did Taillefer, who was among the first to be killed.) The Anglo-Saxons stood their ground. Norman arrows and javelins having made little impression against their shields, they drove the enemy back down the hill in bloody flight. The only significant Norman success was the deaths of Leofwin and Gyrth, Harold's younger brothers and subordinate commanders.

For over two hours the invaders attacked – first the infantry and then the heavy cavalry – but always in vain. The five-foot Anglo-Saxon axes, with their wickedly sharp twelve-inch-wide heads, did terrible damage, slicing through chain mail, cutting off horses' feet. 'The only movement was the dropping of the dead,' wrote a contemporary historian, 'the living stood motionless.'[3] By about 9.45, however, the Bretons on the left started moving back: some grew so unnerved that they ran away, prompting a few of Harold's troops to break ranks to pursue them. Worse still a cry went up that their leader, whom the invaders had twice seen having had his horse killed from under him, was dead. The battle was at its moment of crisis. It seemed that the duke whom posterity calls 'the Conqueror', would in fact become William the Vanquished and that his scheme to invade England would come to naught.

It began over nine months earlier, days after Edward the Confessor, King of England, died on 5 January 1066. Although he married, Edward was too holy a man to consummate the relationship. While this helped him become a saint (after whom Westminster Abbey was to be named), it left his wife unsatisfied, England with a succession problem and Harold Godwinson, Earl of Wessex, with the opportunity to seize the throne. Harold asserted that Edward had left it to him, a claim which the leading nobles promptly accepted at the coronation held with indecent haste the day after Edward died. With the crown on his head, all Harold had to do was keep it there.

The first threat came from Earl Tostig, Harold's brother. The siblings 'were distinctly handsome and graceful persons, similar in strength,' wrote an observer, 'equally brave.' They had fallen out the previous year when rebels, protesting Tostig's iniquitous rule and heavy taxes, drove him out of Northumbria, and Harold refused to help his brother regain the earldom. In May 1066 Tostig arrived off the Isle of Wight with about sixty ships, some of which were from the Orkney Islands, then ruled by Harold Hardrada, King of Norway. Tostig raided the Isle of Thanet and the east coast before withdrawing to Scotland. Although Tostig did little actual damage, he forced Harold to assemble his forces early in the year which meant that by the time the significant invasions came in the autumn, many of his soldiers and most of his ships had been demobilised.

Harold Hardrada was a formidable foe, being described by a contemporary as 'the doughtiest warrior under Heaven'.[4] After being wounded in the Battle of Stikestad, near Trondheim, which was fought during a solar eclipse in 1030, he went to Byzantium, where he led a band of 500 mercenaries, fighting in Greece, Bulgaria, the Holy Land, Sicily and Ireland. He returned home in 1047 to become King of Norway. He brooked no opposition. When some farmers protested his heavy taxes he had their spokesman, Einar, hacked to pieces in his presence, and burned their cottages. 'Flames cured the peasant of disloyalty to Harold,' a bard dryly noted. In 1064 he routed King Sweyn II of Denmark and his fleet at the Battle of Nissa so completely that blood reportedly gushed into the ocean.

So when in September 1066 Harold Hardrada sailed up the River Ouse to land at Riccall in Yorkshire, with 300 ships, and as many as 12,000 Northmen, intent on seizing the English throne, he posed a mortal threat to King Harold and the English. Harold moved with remarkable speed. As the Norwegians beat the local English militia at Gate Fulford on 20 September and occupied York, he marched his army the 210 miles from London in a week to catch the invaders off-guard at Stamford Bridge. Hardrada had drawn his troops up on both sides of the River Derwent, at an important road junction. Hardly pausing for breath, King Harold threw his men against the Northmen on the west side of the river, quickly pushing them back across the Derwent. A single Viking warrior stood on the bridge (about 700 yards downstream from the present structure), defying all to cross. Once soldiers standing in the river underneath killed him with spears thrust through cracks in the planking, the English poured across the Derwent, forcing the invaders back to Battle Flats, a plateau 300 yards east of the river.

At first the Northmen, safe behind their wall of shields, resisted stoutly. A poet recalled:

> *Where battle storm was ringing,*
> *Where arrow storm was singing*
> *Harold stood his ground.*

Unfortunately for Harold Hardrada, at this critical moment, an arrow struck his windpipe and he drowned in his own blood. Shocked, both sides paused. King Harold offered quarter, which Tostig, now leader of the Northmen, contemptuously rejected. In the ensuing mêlée he was killed, just as reinforcements arrived from the ships at Riccall. They came too tired and too late to make any difference, except to augment the casualties. Three hundred ships had brought the invaders to England: twenty-four were enough to take the survivors home.

Harold did not have long in which to savour this resounding victory. Twelve days later, supposedly during the celebratory banquet in York, he was informed that William, Duke of Normandy, had just landed in Pevensey and captured Hastings.

William's road to Hastings was a long and complicated one, which in many ways started at the moment of his conception.

According to a twelfth-century chronicler, Robert, Duke of Normandy fell in love – or at least lust – at first sight with Herleve (sometimes known as Arlette), when he saw the maid washing clothes in the stream which flowed beside her father's tannery at the foot of Falaise Castle. He took her back to his chamber, where that night, having conceived her first child, she dreamed that a tree sprung out of her womb, its branches growing and growing to cover both Normandy and England. There is, of course, no truth to the legend – at least not in the literal sense – if only because Herleve's family was far too prosperous to have her publicly scrub its dirty linen. But of one fact there can be no doubt: that their child, William, born in 1027 or 1028, was illegitimate, and as such had little prospect of ruling Normandy, let alone England.

In 1034 Robert decided to go on a pilgrimage to Jerusalem, and called a meeting of his magnates to accept William as his heir, just in case he did not return. 'He is little,' explained Robert, 'but will grow up if God so wills, and grow better.'[5] After much grumbling, and pressure from Robert, Archbishop of Rouen, the barons acquiesced. After all, going on pilgrimages was a highly regarded activity, and nominating an heir, albeit an illegitimate one, was a reasonable insurance policy.

It turned out to be a valid one. In July 1035 Duke Robert died at Nicea, in Asia Minor, on his way back from Jerusalem. With Archbishop Robert's help the barons accepted William as the Duke of Normandy: more important, so did Henry I, King of France, to whom William may have sworn fealty as a vassal.

Archbishop Robert's death in March 1037 removed the one man who could keep Normandy in order during William's minority. Violence, rebellion, rape, looting and plunder broke out. Many of William's supporters perished. Ralph de Gacé, Archbishop Robert's son, had Gilbert,

Duke Robert's confidant, assassinated. Torold, William's tutor was murdered. Osbern, his steward, was killed in a brawl in the boy's bedroom. Walter, his uncle, spent many a night on guard there, fully armed, and on several occasions baronial plots forced them to seek refuge in peasant hovels. Only luck, and the realisation that William's murder might prompt a French or Angevin invasion, enabled him to survive what one biographer has called 'a terrible childhood', lived during 'one of the darkest periods of Norman History'.[6]

The blackest year was 1047 when William came of age. Seeking to emasculate the duke's power a group of barons, egged on by Guy, Count of Burgundy, attempted to seize William at Valognes. Forewarned the duke escaped, and riding in desperate haste, eluded his pursuers by fording the Vire estuary at low tide to reach the safety of Falaise. He appealed to Henry I, whom he found at Poissy, and, prostrating himself at the French king's feet, claimed the protection which the feudal system accorded all faithful vassals. Worried by the growing lawlessness in Normandy, and perhaps grateful for the help Duke Robert had given him and his mother in 1031 when a similar baronial conspiracy ejected them from France, Henry invaded Normandy in 1047. Marching rapidly via Caen he and William routed the barons at Val-és-Dunes, driving many of the rebels to watery graves in the River Orne.

Although William had fought bravely at Val-és-Dunes, his rule was far from secure, the victory being basically a French one. So he had to pardon all but one of the rebels, and call an ecclesiastical council which proclaimed a Truce of God that forbade war between Wednesday evenings and Monday mornings, and during Pentecost, Lent, Advent and Easter. Even though the truce restored some order to Normandy, William had to spend three years starving Guy of Burgundy out of his citadel at Brionne. He consolidated his hold on the dukedom by building castles, cultivating the church and barons, and making a marriage alliance with Flanders.

William's success excited the envy of neighbours. When Geoffrey of Anjou invaded southern Normandy, William had to thwart his aggression by capturing Alençon and Domfort castles. So Geoffrey formed an alliance with Henry I (who was worried that William had grown too powerful), that resulted in a joint invasion of Normandy in 1052. Two years later William's defeat of Henry at Mortemer ended the French threat, which further diminished in 1060 when both Geoffrey and Henry died, the latter being succeeded by Philip I, who was only eight and a ward of Count Baldwin V of Flanders, William's father-in-law.

By now, after decades of almost constant warfare William had not only secured his position as ruler of Normandy but learned much about ruling his fellow men. 'From my childhood I have been continually involved in numerous troubles,' William recalled. 'The Normans,' he concluded, 'when under the rule of a kind but firm master are most valiant people. But in other circumstances they bring ruin on themselves by rending each other. They are eager for rebellion, ripe for tumults, and ready for any sort of crime.'[7]

In countless skirmishes and in several pitched battles William had proven his courage and leadership, winning a reputation as an effective, albeit cold-blooded general. At Brionne and Domfort he demonstrated a genius for siege warfare. At Alençon he also exhibited a chilling cruelty. During the siege the defenders taunted him by waving skins from the battlement and shouting 'hides for the tanner', a hurtful reference to both his illegitimacy and his mother's supposed humble birth. After capturing the town one source recorded that he had the defenders skinned alive, while another reported he amputated all their limbs. Such ferocity persuaded the nearby garrison of Domfort to surrender immediately.

There is no doubt that William sorely felt the stigma of illegitimacy. Bastardy is a cruel rejection. Having had his pleasure, the bastard's father refuses to do his duty, and by implication asserts that his child and its mother are not good enough for him. By marrying Herleve to Herluin, Vicomte of Conteville, in about 1030, and then going off on a crusade, it could well appear to William that his father was both callous and irresponsible. William's deathbed assertion that 'my father went into voluntary exile, entrusting the Duchy of Normandy to me' makes it clear that for the whole of his life William was reluctant to face up to the truth about his birth and his father's desertion.

When taunted with his illegitimacy William could react with explosive rage – as both the defenders of Alençon and his wife could vouchsafe. According to one chronicler, when he was about eighteen William sent a messenger to ask Count Baldwin of Flanders if he could marry his daughter, Matilda. This high-born young woman, the granddaughter of the king of France, scornfully replied that she would wed no bastard. So William, who was over six feet tall, huge for the times, rode to Bruges, burst into the palace, and forced his way into Matilda's room, where he beat and kicked the petite, four-foot two-inch girl. Overcome by such rough wooing, she took to her bed, vowing she would wed no man but her conqueror. Their marriage was an extremely happy one. William was famous for his fidelity, and intolerance of the peccadilloes of others, a clear repudiation of his father's promiscuity.

William blamed his illegitimacy for an unhappy childhood. 'Calling me a bastard, degenerate, and unworthy to reign,' he fulminated, Guy of Burgundy 'strove to strip me of the whole of Normandy. Thus, while I was yet a beardless youth, I found myself compelled to fight on the plains of Val-és-Dunes.' A few years after he complained that by urging Henry I to invade Normandy his uncles had 'treated me with contempt'.[8]

Illegitimacy may not only deprive a child of a father, but can also deny him his patrimony. William resented the fact that 'My nearest friends, my own kindred, who ought to have defended me at all hazard against the whole world, formed conspiracies against me, and nearly stripped me of the inheritance of my fathers.' Just as his faithfulness to his wife was a compensation for his father's infidelity to his mother, so William's treatment of his legitimate sons (for he had no illegitimate ones) was a reaction against the way Robert had treated him. 'Normandy is mine by hereditary descent,' he told his eldest son, whom he christened Robert after his father, as if to bolster the legitimacy of a dubious succession.[9] On his death, so as not to deny any of his boys their patrimony, William left Normandy to Robert, his eldest son, England to William, and large estates to Henry, the youngest.

William's extreme sensitivity about his illegitimacy, and determination to gain his patrimony, no matter the cost, would not have mattered had he not believed England was rightfully his. Just before the battle of Hastings he told his men that Harold 'will fight to retain what he has wrongfully seized, where we shall fight to regain what we have received as a gift and what we have lawfully acquired.'[10]

All the audience knew that William was referring to the events which started in 1051. What exactly happened in the spring of that year is debatable, the various contenders for the English throne having different versions. But the fact remains that William was convinced that Edward had named him as his successor. The reaction of Godwin, the Earl of Wessex – who denied the story – tends to confirm it. He was so annoyed by Edward that he refused to accept a summons to appear before the royal court to answer charges relating to an affray at Dover, but instead fled to the continent, where he raised an army. Godwin then invaded England and purged Edward's council of all his Norman advisers, except for the Bishop of London and one Ralph the Timid. For the rest of Edward's reign Godwin, and then his son Harold, dominated English affairs.

In 1064 Edward sent Harold to France in order – so William maintained – to confirm the 1051 promise. Adverse winds blew Harold ashore near the mouth of the River Somme, where the local magnate, Count Guy of Ponthieu, arrested him. William intervened to free Harold from Guy's dungeons, personally escorting him to Rouen, where he was treated as an honoured guest. Soon afterwards (the Bayeux Tapestry maintains), Harold swore with one hand on the Bible and the other over a chest of relics to represent William's interests at Edward's court, to maintain garrisons of Norman knights in England, and when Edward died to do all he could to ensure William's succession [Plate 2.1].

William was out hunting in his park at Querville when he heard that Harold had broken his oath by seizing the English throne on Edward's death. He was so angry that only his closest friend, William Fitz Osbern, could talk to him. William took decisive action. According to a Norman chronicler 'the duke at once sent messengers to Harold urging him to desist from this mad policy.'[11] Another chronicler reflected William's fury by having him describe Harold as 'stained with vice, a cruel murderer, purse proud, and puffed up with profits of pillage, an enemy of justice and all good'.[12]

Without doubt William was outraged; his patrimony had been denied. But unlike most bastards, who have to learn to live with life's inequities, William was a proven warrior. Conquering England, however, was far from a proven certainty.

William had to win support at home and abroad by arguing that his cause was both just and profitable. The first argument convinced the pope who gave William a pallium, a special banner signifying the Holy Father's blessing, thus turning a conquest into a crusade. The second rationale convinced many knights from Normandy, as well as Brittany and France, to join him. As a contemporary put it they were 'panting for the spoils of England'.[13]

The snag was getting there. Transporting an army of seven thousand men, plus half as many camp followers, and two thousand horses required a huge fleet. William requisitioned some ships: most of them he built from scratch, a massive undertaking. By mid-August the fleet rendezvoused at Dives on the coast of Normandy, where the huge army had assembled. To be closer to England William moved them north east to St Valéry at the mouth of the Somme. Several ships were lost in the trip (which was far less perilous than the cross-channel passage). William concealed the incidents, and secretly buried the corpses that were washed ashore to maintain his men's morale as they waited (always the hardest part of battle), for a favourable wind.

It came on 27 September. That evening the fleet left for England with William leading aboard the *Mora* (the Latin for 'delay'), a most inappropriate name, for when dawn broke the next morning William's ship had out-sailed the rest of the fleet to find itself alone in the middle of the English Channel. William ordered a sailor to climb the mast to see if he could see any other ships. None were sighted. Calmly the Duke ordered a feast prepared, with several bumpers of spiced wine, and 'dined in good spirits as if he was in a room in his own house'. Eventually the

Plate 2.1 Harold swearing an oath to William © Reading Museum Service (Reading Borough Council).

look-out shouted down he could see four vessels, and soon after reported the whole fleet in sight, 'like a forest of trees bearing sails'.[14]

After making a landfall off Beachy Head William came ashore at Pevensey, where he built a fort on the site of the Roman castle. With a bodyguard of 25 knights he personally reconnoitred the region, deciding to shift camp to Hastings, where he built another castle. In those days Hastings was on a peninsula that was both easily defended, and provided a ready evacuation port.

William knew much about his enemy's movements. Since Edward's death he had sent spies ahead to keep him abreast of events in England. With excellent intelligence about Harold's position, William and his troops left Hastings before dawn on 14 October. They marched north along the London road, to meet Harold in the battle that reached its climax at about a quarter to ten in the morning.

It was at about that time that the Bretons on the left flank of the invader's line started to panic. William had just had a horse killed under him. Many of his troops believed he was dead. Several historians are convinced that if at this moment Harold had seized the initiative by ordering his troops to attack he would have won the day. It was not to be. William quelled the panic by removing his helmet and exposing himself to his men (as well as to the enemy's archers), riding up and down between the two front lines shouting, 'Look at me well. I am still alive, and by the grace of God shall yet prove victor.'[15]

It worked. William's men not only steadied, but rallied enough to advance a little, and mop up a few reckless Anglo-Saxons who had ventured too far in front of their lines.

We know little about the next six or seven hours of the engagement. After both sides had regrouped, 'it was a strange kind of battle,' wrote William of Poitiers, 'one side attacking with all mobility, the other with-standing, as though rooted in the soil.'[16] Each thwarted Norman assault added to the pile of dead and dying in front of the English lines that made a gruesomely effective barrier.

Towards nightfall, at about seven o'clock, perhaps frustrated by their inability to break the enemy lines, the Normans started to retreat. Whether this was a genuine or feigned flight has been a matter for debate. After the battle the Norman chroniclers and the Bayeux Tapestry may have suggested the latter to hide the disgrace of running from the enemy. Yet the retreating soldiers quickly rallied – a very difficult turnabout had the panic been genuine, which suggests that it was a ruse similar to the ones the Normans had used at St Aubin on 1053 and Messina in 1060.

Now, recognising that if he did nothing, and that an inconclusive battle would in fact be a defeat, William ordered his archers to shoot up in the air. While the Anglo-Saxons' shields stopped most arrows fired horizontally, they were ineffective against plunging fire. A lucky arrow hit Harold in the eye, perhaps killing and certainly incapacitating him. Without their leader the Anglo-Saxons panicked. As they ran the Norman cavalry chased them, slashing down, cracking skulls, severing necks, fracturing spines. So headlong was the chase that in the gathering dark some Norman horsemen killed themselves by riding into a steep ravine, known as Malfosse – the 'evil ditch'. In the end it made no difference, for in a single day, noted William of Poitiers, the duke 'took possession of his inheritance by battle'.[17]

The victorious survivors spent that night amid the carnage of battle: the untended wounded lay dying, making that ghastly humming sound survivors of similar catastrophes recall, which by dawn terminated in an even more funereal silence. A grey Sunday morning revealed piles of dead on the ridge. 'The bloodstained battlefield,' William of Poitiers wrote, 'was covered with the corpses of the youth and nobility of England.' The local streams ran red with blood. After looting the enemy dead, the Normans buried their own. William walked through the carnage, looking for the bodies of friends, whom he ordered buried with special respect. After Bishop Eure had sung a mass for the souls of the departed, the Conqueror permitted the local Anglo-Saxon women to retrieve and inter their fathers, sons and husbands. Edith Swan-necked, Harold's mistress of many years, recognised his disembowelled and mangled corpse by a birthmark in a place that only a lover could know. Not all the corpses were buried: seventy years after the battle piles of bones could still be seen strewn along the ridge.

For five days William and his troops remained in the Battle area. Then they moved east, punishing the inhabitants of Romney so savagely for attacking a Norman reconnaissance party that Dover surrendered without a fight. Canterbury was just as compliant. A shortage of food added to the usual stresses of campaigning caused an outbreak of dysentery in the Norman army. William's bout was so bad that he could not move for five weeks. The delay allowed news of his victory and the harsh way in which he treated resistance to spread throughout England, prompting Edith, Edward the Confessor's widow, to surrender Winchester, which gave William control of the South East.

London was the key. So William moved north to Southwark, where he routed an Anglo-Saxon force that sallied out across London Bridge. After setting fire to Southwark he moved through Hampshire and Berkshire, laying waste on the way, crossing the Thames at Wallingford. William's brutality paid off. The few leading Anglo-Saxon nobles left alive, plus Archbishop Aldred of York, came to surrender London to the

Duke, whom Aldred crowned King of England in Westminster Abbey on Christmas Day.

Even though William conquered the English at Hastings in one of the world's most decisive battles, he had to spend the rest of his life making good his victory. Only three of his next seventeen years were free of fighting. Soon after he returned to Normandy in March 1067 a revolt broke out in the Welsh Borders led by one Eric the Wild, a shadowy figure about whom little is known except for his claim one night to have come across a group of fairies, one of whom he married. Thus is it not surprising that Eric failed to capture the Norman strong point at Hereford.

Far more serious were the problems which faced William when he returned to England in December 1067. He marched to the south west to quell a rebellion centred in Exeter, which surrendered after an eighteen-day siege. In the summer and autumn of 1068 he had to put down rebellions in the Midlands and the North.

The following year William had to face the most serious challenge to his rule, a rising in the north of England led by Robert Commines, the Earl of Northumberland, who had burned 900 of William's men to death in the Bishop's Palace in Durham. William harried the north, wreaking such destruction that even his friend William of Poitiers had to admit 'such barbarous homicide should not go unpunished'.[18] Hundreds were hanged, thousands died of starvation and exposure. It took over a generation for the north to recover. By Easter of the following year William was back in the south quelling rebellions in Dorset and Somerset, instigated by two of Harold's sons. Next he had to deal with revolts in North Wales, Shropshire and Chester.

In the autumn of 1069 King Sweyn Estrithson of Norway sent a large invasion force led by his two sons, Harold and Canute, which landed at the mouth of the River Humber. With considerable local support – a sign that many Anglo-Saxons still had not accepted the conquest – the Norsemen managed to capture York on 20 September. Once more William acted with characteristic resolve. He drove the invaders out of Lincolnshire, turned west to quickly suppress a rising in the Borders led by Eric the Wild, before shifting north to capture York, where he spent Christmas. The following spring he crossed the Pennines, scorching its earth with his usual ferocity.

Once again Sweyn sent an invasion fleet which landed in Lincolnshire, meeting up with Hereward the Wake, an Anglo-Saxon guerrilla leader based in the Fens. They sacked Peterborough and captured Ely. By making a peace with William in June, Sweyn deserted Hereward, who continued his irregular warfare for several years. William next turned his attention to Scotland. He crossed the border in August, and supplied by a fleet sailing along the east coast, forced King Malcolm to sign the Peace of Abernethy.

The peace did not end the war. William had to return to France straightaway where he fought a series of campaigns in Normandy and Maine, as well as a revolt hatched by his eldest son, Robert. He died in the saddle in 1087, while fighting the King of France. After capturing Mantes, thirty miles from Paris, his troops sacked the town with a ferocity intense even by their brutal standards. Riding through the town's burning ruins, hardly any of whose inhabitants had survived, William's horse was startled by some frightful sight. It threw the king (who had put on so much weight in the last few years that the King of France jeered that he had the belly of a pregnant woman), against the pommel of his saddle, fatally rupturing him.

Six weeks later, as he lay dying in St. Gervaise Priory, just outside Rouen, William bequeathed Normandy to his eldest son, Robert, and England, which he admitted was his by right of conquest, to his second son, William. 'My friends, I tremble,' his biographer Ordericus Vitalis, has him say, 'when I reflect on the grievous sins which burden my conscience, and now, about to be summoned before the awful tribunal of God, I know not what I ought to do. I was bred to arms since childhood, and am stained with the rivers of blood I have shed.'[19]

Like most successful military commanders who have shed gallons of blood, William was not an especially attractive man. Tall and energetic, he fought with great vigour wearing heavy chain armour. With both hands he could fire a long bow on horseback, a skill that required immensely strong leg muscles to grip the horse. William preferred indirect tactics, Hastings being his first pitched battle. When Henry I invaded his realm, William harassed the French king's army, wearing them down until they were forced to withdraw. Rather than defeat the enemy head on, he used fear to make them submit. 'He sowed terror in the land,' wrote William of Poitiers about his conquest of Maine, 'he devastated vineyards, fields and estates.'[20]

Behind this ruthlessness was an intense drive. William admitted as much in his deathbed confession: 'I am prey to cruel fears and anxieties.' In part these came from his illegitimacy, a subject about which he was acutely sensitive, and which made him fight for what he considered was his rightful patrimony. William was one of those great men who are driven by some paternal curse with which they must live and which they must live down. 'I am ready to wager my life,' he declared a few days before Hastings, in order to conquer England which 'by right falls to me'.[21] During the battle he symbolically expressed this conviction in two ways. First, by flying the pallium, the flag given him by the pope – a father figure if ever there was one. Second, by wearing under his armour some of the relics on which Harold had sworn to support his claim to the throne.

Paradoxically illegitimacy may well have given William a sense of self-confidence, for it is clear that his mother doted on him. Herleve might have endowed her favourite child with 'the feeling of a conqueror, that confidence of success that often induces real success', which Sigmund Freud called 'the legacy of a mother's favour'.[22]

William became Duke of Normandy and then King of England not because of the chance of inheritance, but through his abilities as a soldier. Long before 1066 he had shown himself one of the best generals in Europe – which explains why so many freebooters decided to join the Norman invasion. He not only recruited good men, but appointed good lieutenants. He led by example, 'more often commanding men to follow than urging them on from the rear'.[23] William had great logistical and administrative skills. Before the invasion he supplied a huge army at Dives and then at St Valéry-sur-Somme, which needed about 9,000 wagon loads of food a month, without despoiling the local inhabitants. He developed an effective intelligence system, with spies from across the Channel telling him of Harold's every move. He proved the veracity of the old military maxim, 'time spent in reconnaissance is time never wasted', by using his cavalry to scout the enemy. Before battle William protected his bases by building castles, often a simple wooden structure erected on a mound of hastily dug earth. After victory he used castles, usually more elaborate stone buildings, to hold the land he had gained. Following the Conquest he built some 80 castles in England.

But above all the key to William's success as a royal warrior was his outstanding physical courage. William of Poitiers recalls him as a young man.[24]

> Armed and mounted he had no equal in all Gaul. It was a sight both delightful and terrible to see him managing his horse, girt with sword, his shield gleaming, his helmet and lance alike menacing . . . in him courage and virtue shone forth.

Replete with valour William had no doubt about its value. 'Wars are won by the courage rather than the number of soldiers,' he assured his men just before the Battle of Hastings.[25]

William's genius as a royal warrior reached its zenith at Hastings, which was not a foregone conclusion. Normandy was smaller than England. Crossing the Channel, particularly against the prevailing winds, was a risky venture. If only Harold had fought at Hastings with the originality he had shown three weeks earlier at Stamford Bridge he could well have won. In fact Harold's victory in the north was the root cause of his defeat in the south. He repeated the tactics which had worked against Harold Hardrada – a fast march against the enemy to force a decisive battle at the first possible opportunity, catching the enemy by surprise. William astutely provoked him into doing so by ravaging the area around Hastings, forcing Harold to fulfil his feudal obligation to rescue his vassals as soon as he could. This meant that the Anglo-Saxon forces arrived piecemeal at Hastings, tired and late at night, having scant time to rest before fighting began at dawn. Harold had few archers (the Bayeux Tapestry depicts but one), and had left as many as a third of his troops behind in the rush to fight and win another Stamford Bridge.

Nonetheless the army that Harold commanded at Hastings was the largest any Anglo-Saxon monarch had ever led into battle. The problem was that Harold's control was severely limited. William divided his army into three, the Normans, the Bretons and the French, facilitating his ability to command. Harold kept his in one long line, his personal house-carls intermingled with the local fyrd, severely restricting his ability to direct events.

Perhaps this, plus Harold's better defensive position, helps explain why William took the offensive: he knew that he must win a decisive engagement before disease eroded his army, and reinforcements could join Harold's. The cunning of the feigned retreat, the luck of Harold's death, his own personal valour, and a military character and skills forged since childhood, brought William victory. Had he not won decisively at Hastings, had the day ended with no clear-cut winner, then the invasion would have surely failed.

It succeeded, and for the English the results were profound, some might say devastating. Ordericus Vitalis, the duke's apologist, admitted as much:[26]

> The native inhabitants were crushed, imprisoned, disinherited, banished and scattered beyond the limits of the country; while his own vassals and adherents were exalted in wealth and honours and raised to all offices of state.

Ever since the conquest historians have debated its effects. 'Without the Normans what had it ever been?' sneered Thomas Carlyle in 1858. Few accepted his answer, 'A gluttonous nation of Jutes and Anglos capable of no great combinations', preferring instead Maurice Ashley's conclusion that 'the conquest was purchased at a terrible cost out of all proportion to the benefits it conferred.'[27]

A few benefited – those Norman freebooters to whom William awarded about half of England which he claimed by right of conquest. Many suffered grievously including the Anglo-Saxon élite, most of whom perished at Hastings or during later rebellions, or were driven into exile.

The Norman conquest changed the direction of English history away from a Scandinavian nexus towards continental Europe. The introduction of Norman French on top of the old Anglo-Saxon foundation helped produce a language whose rich vocabulary still reflects social nuances. William invaded with the support of the Catholic church: his troops fought under a banner the pope had specially sent. So it is not surprising that after 1066 the church became stronger in England, and the links with Rome remained vibrant for nearly 500 years until the Reformation. Because the rulers spoke Norman-French and the peasants Anglo-Saxon the language barrier widened the gap between the conquerors and vanquished. After the conquest England and Normandy had common rulers, the Channel being both a bridge and divide between the two parts of the same realm that was both a source of strength and weakness. Until Mary Tudor finally lost Calais in 1558 England was constantly involved with trying to defend and expand its possessions on the continent. Since the king could not be in both parts of his realm at the same time, he had to develop systems to administer his dominions in his absence.

The most important change introduced by the conquest was the feudal system. Although the term was not coined until the eighteenth century, at the time everyone in England knew what was involved. Perhaps parts of the feudal system had been developed by the Anglo-Saxons before 1066. Afterwards it was far more cohesive and regular, because William, by right of conquest, imposed it rapidly from the top down.

The system was designed for war in an age when money to raise and pay soldiers was in short supply. Instead of paying taxes individuals became vassals to a lord, to whom they owed allegiance and military service receiving protection and land in return. At the apex was the king, who kept as much as a quarter of the land in England for himself, gave a quarter to the church, and half to several thousand knights, of whom no more than a couple of dozen got the lion's share. They paid their rent, as it were, in military service, providing the king with a set number of knights for so many days a year, based on the amount of land they received. They might divide their land amongst other tenants, who agreed to provide them with military service. At the bottom of the system was the individual serf who, tied to the land the local lord of the manor had given him, was obliged to pay for it by working on his master's fields.

In many ways this system was designed to produce heavily armed knights, protected by a screen of lower-class infantry. The knights spent much time in training to fight on horseback, imbuing the traditions of a warrior caste. In fact the knight was less significant than the emphasis on him would warrant. Battles, which were exceedingly rare, were usually won by foot soldiers, not heavy cavalry, while the hastily built motte and bailey castles, of wood constructed on an earthen mound, needed small garrisons of foot soldiers.

A warrior ethos often becomes stronger as that warrior's military importance declines. If feudal society was a society geared for war, the knight was its main driving force. They were 'a class', observed William of Malmesbury, the twelfth-century historian, 'full of greed and violence'.[28] Thus they developed a form of warfare which for them, at least, was fairly safe. Of course fighting on horseback is intrinsically far less dangerous than on foot, if only because your mount's four feet can let you escape far faster than your own two. A horseman can carry more armour than a foot soldier, who was given the most hazardous duties. War was even more harmful for civilians. 'First waste the land, and then deal with the foe,' Philip, Count of Flanders advised King David of Scotland in 1174, underscoring the reality that most armies were not defeated in battles or even sieges, but instead were starved into submission.[29]

In contrast to the knightly ethos, in which war, honour, courage and even rebellion were the main motivations for the élite, feudalism helped construct a strong centralised government that produced domestic stability. William the Conqueror's successors developed efficient legal systems that kept the king's peace, effective financial institutions that collected ever increasing taxes, and strengthened relations with the church that provided literate officials to do the king's bidding. The king's mightiest subjects, the nobility and barons, resisted this growth in royal power because it came at the expense of their own. As royal power grew, a reaction developed, producing the anarchy of weak central rule and even civil war, which in its turn produced the counter-reaction of a strong monarch.

Even though king and barons conflicted, they shared the same warrior ethos – or if the king did not he was in serious trouble. This meant that they had to satisfy their desire for glory, which only war could provide, by fighting overseas. Such of course was expensive and well beyond the capabilities of the feudal system, which with its limited military service, normally of 40 days, was designed for home defence. So paradoxically the needs of those royal warriors who developed feudalism in England led to the use of mercenary troops for foreign wars, which in its turn contributed to the end of feudalism. To put it crudely, until the waging of war became the responsibility of the institution of the crown in the eighteenth century, a king could fight or rule, but rarely could he do both. But during the middle ages being a great warrior was far more important than being a great ruler.

William II (1089–1100), known as Rufus for his red hair, was by all accounts a brave warrior. As a young man he had been wounded fighting for his father outside Gerberoy in Normandy. Only two of the ten years of his reign were ones of peace: he put down a baronial rebellion, invaded Scotland twice and Wales once, and fought four campaigns in France. A brave man, fully conversant with the business of war, he was a warrior king. He could well have been a homosexual, which endeared him in the man's world of war, even if it caused churchmen (who wrote the history) to despise him. They were convinced that his death during a hunting accident in the New Forest in December 1100 was more than an accident: it was divine punishment.

His younger brother, Henry I (1100–1135), who on their father's death eleven years before had been left some money and a few scattered estates, did not pause to ponder the issue. Within a day he seized the treasury at Winchester and three days later had himself crowned king of both England and Normandy, which the Conqueror had bequeathed to his older brother Robert, who at the time was away on a crusade. On his return Robert invaded England, but failed to regain the kingdom. Five years later Henry I attacked Normandy, and defeated his brother at the Battle of Tinchebray, keeping him prisoner until he died in Cardiff Castle eighteen years later. Robert was not the only man to feel Henry's anger. He once had a captured knight blinded because, the king explained, he was a 'facetious joker', who 'wrote scurrilous songs about me, and sang them in public'.[30] Henry was something of a puritan. Before the Battle of Tinchebray Serlo, the Bishop of Séez, preached a sermon before Henry's troops condemning degenerate affectations such as long hair and pointed shoes. Henry not only endorsed the sentiments, but was the first to volunteer for a short back and sides administered by the bishop (who just happened to have a pair of shears with him). The rest of the royal household knights followed suit although with far less enthusiasm.[31]

Although only eleven of the first twenty-four years of Henry I's reign were peaceful, he was not an especially great warrior, preferring instead to buy off his enemies, and build castles to prevent revolts by nobles. By developing machinery to collect taxes and laying the foundations for the system of royal justice and judges, Henry strengthened the monarchy. He was, however, unable to provide the one thing to ensure dynastic stability, a live male heir.

He was not, however, without issue. His twenty-one bastards are the record for any British king. But Henry I had only one legitimate son, William the Atheling, who was drowned in November 1120 when the *White Ship* sunk. On their way back to England for Christmas the crew and passengers anticipated the festive season by getting so drunk that they ran into a rock in Harfleur Harbour. Only two of the three hundred aboard survived. The disaster left Henry with only one legitimate heir, Matilda, who was married to the Emperor Henry V of Germany. Fully aware of English prejudices against women (not to say those against German emperors), Henry thrice got his barons to swear that they would accept Matilda as his successor and, to ensure their continued acceptance after Emperor Henry died, remarried her to Geoffrey, Count of Anjou.

It did not work. When Henry died in December 1135 having defied his doctor's orders by eating a surfeit of lampreys, the small eels of which he was fatally fond, Stephen of Blois, who was the Conqueror's grandson, moved swiftly to take over the throne – just as Henry I had done 35 years before. Stephen's brother, Henry, the Bishop of Winchester, claimed that on his deathbed Henry I had changed his mind: instead of leaving the throne to his daughter, Matilda, he had actually conveyed it to Stephen. This persuaded the Archbishop of Canterbury to crown him in December. Many of the barons rallied to his side hoping that Stephen would be a weak king under whom they could become more powerful. His martial reputation was stained by the cowardice of his father, Stephen, Count of Chartres, whom most people believed had during the First Crusade sneaked away from the Siege of Antioch in 1098 by sliding down a rope from the walls at night, and scarpering home. Some barons took the opportunity of Stephen's accession to rebel, but he easily crushed Baldwin de Redver's rising in Exeter, and Hugh Bigod's in East Anglia. To take control of the machinery of government Stephen arrested the Bishops of Ely, Lincoln and Salisbury, Henry I's chief administrators. After his troops had routed a Scots invasion force led by King David at the Battle of the Standard in August 1138, it seemed that the crown had never sat more securely on Stephen's head.

His mistake, however, was to break with Robert, Earl of Gloucester, the oldest and favourite of Henry I's illegitimate children. Robert joined his half-sister Matilda on the continent and together they landed at Arundel Castle in August of 1139 with 140 knights. Stephen moved rapidly against them, but allowed Robert to slip out of the castle to make his way to Bristol, and – more serious – permitted Matilda to join him there. This error resulted in desultory siege warfare continuing until early 1141 when Stephen's efforts to capture Lincoln Castle, where Robert of Gloucester's daughter had taken refuge, prompted a rare battle. Robert naturally raced to his daughter's aid, and Stephen, surprisingly, took the unusual risk of agreeing to do battle. At Lincoln on 2 February he was defeated and captured.

It was 'at this very moment Stephen, King of England, languished wretchedly in a dungeon,' recalled Ordericus Vitalis, that Matilda made peace with Henry, Bishop of Winchester, who had fallen out with his older brother Stephen after the king arrested the bishops of Ely, Lincoln and Salisbury. Bishop Henry persuaded the church to proclaim Matilda 'Lady of England'.[32]

England's lady straightaway snatched defeat from the jaws of victory. She behaved, one commentator recalled, like 'a virago'. Perhaps Matilda could not forget that she had once been empress of Germany: years later after old age had mellowed the sharpness of her character, Nicholas of St Jacques nonetheless described Matilda as 'of the stock of tyrants'.[33] She treated allies with public disdain, not deigning to rise to greet Henry of Winchester, instead reproving him with 'harsh and insulting language'. When a deputation of Londoners petitioned her to lower taxes, 'She, with a grim look, her forehead wrinkled in a frown, every trace of a woman's gentleness removed from her face, blazed with unbearable fury.' Worse still she threatened to remove London's privileged status as a commune. Outraged, its citizens spontaneously rebelled, driving Matilda and Robert of Gloucester to seek refuge in Bristol.

From here she moved against Bishop Henry, who was holding Winchester Castle. After two months of complicated fighting, in which the city was burned and its inhabitants plundered, Matilda was forced to escape back to Bristol, while her half-brother, who stayed behind to enable her to do so, was taken prisoner. In December he was exchanged for the king, and all hope of one side or the other winning a rapid victory was lost.

For the next five years England was the scene of considerable fighting as each side built, besieged and surrendered castles. Stephen invested Matilda in Oxford Castle for three months before she escaped just before Christmas 1142, some say by being lowered down the wall by rope in the night. She made her way through the snow with only four companions to the safety of the West Country. Tired and defeated Matilda eventually left England in 1147.

That did not mean that the hopes of her party, the Angevins, absconded with her. The same year Henry, her son by Geoffrey of Anjou, invaded England with the help of King David of Scotland. Although his assault failed, he managed to avoid capture, returning to Normandy in 1152. On 6 January of the following year he returned to England with an invasion force of 140 knights, and 3,000 infantry. After inconclusive fighting around Malmesbury and Wallington, in which neither side was willing to risk a pitched battle, Henry and Stephen made a truce, which by the end of the year had become the formal Peace of Winchester. In it Henry swore fealty to Stephen, who in return agreed to accept him as the next king of England when he died, which he did less than a year later in October 1154.

Few mourned Stephen then and fewer have since. Why? Stephen was not without his military virtues. He could act decisively and move fast. He used terror to persuade castles to surrender. Undoubtedly he was brave. At the battle of Lincoln he fought 'like a lion, grinding his teeth and foaming at the mouth like a boar',[34] swinging an axe after his sword broke in the frenzy of combat. Yet notwithstanding his courage Stephen was taken prisoner in a battle which he should never have joined in the first place. Outnumbered, he fought at Lincoln because 'he refused to sully his fame by the disgrace of flight', explained the *Gesta Stephani*, the contemporary royalist history. 'The Willful prince,' Ordericus Vitalis agreed, 'judged it dishonourable to put off battle for any reason.'[35] Both are clear references to his father, whose cowardice at Antioch haunted Stephen's military career.

Perhaps this fear enhanced Stephen's insecurity, making him terrified of being dominated by anyone whose talents exceeded his own. He arrested the bishops of Ely, Lincoln and Salisbury on charges as flimsy as those he later used to imprison the earl of Chester, and Geoffrey de Mandeville, two magnates with large baronial followings. All too often decisiveness became impulsiveness. His failure to follow Henry's practice of using sheriffs as sources of intelligence led to disaster. He lacked the generosity of spirit to win men's loyalty. In 1137, for instance, the combined Norman/Flemish army he commanded disintegrated due to a drunken brawl in which several men were killed.

Stephen's failures would have mattered less had they not been matched by Matilda's. Neither could bring the war to a close. She captured him at Lincoln; he surrounded her at Oxford. But on both occasions each of them got away to fight another day in a war of sieges that were protracted, bloody and inconclusive.

Unlike the other great civil war of the seventeenth century, in which battles were the decisive military events, that of the twelfth century was one of sieges, which by their nature tend to drag on, producing no clear result. They do, of course, produce immense casualties, particularly among civilians whose land is wasted in order to starve nearby castles into surrendering. Since castles were increasingly being built of stone, and their foundations were sunk further into the ground to frustrate mining operations, siege warfare became more drawn out.

Understandably Stephen's reign has been seen as one of anarchy. Some of the troubles were bearable. When the well in Exeter Castle dried up after a three-month siege the defenders had to drink wine and even boil their food in it! Most ordeals were far worse, largely because the feudal system which was designed to provide heavy cavalry for a short term could not support mercenaries over the long one, forcing them to plunder.

'It is not surprising that I take things from other people,' Brian fitzCount justified his looting of merchants, 'in order to sustain my life and the lives of my men.'[36] Pillage grew increasingly heartless near castles, where stationary garrisons had to support themselves over the long run. *The Peterborough Chronicle* (1070–1154) relates:[37]

> When the castles were built . . . they filled them with devils and wicked men . . . they took those people who had any goods . . . and put them in prison and tortured them . . . to extort gold and silver . . . they hung them by the thumbs or by the head . . . knotted ropes were put round their head and twisted till they penetrated the brain. They put them in prisons where there were adders and snakes and toads. . . . When the wretched people had no money to give, they robbed and burned all the villages, so you could easily go a whole day's journey and never find anyone occupying a village, and no land tilled . . . it was openly said that Christ and his saints slept. Such things we have suffered nineteen winters for our sins.

Historians have debated the extent of this anarchy, pointing out that Peterborough was in a particularly hard hit area. But folk had no doubt that during Stephen's reign they had survived a terrible time which they had no wish to repeat. So when Henry II became king in 1135 they were ready to support the establishment of a strong monarchy, which was able to survive the reign of an equally flawed warrior, yet a king of unsurpassed reputation – a royal hero.

Richard I (1189–99) was only fifteen when he first saw combat in 1173, fighting against his father, Henry II, in France. Only one of the remaining twenty-six years of his life was peaceful. After coming to terms with his father he fought for him, often against the king of France, and occasionally against his elder brother, Henry. The latter's death in 1183 enabled him to inherit the throne when his father passed away in July 1189.

On becoming king Richard wasted no time in setting out on a crusade, the finest mission any Christian knight could perform. Ever since the Muslims captured Jerusalem in 1187 the church had encouraged people to fight to regain the city of Our Lord's death and resurrection. The crusades were an outlet for the violence that was endemic to feudalism. They were also directed against infidels, whom Christians believed were unworthy of God's love. After raising as much money as he could, Richard set sail for Calais in December, and made an alliance with the French king, Philip Augustus. By the following September they were in Sicily where the two kings fell out, largely because Richard refused to marry Alice, Philip's sister, to whom he had been betrothed for a quarter of a century. The following April the monarchs, having patched up their differences, set sail for Acre. A storm diverted Richard's fleet to Cyprus, whose tyrannical ruler, Isaac Comnenus, insulted Richard's sister, Joan, and Berengaria, his prospective bride and the daughter of the king of Navarre. So Richard attacked Cyprus, overrunning the island in just under three weeks. Thus he acquired a secure base for the invasion of the Holy Land.

On 8 June Richard and Philip Augustus landed at Acre and besieged the citadel. On 12 July, five days after promising Saladin, the Arab leader, that they would hold out to the death, the garrison surrendered. At this point, Philip Augustus, whose relations with Richard had become intolerable, went home. Unable to come to terms with Saladin, and unwilling to leave so many enemy unguarded in his rear, on August 20 Richard had the 3,000 garrison slaughtered in cold blood, an atrocity which even the king's most ardent defenders have found hard to excuse [Plate 2.2 – colour]. Five days later, fully rested from their exertions, the Crusaders set out for Jaffa.

As they marched south along the coast road, being supplied from ships, the Crusaders had to beat off enemy skirmishers. Richard was slightly wounded leading a counter-attack. By 7 September they reached Arsuf, just north of Jaffa, where a Muslim army 30,000 strong waited. Richard drew his men up in a defensive formation. He allowed the enemy to attack first, squandering their strength against his defences. Toward nightfall, however, the Knights Hospitalers could stay still no longer, and charged. The battle hung in the balance as both sides assaulted each other in confused array, until Richard himself led the final charge that put the enemy to flight.

Arsuf was the climax of Richard's military career. Within four months he was to see its nadir. Since the objective of the Crusades was to restore Jerusalem to Christian rule, Richard moved east from Jaffa arriving at Beit-Nuba, only twelve miles from the Holy City, on 11 December. It was the closest Richard got to his goal. Some say he refused to look, closing his eyes on the prize which he realised he could never win. Lacking the supplies for a successful siege, Richard turned his attention to building a firm base on the Mediterranean coast so those who followed might have better fortune. He personally led several small reconnaissance patrols disguised as Bedouin, often coming close to being captured. In June he discovered a large caravan carrying gold for Saladin's army, went back for reinforcements, and personally led a successful attack. Two months later, after the Muslims captured Jaffa, Richard sailed to relieve the citadel, running his ship on the beach, being the first to land. Within an hour his whole army was ashore, and drove the enemy out of the harbour. Three days later Saladin arrived with a relief force, which Richard, with only 17 knights and 300 infantry, cowed into submission. The king personally rode in front of the Muslims, taunting them to fight. None dared. One confessed, 'We never had among our enemies a man bolder or more crafty than he.'[38] A month after making a truce with Saladin in September Richard sailed for home, aware that after so long an absence affairs in Normandy and England urgently required his presence.

On the way back Richard was shipwrecked near Trieste. On the run for several weeks, Leopold of Austria captured him outside Vienna just before Christmas 1192, holding Richard in Dürnstein Castle on the Danube before selling him to the Emperor of Germany, Henry VI, for half the anticipated ransom of 100,000 marks. While back home his brother John did all he could to prevent the collection of this huge amount – equal to two years' annual revenue for the crown – and even swore fealty to Philip Augustus, Richard's ministers raised the money with a 25 per cent tax on income and movable property. The king was released in February 1194, arriving in England six weeks later.

Throughout this ordeal Richard behaved with honest fortitude. The legend of his faithful minstrel, Blondel, who roamed Europe, standing outside castles singing a song that only the two of them knew, until he found his master who sang back from a dungeon, only added to Richard's romantic aura. Contemporaries were convinced he had behaved heroically. 'No tribulation could cloud the countenance of this serene prince,' wrote Ralph of Coggeshall, 'His words remained cheerful and jocund, his actions fierce and most courageous.'[39]

People did not feel the same about Leopold. The pope excommunicated him for kidnapping a crusader, a soldier of Christ under the church's protection. More efficacious than the Holy Father was Leopold's horse, which in December 1194 stumbled, trapping the duke. His foot turned gangrenous. No surgeon dared amputate. So the Duke Leopold had to hold an axe close to his leg, ordering a servant to smite it with a mallet. After the third blow the operation was over: after five days the duke was dead.

Richard spent two months in England before returning to France. He passed the next five years waging a long and complicated series of wars to deal with rebels, incited by his brother John and Philip Augustus who had taken advantage of his imprisonment to conquer territory in Eastern Normandy and Poitou. To regain his lands Richard used two techniques. First, he employed mercenaries. While well trained and highly manoeuvrable, they were expensive and rapacious, and thus alienated many of Richard's French subjects. Second, he built castles, such as that at Gaillard overlooking the River Seine. It was exceedingly expensive, costing £12,000, being laid out so that an enemy could not approach without coming under intense fire. Even if the walls had been made of butter, Richard boasted, he could have held the Gaillard Castle against all comers.

While Richard was besieging Chalus Castle, near Limoges, in March 1199 a crossbowman, who had been braving showers of arrows, shot at the king. Admiring the fellow's courage, Richard neglected to raise his shield, and was hit in the shoulder. He tried to pull the bolt out, but the shaft broke. By candle-light a local surgeon hacked out the iron head, a long as a man's palm, but the wound turned septic. Doubling every forty minutes the bacteria soon destroyed the body's main organs. As Richard lay dying the castle was captured and its garrison hanged except for the sniper, one Bertrand de Gurdon, who was brought to the royal tent.

'What wrong have I done to you that you should kill me?' asked the king.

Bertrand, who explained that his father and two bothers had died fighting Richard, scornfully replied, 'Take your revenge anyway you like. Now that I have seen you on your death bed I shall gladly endure any torment you may devise.' So impressed was Richard by the fellow's boldness that he ordered him freed.

Richard's followers (who were not as forgiving, for they skinned Bertrand alive), were distraught. 'O death! Do you realise what you have snatched from out,' lamented Geoffrey of Vinsauf, 'He was the lord of warriors, the glory of kings, the delight of the world.'[40] This herculean view of Richard was widely shared until the Victorian age, when the historian, Bishop William Stubbs deemed him 'a man of blood . . . a bad son, a bad husband, a selfish ruler, and a vicious man'.[41] To be sure, by killing three thousand Muslim prisoners he was a man of blood. Admittedly he did rebel against his father, yet he spent much longer fighting for Henry II, so by the standards of his age he was not a particularly bad son. Richard was a far worse husband. He spent little time with Berengaria, having no children by her. Stories about his promiscuity with both sexes abound – which upset the Victorians far more than murdering thousands of heathen. While Richard was probably not a homosexual, he was credited with avaricious appetites. It was said that while a prisoner he seduced Margery, Henry VI's daughter. Once he threatened, so another story goes, to burn down a nunnery if they did not let him have his way with a particular nun. Asked what attracted him most to the woman, he replied her eyes. So the nun cut them out and sent them to him to protect her honour.

Chief among the criticisms of Richard is that he spent only six months of his ten-year reign in England. As *1066 and All That* (a sure guide to popular misconceptions about history), observed, 'Whenever he returned to England he always set out immediately for the Mediterranean and was therefore known as Richard Gare de Lyon.'[42]

Such observations were designed to be humorous. That of J. A. Brundage, who as recently as 1974 described Richard as 'certainly one of the worst rulers that England has ever had', were not.[43] To be sure he failed to capture Jerusalem. Yet the second Crusade was not a complete failure. By putting the eastern seaboard of the Holy Land firmly under Christian control he ensured the enclave's survival for another century, while his capture of Cyprus facilitated the introduction of Arabic goods and ideas into the West.

In the last couple of decades historians have agreed with the verdict of Richard's contemporaries. 'He had the valour of Hector, the magnanimity of Achilles; in courage he was equal to Alexander and Roland,' thought Ambroise, the Anglo-Norman minstrel who accompanied the king on the crusade.[44] 'Sir, I say with pride,' his Archbishop of Canterbury, Hubert Walter, boasted to Saladin, 'That my Lord is the finest knight on earth.'[45] The Muslim leader qualified his agreement: 'Your king is a man of honour and very brave, but he is imprudent, indeed absurdly so, in the way he plunges into the middle of danger and in his reckless indifference to his own safety.'[46]

Yet it was this reckless courage that endeared Richard to his followers and terrified his opponents. In 1194, on learning that Richard had been freed from prison and was back in England, Henry de Pommeroy, governor of the rebels in St Michael's Mount, dropped dead of shock. He knew two things. First, that the presence of the king in war at the head of his army was worth thousands of fighting men, and, second, that for a medieval monarch there was no higher calling than being an effective royal warrior.

Notes

1. J. H. Robinson (ed.), *Readings in European History* (Boston: Ginn and Co., 1904), 224–9.
2. William of Poitiers, 'The Deeds of William, Duke of the Normans and King of the English', in David C. Douglas and George W. Greenaway, *English Historical Documents, 1042–1189* (London: Eyre Methuen, 1981), II, 239.
3. William of Poitiers, quoted by P. Young and J. Adair, *Hastings to Culloden: Battles of Britain* (Stroud: Sutton, 1996), 18.
4. Robert fitz Wimarch, quoted by William of Poitiers, *Histoire de Guillaume le Conquérant* (Paris: 1962), 170.
5. Quoted by H. R. Loyn, *The Norman Conquest* (New York: Norton, 1967), 34.

6. D. C. Douglas, *William the Conqueror: the Norman Impact on England* (London: Eyre Methuen, 1964), 374.
7. William of Jumièges, in Douglas and Greenaway, *op. cit.*, II, 229.
8. Ibid., II, 307.
9. Quoted by M. Ashley, *The Life and Times of William I* (London: Weidenfeld and Nicolson, 1973), 94.
10. William of Poitiers, in Douglas and Greenaway, *op. cit.*, II, 234.
11. William of Jumièges, in ibid., II, 229.
12. William of Poitiers, in ibid., II, 236.
13. Ordericus Vitalis, quoted by James Bradbury, *The Battle of Hastings* (Stroud: Sutton, 1998), 135.
14. William of Poitiers, in Douglas and Greenaway, *op. cit.*, II, 162–4.
15. Ibid., II, 240.
16. Quoted in R. A. Brown, 'The Battle of Hastings', *Proceedings of the Battle Conference* (Woodbridge: Boydell, 1983), 11.
17. William of Poitiers, in Douglas and Greenaway, *op. cit.*, II, 246.
18. Quoted by Douglas, *op. cit.*, 221.
19. Ibid., II, 306.
20. Quoted by J. Gillingham, 'William the Bastard at War,' in S. Morillo, *The Battle of Hastings* (Woodbridge: Boydell, 1996), 102.
21. William of Poitiers, in Douglas and Greenaway, *op. cit.*, II, 179–80.
22. Sigmund Freud, *Collected Papers* (London: The International Psycho-Analytic Library, 1952), 367.
23. William of Poitiers, in Douglas and Greenway, *op. cit.*, II, 200–4.
24. William of Poitiers, *Histoire de Guilliame le Conquérant*, 12–14.
25. Ibid., 157.
26. Quoted by Ashley, *op. cit.*, 207.
27. Carlyle quoted in Douglas, *op. cit.* 6. Ashley, *op. cit.*, 216.
28. C. Holdsworth, 'War and Peace in the Twelfth Century: The Reign of Stephen Reconsidered', in B. P. McGuire, *War and Peace in the Middle Ages* (Copenhagen: Reitzel, 1987), 76.
29. Quoted by W. L. Warren, *Henry II* (Berkeley and Los Angeles: University of California Press, 1973), 231.
30. C. W. Hollister, *Monarchy, Magnates and Institutions in the Anglo-Norman World* (London: Hambledon Press, 1980), 291.
31. J. O. Prestwick, 'The Military Household of the Norman Kings', *English Historical Review*, 96 (1981), 29–30.
32. J. Bradbury, *Stephen and Matilda, and the Civil War of 1139–53* (Stroud: Sutton, 1996), 100.
33. M. Chibnal, *The Empress Matilda* (Oxford: Oxford University Press, 1991), 204.
34. Robert of Torigny, quoted by Bradbury, *op. cit.*, 97.
35. Ibid., 91.
36. R. H. C. Davis, *King Stephen, 1135–54* (Harlow: Longmans, 1990), 64.
37. H. A. Cronne, *The Reign of King Stephen: Anarchy in England, 1135–54* (London: Weidenfeld and Nicolson, 1970), 13.
38. Quoted by J. Gillingham, *Richard I* (New Haven: Yale University Press, 1999), 19.

39. Quoted by Gillingham, *op. cit.*, 254.
40. Ibid., 321.
41. A. Bridge, *Richard the Lionheart* (London: Grafton, 1989), 244.
42. W. C. Sellar and R. J. Yeatman, *1066 and All That* (London: Magnum, 1980), 23.
43. J. A. Brundage, *Richard Lionheart* (New York: Scribner, 1974), 262.
44. J. Gillingham, 'The Art of Kingship, Richard I, 1189–99', *History Today*, 35/4 (1985), 27.
45. Ibid., 16.
46. J. Matthews, *Warriors in Ancient Times* (Poole: Firebird, 1993), 174.

chapter 3

WITH GRACE AND MIGHT
OF CHIVALRY

> *Our king went forth to Normandy,*
> *With grace and might of chivalry.*
> *There God for him wrought marvelously*
> *Deo gracias*
> *Deo gracias Anglia*
> *Rede pro victoria.*
>   *Anon.*, The Agincourt Carol, *c. 1415.*

Nowadays people increasingly get their view of the past not from history books but from film and television. Ask anyone what they associate with Henry V (1413–22), and they will most likely answer the Shakespearian view of the heroic warrior king, portrayed by Laurence Olivier in his 1944 film or by Kenneth Branagh in that of 1989. According to the king's most recent biographer, 'Shakespeare was to create a Henry V destined to become part of England's cultural heritage'[1] [Plate 3.1].

Why is this so? In one sense the answer is very simple. The story of Henry's invasion of France, his victory at Agincourt and rough wooing of Princess Katharine, the king of France's daughter, is an attractive one, told by England's greatest dramatist. Certainly Henry was also personally brave, a quality that all people treasure in their leaders. The transformation of the irresponsible, hell-rousing Prince Hal into the sober, virtuous King Henry is one for which the parents of many an adolescent male pray. Admittedly Jack Falstaff is treated shabbily, but few of us are generous to those whom we blame for corrupting our children. On the stage the courtship of Katharine is a romantic ending to a bloody saga. In reality Henry may have been more influenced by her dowry of a million gold crowns than by her beauty, for after only two days' honeymoon he returned to campaigning. Many of us, who

Plate 3.1   Olivier in Henry V © Corbis

(I suspect) form a majority of males, find the unsophisticated wooing of Katharine reassuring. No matter if we lack the patter, the continental, slightly smarmy hand-kissing of a Don Juan or Casanova (both foreigners), as honest-no-nonsense Brits we too can get the girl in the last reel.

Shakespeare's Henry V is a great patriotic icon who epitomised the national virtues by fairly beating the traditional enemy, France, in both love and war. The English have portrayed Agincourt as one of those sublime deciding events – like the Armada, Trafalgar or the Battle of Britain – when, backs to the wall, the happy few did what England has always expected – saving a more civilised way of life. According to the jingoistic myth they were ordinary men. Those few, that band of brothers who fought at Agincourt were ancestors of the Tommies, Jocks, Taffs and Micks who formed squares at Waterloo, went over the top at the Somme, jumped at Arnhem, or yomped across the Falklands. If the English slaughtered a few French prisoners after Agincourt, the atrocity is ignored, or justified as righteous revenge done in hot blood for the murder of the unarmed boys who were left out of battle to guard the baggage train.

The heroic view of Henry V has remained constant over the centuries. Shakespeare created it to bring the paying public to the Globe, as well as to attract royal patronage. Henry VIII, Queen Elizabeth's father, had tried to emulate – even exceed – Henry V's achievements by twice invading France, and if his efforts were ignominious failures, the bard was certainly not going to point it out. John Churchill, the duke of Marlborough, the great scourge of the French during the early eighteenth century, admitted that Shakespeare's plays were 'the only English History I ever read'. During the Napoleonic Wars recruiting posters appealed to the glorious memory of Agincourt. The French remained the enemy: and thus Henry's fame as their devastator lasted for four and a half centuries. 'A true English heart breathes, calm and strong, throughout the whole business,' Thomas Carlyle wrote in 1841 about Shakespeare's hero.[2] For the Victorians Henry V became the best sort of public school boy. 'He was religious, pure in life, temperate, liberal, careful and yet splendid,' wrote Bishop William Stubbs, 'merciful, truthful, honourable, direct in word, provident in council, prudent in judgment, modest in looks, magnanimous in acts, a true Englishman.'[3] Safe from all temptations, his God-given goal was, apparently, to invade other nations.

Winston Churchill, who helped direct a more recent invasion of Normandy, called Henry V 'the gleaming king'. To bring that view to the attention of the general public he ensured that the few reels of technicolour film available in England in 1943 were used to make Laurence Olivier's version of the play. (The fact that the role of the British Army was played by the Irish Army, the British one having a more pressing engagement, was kept unsurprisingly quiet.) Those British and American soldiers who saw the film on its first run found it inspiring, although one GI recalled that halfway through a group of Free French soldiers in the row behind noisily walked out of the cinema.[4] Before the invasion Generals Eisenhower and Montgomery talked informally to their ordinary soldiers a little like 'Harry in the night', reassuring Privates Bates, Court and Williams. On D-Day over the loudspeakers of some landing craft the great speech about going once more into the breach was read to the troops, some of whom were within a few hours to become the English dead that would fill up the Atlantic Wall. Henry was as con-vinced as the allies would be of the rightness of his cause. He was certain that the Salic Law, which prevented inheritance descending through the female line, had unjustly deprived him of the throne of France. Such resentment might (like William the Conqueror's), have compelled him to mount an invasion. Certainly Henry protested – some might say he did so too much – that justice was on his side, and got the English church's approval before shedding a drop of blood. Had Henry V written his memoirs of the Norman invasion he might well have chosen the same title that General Eisenhower selected for his – *Crusade in Europe*.

One suspects too that had Kenneth Branagh's 1989 version of *Henry V* been shown in 1944 many soldiers might have deserted for fear joining England's dead. The differences between Olivier's and Branagh's interpretations of the play reflect how in half a century attitudes to portraying war have changed. A nuclear holocaust can never become a crusade. The study of war has altered, focusing on battle's ugly face, where there is little room for a romanticised Shakespearian hero. Much of the widely perceived image of Henry V is false. But that does not mean that Henry was a disastrous monarch. Far from it. 'Whether we like it or not, leadership in war was a vital aspect of kingship,' Professor Gillingham has written, 'and successful leadership required many qualities beside those of brute courage and physical strength.'[5]

If Henry V would rank among the most heroic of England's monarchs, there is no doubt that King John (1199–1216) and King Edward II (1307–27) would be cast as villains. Paradoxically their failures helped bring about the victory at Agincourt:

> *Our king went forth to Normandy,*
> *With grace and might of chivalry.*

Everyone knows that John was the 'bad king' who sealed (not signed, for he could not write) Magna Carta. According to Sir Edward Coke, the great seventeenth-century common lawyer, Magna Carta was 'the Charter of Liberty, because it maketh freemen'.[6] At the time it was a peace treaty that failed to make a peace. It had far more to do with King John's failures as a royal warrior than the barons' desire to establish the liberties due all free-born Englishmen.

Long before he became king in 1199 many had serious reservations about John's character and ability to rule. In 1185 when he was nineteen his father, Henry II, sent him to Ireland to learn about war. Instead of listening to the veterans, he laughed at the Irish with their shaggy beards and uncouth ways. After eight months John was sent home as a failure. Half a decade later, when John's elder brother Richard I went off on a crusade in 1189, he appointed William Longchamp, the Bishop of Ely, to run the realm in his absence, and ordered John to stay out of England for four years. On reaching Sicily, Richard designated his nephew Arthur, and not John, as his successor. His wariness was well founded. In 1190 John returned to England and managed to depose Longchamp, and the following year formed an alliance with King Philip Augustus of France, the two of them doing all they could to prevent the payment of Richard's ransom and return to England. On arriving home Richard forgave his brother's treachery with humiliating condescension: 'Think no more of it John, you are only a child who has had evil counsellors.' For the next half dozen years John faithfully fought for his brother in France. This, however, won him little support in England, where he was compared unfavourably to Richard Coeur de Lion: some called him John le Coeur de pouppée – the doll-hearted.[7] 'What hope remains to us now?' wondered Hubert Walter, the Archbishop of Canterbury, on learning of Richard's death in 1199, 'I can see no successor able to defend the kingdom.'[8]

King John's main problem was that he could not defend his French possessions. In 1200 John and Philip Augustus, the French king, made a peace treaty at Le Goulet in which he gave away so much – including an annual payment of 20,000 marks – that he earned the nickname, 'John Softsword'. The treaty did not hold, largely because John married Isabella of Angoulême, a rich heiress who was already betrothed to Hugh le Brun, one of Philip Augustus's vassals. So when the French king ordered John to appear before his court in Paris, John naturally refused, giving Philip Augustus an excuse to go to war. At first things went well for John, who managed to capture his nephew, Arthur of Brittany, who had sided with the French at Mirebeau. The turning point came in April 1203 when Arthur was murdered, some believed by John, who in a drunken rage threw a javelin at him, pinning his nephew against a wall. Arthur certainly died on John's orders, the corpse being thrown into the Seine in a sack weighted with stones. John's support on both sides of the Channel evaporated. In early 1204 Philip Augustus captured the strategically vital castle at Gaillard, which Richard had built boasting it was impregnable. By the end of the year John had lost the whole of Normandy.

The reaction to this humiliating defeat was bitter. 'Foul as it is, hell itself is defouled by the foul presence of John,' excoriated Matthew Paris, the contemporary historian.[9] John's failure as a military leader defined the rest of his reign, bringing about a second defeat in France, the sealing of Magna Carta, and a civil war.

After dealing with uprisings in Ireland, Scotland and Wales, and making peace with the Pope, John turned his attention back to recovering Normandy. On 30 May 1213 an Anglo-Flanders fleet of some 500 ships commanded by his half-brother William Longsword annihilated the armada which Philip Augustus had assembled at Bruges to invade England. In February 1214 John invaded southern France with a large army, but failed to do much damage to Philip Augustus, whose crushing victory at Bouvignes against the Flemish made John's position untenable, forcing him back to England in ignominy.

It was not just the shame but the cost of defeat which angered the barons, who resented being excluded from power. In early 1215 they and the king started preparing for civil war. Unable to find much support in France, John agreed to make peace with the barons at Runneymede in June. Magna Carta attempted to solve the feudal disputes between the king and his leading subjects. It failed – at least in the short term.

During October and November John skilfully besieged Rochester Castle. He used five stone-slinging engines to batter the garrison, and built mines under a corner tower, which he collapsed by burning down its wooden props with a fire fuelled by the fat from forty plump pigs. After John's successful sieges a monk from Cambridgeshire sardonically observed, 'Few cared to put their trust in castles.'[10]

Most of John's English subjects preferred instead to put their trust in the king of France. At the invitation of a group of barons the French invaded England in May 1216, and when Philip Augustus' troops entered London they were greeted as liberators. Meanwhile John divided his forces, and after campaigning in the north returned to go on the offensive in September capturing Cambridge and King's Lynn. Here he became ill, and after riding in great pain died at Newark on 18 October, having just lost the crown jewels in the Wash when a fast tide covered his slow-moving baggage train [Plate 3.2].

John – to put it simply – was a loser. In the seventeenth and eighteenth centuries when Magna Carta became the rallying point for the defence of the liberty first in England and then in the American colonies, John was seen as a tyrant, whose despotism justified revolution. The Victorians stressed his malice and promiscuity. 'His punishments were refinements of cruelty,' wrote J. R. Green, the best-selling historian, in 1874, 'his courts were a brothel where no woman was safe from a man's lust.'[11] Recently historians have praised the king's administrative achievements – the first continuous run of public records start in his reign. But these records were mainly for the taxes which John both invented and collected with great rigour in order to pay for the wars, which he lost.

Plate 3.2   King John out hunting (Cott. Claud. D.II. Folio No: 116. Min)
© By permission of the British Library

In part he lost them because France had superior resources: yet this does not explain why he precipitated a civil war. John's fundamental weaknesses were those of personality. He could not resist the temptation of kicking a man when he was down: he threw away his victory at Mirebeau in 1202 by starving forty captured knights to death. Uncertain in defeat, he was arrogant in victory. Treacherous himself, he was always on the lookout for treachery in others. Contemporaries stressed John's failures as a soldier. 'He was more given to luxurious ease than warlike exercise', concluded Gerald of Wales.[12] William le Breton reported that on learning the French had invaded Normandy John vowed, 'I will stay in a safe place with my dog.' Another chronicler reported that John failed to relieve the siege of Galliard Castle because he 'was enjoying all the pleasure of life with his queen'.[13]

Had Edward II (1307–27) enjoyed more of life's pleasures with Queen Isabella, his reign would not have been as great a failure as John's.

Edward has been rightly described as 'one of the most unsuccessful kings ever to rule England, whose reign was a series of political failures punctuated by acts of horrific violence' that were closely linked with his incompetence as a royal warrior.[14] Physically strong, even attractive, he could be lavish, unstable and cruel. The Victorians coyly described Edward II as 'eccentric'. He was a dilettante, dabbling in farming and horse breeding, thatching, hedging and ditching – uncouth, unmanly tasks fit for a peasant, not a king. Equally damaging was his homosexuality, an inclination which in the thirteenth century was associated with heresy. To compound the damage Edward chose as his lovers unsuitable arrogant young men, like the Gascon, Piers Gaveston.

The two met when Edward was sixteen and about to go on campaign with his father, Edward I, against the Scots; instead he preferred to spend a week with his friend at Bury St Edmunds monastery, rather than march north to the border. After he arrived in Scotland a local poet described the heir as:[15]

> *A Youth of Seventeen years of age*
> *And newly bearing arms,*
> *He was a well proportioned and handsome prince*
> *Of a certain disposition.*

Edward I, a successful soldier who had conquered Wales and much of Scotland, resented Gaveston's relationship with his son, which contemporaries described as 'beyond the bounds of moderation', and as 'wicked and forbidden', because the two youths took 'too much delight in sodomy'.[16] Early in 1307 Edward I banished Gaveston to Gascony. Six months later, on the death of his father, Edward II invited his friend back to England, showing him so much favour and showering him with so many goods that parliament insisted that he be exiled to Ireland. Once parliament dissolved, Piers returned, and a civil war broke out in which a group of barons captured and executed Gaveston. They left his headless corpse on the ground (to be rescued and sewn back together by four local cobblers), and Edward with an unbridled desire for revenge.

In an attempt to regain the support of his leading subjects so he would be powerful enough to punish his enemies Edward decided to complete his father's conquest of Scotland. In the summer of 1314 he led an army of 18,000 foot and 2,000 horse towards Stirling Castle, whose English garrison had agreed to surrender if not relieved by 24 June. On the 23rd, at Bannockburn, a couple of miles from his destination, Edward confronted the Scots army under King Robert the Bruce. The English were cocksure: a contemporary poet called them as 'too showy and pompous', while a chronicler described their leader as 'ablaze with strident anger'.

In contrast Robert the Bruce was an experienced general who chose to fight at his own time on his own ground and, as a contemporary poet put it:[17]

> *... for our lives*
> *And for our children and our wives,*
> *And for our freedom and our land.*
> *In battle we are forced to stand.*

The Battle of Bannockburn was unusual because it took place over two days. On the first Edward sent a small party of about 600 men to try and outflank the Scots on his right. When they were repulsed he ordered a frontal attack in which Sir Henry de Bohun personally challenged Robert the Bruce, who slew him with a single blow of a battle axe, shattering both the English army's morale and Sir Henry's skull. That evening, after the two sides pulled apart, Edward moved his forces to the Scot's left flank, neatly trapping himself in the 'V' formed by the branches of Bannockburn and Pelstreamburn. That night English spirits plummeted: those of the Scots soared for they had repulsed an army three times their size.

The following morning the Scots knelt in prayer before going into the attack. 'Those men kneel to ask for mercy,' Edward observed. 'You are right,' replied Sir Ingram de Umfravillc, 'they ask for mercy, but not from you.' The Scots did not need it. The English cavalry charges failed to break their infantry, who were armed with fourteen-foot pikes. Men and animals were impaled, riderless horses frenzied with fear added to the confusion. Each wave of attackers piled up on the bodies, some wounded, others dead, of those who had just been repulsed. When the earl of Gloucester urged caution, the king accused him of cowardice. So the earl, single-handed, charged the enemy in such a fury and so precipitously that he neglected to put on his armoured surcoat. His death broke the invaders' morale. The earl of Pembroke insisted the king, who had fought bravely, having already had one horse killed beneath him, leave the field of battle, lest he be captured and England forced to sign a humiliating peace and pay a huge ransom. Most of his army were not so lucky. Many panic-stricken Englishmen drowned in the Bannockburn and River Forth: still more fell victim to the blood lust of the Scots.

It was a decisive victory both for the Scots and for the infantry. 'Indeed I think it is unheard of in our time for such an army to be scattered so suddenly by infantry,' observed the *Vita Edward Secundi*.[18] Twenty years earlier Edward I's knights had crushed the closely packed Scots foot at the Battle of Dunbar. At Bannockburn the tables were turned. Even though guerrilla warfare dragged on for fifteen years, and Edward tried, but failed, to regain Scotland in 1322, Bannockburn gave that nation three hundred years of independence. For the English, it was, to quote a chronicler, 'an evil, miserable and calamitous day'.[19]

Bannockburn set the tone for the rest of Edward II's reign. While Edward managed to defeat the barons, executing their leader, the earl of Lancaster in 1321, he over-played his hand, extracting so severe a revenge, and showing so much favour to his new lover, Hugh Despenser, that he provoked another civil war. It was led by his wife, Queen Isabella and her lover, Roger Mortimer, the earl of Lancaster's son. Both had reason to hate the king and his favourite. When they captured Despenser they had him castrated before his heart was ripped out, his head was cut off and his body cut into quarters. After Edward abdicated they had him murdered in a most horrible – and some might say appropriate fashion – at Berkeley Castle.

It is ironic that the lessons of Edward II's defeat at Bannockburn were well learned by his son and heir Edward III (1327–77). He was a successful warrior, who helped bring about such a transformation in English warfare that some have called it a military revolution.[20]

Plutarch, the contemporary Italian poet, noticed the change. The English, he wrote in 1360, used to be 'the meekest of barbarians': now they were 'a fiercely bellicose nation'.[21] Major General J. F. C. Fuller agreed that the change 'made the English a military nation'.[22] The basic reason for this turnabout was the collapse of feudalism. William the Conqueror imposed a strong feudal system based on land holding to raise knights for the defence of the realm. The difficulty was that they could only serve forty days a year, and that the system raised fewer and fewer knights – less than 600 by Edward II's reign. For both cavalry and infantry feudal service was becoming more unpopular. One archer ordered to fight north of the border in 1300, turned up equipped with a bow and a single arrow, which he fired at the first Scot he came across. He missed, and then announced that duty done he was going home.

The weapon which did the most to end feudalism was the longbow. Six foot long, made from the heart of ash or yew, it was a formidable weapon that fired thirty-inch-long arrows tipped with an iron head that could be needle sharp, or barbed, making them hard to pull out. An archer could fire ten, perhaps twelve times a minute, producing a hail of arrows, recalled Jean Froissart, 'so thick and fast that it seemed like snow'. Unlike snow the arrows did terrible damage. At sixty yards they penetrated armour or three inches of oak, at a hundred they decimated the enemy, and at three hundred killed many and wounded even more. Until the introduction of the bolt-action magazine rifle in the late nineteenth century, the longbow was the most effective weapon an infantryman could carry. Unlike the rifle, and its predecessor, the musket, the longbow took years of training to master. Only the strongest could pull an 80–100 lb bow. Such men tended to come from poorer marginal areas, such as Cheshire and Wales. Dressed in rough deerskin jerkins, reinforced with steel plates, and wearing metal pots on their heads, they were so formidable a foe that if captured they were lucky to escape alive with the first two fingers of their right hands cut off so they could never again ply their lethal trade.

Equally hated were gunners, whose noisome weapons were generally regarded as the devil's spawn. Although the English first used cannon in 1327, initially they were very ineffective. During the English siege of Calais in 1347 a balladeer sneered:[23]

> Gunners, to show their art
> Into the town in many a part
> Shot many a full great stone.
> Thanked by God and Mary Mild,
> They hurt neither man, woman nor child.

Artillery was not to become a potent weapon for over a century, and then mainly in siege warfare.

In order to overcome the forty-day limit on feudal service kings came to rely on mercenaries recruited under contracts. This necessitated raising more taxes which helped parliament develop as a constitutional body, obliged the king to encourage trade so he could collect more customs duties, and led to the growth of towns. The monarch contracted with individuals to raise so many men for a set period at a set sum. Thus in 1415 Humphrey, the duke of Gloucester, agreed to provide 199 horsemen and 600 archers, while Thomas Chaucer (the poet's brother), promised 14 men-at-arms and 122 bowmen.

The feudal knight did not accept these changes without a fight. After all war, and winning honour in battle, was his *raison d'être*. War was an antidote to boredom. It was enjoyable. 'We are going to have some fun', declared Baron Bertrand Du Bon, a French knight as he charged into battle, pretty confident that he would emerge unharmed. For a heavily armed cavalryman combat had been a pretty safe adventure. Girded by armour he was secure from poorly armed spearmen, and if dismounted and captured could expect quarter from his fellows. 'If you are compelled to go into combat with another knight [and] if you gain the upper hand,' advised Chrétien de Tours in the late thirteenth century, in his edition of the Arthurian Romances, 'you must grant him mercy rather than killing him.'[24]

As the legend of Arthur, that icon of chivalry, became more popular, combat became more brutal and dangerous even for knights. In 1141 only four knights were killed and 400 captured at the battle of Lincoln: 200 years later at Crécy 1,500 were slain – many by longbowmen. The heavy cavalry responded by becoming heavier, wearing up to 80 lbs of armour. This decreased a knight's manoeuvrability in combat, required a stronger, and thus heavier and slower horse, and meant that dismounted he would, if stunned, wounded or exhausted, find it hard to regain his feet, becoming highly vulnerable to foot soldiers. Ultimately a horse could never carry enough armour to protect itself from arrows. Even if the knight decided to fight as a man-at-arms on foot, he was still slow and cumbersome. With the visor of his helmet down he could hear little and had minimal vision, particularly to the sides, from which nimble infantry could attack, shoving daggers into eyes, groin or armpits, gaps armour did not protect.

The infantry did so with increasing relish, for war was becoming much more malicious. To be sure it had never been a picnic for those on the racial margins, such as the Welsh, Irish, Scots and Arabs. Peasants had always suffered the burden of rape, loot and plunder. But during the late middle ages such atrocities become systematised into what was called the chevauchée, a scorched-earth policy that destroyed an enemy's economic base, starving his castles – which were hard to capture – of supplies. Some questioned the contradictions between the chevauchée and chivalry. 'Shame on the knight who proceeds to pay court to a lady,' wrote the troubadour Giraut de Borneil (bitter at having just been pillaged), 'after he lays his hand on bleating sheep and robs churches.'[25] Most Englishmen profited from chevauchées, for there was hardly a house back home that was not graced with fine French clothing, linen or silver. Their new owners agreed with Vegetius, the Roman military thinker, whose works were being rediscovered; 'It is preferable to subdue an enemy by famine, raids and terror than by battle where fortune tends to have more influence than bravery.'[26]

Suffering a chevauchée was such an affront to the honour of a king, who had so strong an obligation to protect his subjects that he (like Harold at Hastings), might be forced to fight a battle against his better judgement. The medieval military revolution did not, however, change his role there. Indeed until the improvement of communications in the eighteen century a general exercised little command and control during a battle. He was supposed to be the heroic leader who, like Boadicea, Alfred and William the Conqueror, drew up and inspired the troops before the fight. Once it started he was expected to be in the thick of the fray. As the veteran Sir John Fastolf (a model for Shakespeare's Falstaff), observed in 1450, a king must be 'a chieftain of noble and great estate, having knowledge and experience of the wars.'[27]

In many ways these changes in warfare reached their epitome at the Battle of Agincourt in 1415.

The Hundred Years War began in 1337 when Edward III claimed the French throne through his mother, Isabella, the King of France's daughter, rejecting the French contention that by Salic law inheritance could not descend through the female line. Even though the French outnumbered the English population six to one, Edward was able to win a resounding victory at Crécy in 1346, and his son Edward, the Black Prince, an equally overwhelming one at Poitiers ten years later, due largely to the devastating firepower of their longbowmen. So when Henry V sent out to invade France in the spring of 1415 the auguries were on his side.

He was born in 1386. After his mother died when he was eight, Henry was brought up in the court of Richard II (1377–99), a surprisingly cultured nursery for a warrior, being filled with artists and poets, such as Geoffrey Chaucer. He first saw action in Ireland in 1399. Later that year his father, the duke of Lancaster, deposed and murdered Richard, usurping the throne as Henry IV (1399–1413). At fourteen Henry accompanied his father on an expedition into Scotland in 1400, where he commanded a company of 17 men-at-arms and 99 archers. Two years later he led a much larger force against the Welsh. On 21 July 1403 he commanded the left flank of his father's army at the Battle of Shrewsbury, and although severely wounded in the face by an arrow, continued to fight courageously. After the battle Henry was lucky to be treated by John Bradmoor, one of the finest surgeons of the age. Bradmoor designed a special metal tool which he inserted through the entrance to the wound into the hole at the back of the arrow head in which the wooden shaft had fitted. Turning a screw the surgeon expanded the end of the probe to grip the arrow head allowing him to remove it. Bradmoor used honey as an antiseptic. It was a remarkably delicate operation conducted without anaesthetics, a tribute to the prince's stoicism and the surgeon's skill.

During the next five years he campaigned in Wales, crushing Owen Glendower's revolt. It was a brutal war. Welsh women would mutilate English corpses, stuffing their private parts into their mouths: many Welsh garrisons preferred to starve to death rather than surrender. So by 1415 Henry V was an experienced warrior, honed by combat, respected by the ten thousand men who set sail with him from Southampton on 11 August.

Fair stood the wind for France,
When we our sails advance,
Nor now to prove our chance,
Longer will tarry;
But putting to the main,
At Caux, the mouth of Seine,
With all his martial train,
Landed King Harry.[28]

Immediately afterwards Henry started to besiege Harfleur, a well-fortified town, protected by strong walls and 26 towers and almost entirely surrounded by water. After six weeks the garrison surrendered, the English having lost 2,000 men, most to dysentery, while an equal number had been sent home too ill to fight.

After spending a month at Harfleur, Henry decided on a chevauchée, marching across northern France to the English base at Calais. His force, roughly 6,000 strong, left Harfleur on 8 October carrying eight days' rations. Four days later they arrived at Blantchetacque at the mouth of the Somme to find a French force of equal size blocking the river. So they had to march east, down river and into enemy territory for six days before they were able to cross at Voyennes. Some men had dysentery so badly that they cut away their breeches so they could relieve themselves as they marched. Morale plummeted so severely that the king hung in front of the army a looter for stealing a cheap copper pyx containing the host from a church. We 'were very few,' recalled an English chaplain, 'and wearied with much fatigue, and weak from lack of food'.[29]

In such a mood the English were cut off by the French on 25 October just east of the village of Agincourt. A cold wet night, disturbed by the sounds of the enemy celebrating their certain victory added to the miseries of this unhappy few: the 800 English men-at-arms and 5,000 archers were outnumbered five to one by the pride of French chivalry.

The two sides started to assemble at dawn. The English were drawn up a thin line with men-at-arms in the centre, and bowmen equally divided on either flank. The French were in three divisions, one behind the other, each roughly eight thousand men strong. The dense, almost impenetrable, forests on both sides of the battlefield prevented either side from outflanking the other, forcing them to make frontal attacks. By eight in the morning each army was arrayed some 700 yards apart. They waited four hours before Henry ordered his men to advance, in the names of Jesus, Mary and St George. Many kneeled to kiss the earth, beneath which they feared they would soon be buried. The English moved forward, not in step, but in a slow shuffle, trying to keep their dressing on the muddy field. They paused before hammering six-foot

Plate 3.3   MS 6 f.243, Battle of Agincourt, 1415, English with Flemish illuminations, St Alban's chronicle, Lambeth Palace Library/Bridgeman Art Library

sharpened wooden stakes into the ground to their front. Then they stuck the arrows into the ground so they could quickly pick them up and fire them. This meant that the points had traces of soil from the Somme region, which, as doctors would discover 500 years later during the First World War, had bacteria which was especially conducive to producing gangrenous wounds.

Whether the French cavalry on both flanks advanced first of their own initiative, or the volleys of English arrows goaded them into doing so is debated. Carrying as much as 300 lb over ground which was getting muddier by the minute, the French horses could only move at ten miles an hour, taking forty or so seconds to reach the English lines. During this time mathematically the 5,000 English bowmen could have fired 40,000 arrows, an average of ten per target. Some of the arrows ricocheted off the knights' oblique-shaped armour. Others penetrated cracks in armpits and groins. Many hit the horses, which fell, throwing their riders to the ground, or impaled themselves on the stakes, or galloped, terrified, back to crash into the second line of French men-at-arms [Plate 3.3].

Unaware of the disaster unfolding to their front, the second French division moved forward. Because the forests on either side narrowed into a funnel about a thousand yards wide, the files of the second division were compressed in on themselves. They collided with the re-treating knights and frightened riderless horses. Those who continued or were pushed forward impaled themselves on the sharpened wooden stakes, behind which stood a thin line of men-at-arms. Squeezed on both sides, as well as from the front and rear, the bodies piled on top of each other. It was rather like a terrified crowd caught in a football stadium or underpass. Some of the French drowned in the mud, many more suffocated in the mound of bodies, which an observer alleged were as high as a man. Those on top were not safe. English and Welsh infantry leapt on this heap, shoving daggers into gaps in French armour, and with a twist killed indiscriminately.

All around this heap small groups of men, mostly on foot, fought in desperate brawls, the French to regain their honour, the English to survive. Henry stood out. His armour flaunted the royal coat of arms. Though wounded he continued to fight, killing enemy knights who had vowed to slay him.

After what must have seemed like an aeon, but was probably no more than half an hour, fighting faded away. Those who were still alive were too tired to continue. Hearing that the local peasants were plundering his baggage train to the rear near the village of Maisoncelle, Henry rushed from the front line and ordered 200 of his archers to fire into the 3,000 French prisoners collected there. Some refused, not out of humanitarian considerations (for they hated the haughty French nobility from whom they could expect no mercy), but from financial ones. They did not want to squander such a rich source of ransom. So the king threatened to hang anyone who refused to open fire, and set alight a barn in which many captives had been confined.

No wonder the French called the hero of Shakespeare's history 'Henry the cut throat'. Though Shakespeare justified the killing as a righteous revenge for the murder of the boys sent back to the baggage train as too young to fight, there is no truth in this explanation. Even by the standards of the time the murder of the French prisoners was a cruel and wanton blight on an amazing victory.

The French had lost three dukes, eight counts, fifteen hundred knights and between four and five thousand soldiers. The English lost but three hundred men, including a duke and an earl, and seven knights. After spending the night sleeping amongst the carnage of the field, the next day Henry's men set off for Calais escorting as many as three thousand prisoners. They carried as much booty as they could strip from the

French dead, who were so numerous that it took five burial pits to hold them all.

In July of 1417, after making an alliance with the Emperor Sigismund of Germany, Henry landed once more at Harfleur with 10,000 men to conquer Normandy, and then perhaps the whole of France. After a bloody siege, in which prisoners were killed, he stormed Caen, sparing few of the defenders. In November he invested Falaise, which fell in the following February. By April of the next year all of Normandy was in English hands. The French agreed to sign the treaty of Troyes by which Henry married Katharine, the heiress to the French throne, with the proviso that their heir would rule both England and France. But after fighting a third French campaign in 1421, Henry died of dysentery aged only thirty-five the following August, leaving a son, Henry VI who, less than a year old, was far too young to retain the crown of both kingdoms.

Ever since Agincourt Henry V has been fulsomely praised. 'The greatest man ever to rule England,' K. B. Mcfarland, concluded. 'England's greatest soldier,' claimed Christopher Hibbert.[30] He regained the trust between crown and nobility that Richard lost and his father had never enjoyed. He worked closely with parliament, persuading the members to vote taxes for his wars on the grounds that they were somehow a crusade, in which the English had some special, even divine mission. He was convinced that God had called him to root out Lollardry, the heresy started by John Wycliffe which in many ways anticipated Luther's teachings by over a hundred years. He personally supervised the burning of John Badby for denying transubstantiation, the orthodoxy that during the mass the priest literally turned the bread and wine into Christ's body and blood. When Badby started to scream the king had him pulled from the flames, offering the Lollard a pension if he would recant. When he refused Henry ordered the heretic tossed back into the fire. No wonder a French astrologer who met him at this time thought the king more like a priest than a soldier.

Yet Henry's reputation rested on his career as a soldier, and on the victory of Agincourt in particular. Henry did not want to fight that battle, being forced into doing so because he failed to reconnoitre the crossing of the Somme and did not bring sufficient supplies. His negligence turned a glorious chevauchée across Northern France into a miserable retreat, that turned into a famous victory. He deliberately set out to create a public image of himself as the chivalrous Christian warrior [Plate 3.4 – colour]. In truth he was a cold killer, priggishly cruel, savagely self-certain, hanging prisoners, starving women and children, if he felt it was in his interests. Certain he was right, he did much wrong.

Not until the German occupation of the Second World War would Normandy and Pas de Calais suffer so badly as it did under Henry V.

France survived both Hitler and Henry, neither of whom had realistic objectives. To be sure Henry V was unlucky to die young leaving an infant as his heir. Yet even had he lived his goal of a long-term English conquest of France was unachievable. France was much larger than England, the French devised tactics to counter English archers, and were developing a sense of nationalism which Joan of Arc exploited to expel the invaders. In April 1450, a generation after Agincourt, on learning that the French had won a far more decisive battle at Formigny in which they used cannon to annihilate the English archers, William Paston, a Norfolk gentleman, wrote in his diary, 'We have now not a foot of land in Normandy'.[31] It was no accident that five years later the Wars of the Roses began.

The causes of the Wars of the Roses go way beyond the defeat in France, after which thousands of veterans returned home to England to continue the violence they had learned abroad. The French wars had also damaged England's economy, the devastation in France decimating exports and the customs they produced for the king's coffers. The decline in revenue lessened royal power, while the Black Death of 1348–51 killed a third of the population in England producing a labour shortage which ended serfdom: able to demand wages peasants were no longer tied to the land. When their lords tried to prevent this from happening and imposed a poll tax upon them, the peasants revolted in 1381, and took their grievances to King Richard II in person.

In his play of the same name Shakespeare argues that the problems that bedevilled England in the following century were due to the usurpation of Richard II in 1399.[32]

> *The blood of England shall manure the ground,*
> *And future ages groan for this foul deed.*

For Shakespeare, and for the historians such as Polydore Virgil, Ralph Holinshed, John Stowe and Edward Hall from whom he lifted his plots, the crisis of the fifteenth century was divine punishment for the foulest deed men could commit, the deposition of an anointed monarch. This engendered the bloody wars between the houses of York and Lancaster, the former symbolised by the white rose and the latter by the red. The breakdown lasted nearly a century, being ended in 1485 when Henry Tudor, a Lancastrian, won the Battle of Bosworth Field and united both houses by marrying Elizabeth of York.

England hath long since been mad, and scarr'd herself:
The brother blindly shed the brother's blood.
The father rashly slaughter'd his own son.

So Shakespeare has the victorious monarch say at Bosworth; afterwards, the bard reassured his audience, under the Tudors all would be sane again, 'With smiling plenty, and fair prosperous days.'[33]

The crises of the fifteenth century, of which the Wars of the Roses were the apex, were due less to the failure of kingship, and more to that of individual kings. Had Henry V not died so young he might have given his son Henry VI (1422–71), time to mature into an effective leader. Although Henry VI was an upright decent man, he was too pious for his own good, and too prim and uxorious for his country's. Once during a court festivity when some young women danced bare-breasted before him, the king left the room muttering, 'Fy, fy for shame, forsooth ye are to blame.'[34] Not the behaviour, and certainly not the language of a warrior king. Henry VI was the first monarch since the Conqueror who did not lead an army into battle.

Ironically Henry V's greatest diplomatic triumph, his marriage to Princess Katharine of France, led to the demise of his line. Henry VI almost certainly inherited from his grandfather Charles VI the gene that produced his mental breakdown in August 1452. Without warning the king withdrew into himself. He neither spoke nor acknowledged any who tried to speak to him. He showed no reaction on being presented with his newborn son and heir a couple of months later, and refused to respond to a deputation from the House of Lords which came to see him in March 1453. Modern scholars have described the breakdown as catatonic schizophrenia. The duke of York was less kind, describing the mad king as 'an idiot and by God's dom of small intelligence'.[35]

Richard, duke of York had good cause for making such a diagnosis for immediately after seeing the addled king the House of Lords appointed York Lord Protector. When Henry recovered his wits in early 1455 the duke of York fought to keep his powers. He was beaten at the Battle of St Albans, a comparatively bloodless affray – little more than a street brawl that was over within half an hour, and in which Henry VI, a bystander, suffered a flesh wound in the neck. His queen, Margaret, used this victory and her husband's injury to take over power, a step which York accepted for five years, before trying to regain it. Soon afterwards in 1460 he was killed in a minor skirmish. His son Edward continued his father's claim, but Margaret's forces routed his at the second Battle of St Albans on 17 February 1461. For some reason (and historians can only speculate that Margaret lost her nerve, or her husband recovered enough sanity to tell her to stop), she did not march on London, but permitted the duke of York to seize the city, and have himself proclaimed Edward IV. With remarkable speed the new king went on the offensive, catching the Lancastrian forces at Towton, ten miles east of Leeds, on 29 March. It was the bloodiest battle of the whole war, with perhaps as many as 80,000 troops present. Fought from ten in the morning to eight at night – long after sunset – it took place during a snowstorm. Neither side used much subtlety. Drawn up in three divisions opposite each other, the infantry waded in, with reinforcements scrabbling over the piles of dead and dying to reach the foe. Eventually, and far later than reason might excuse, the Lancastrians broke, fleeing towards the River Cock, in whose freezing waters so many died that it was said the survivors scrambled to safety across a dam of corpses.

Towton was a decisive victory. Edward IV had seized the crown, which seemed to sit secure on his head until the remarkable reversal of 1469, when he fell out with Richard Neville, the earl of Warwick, the so-called 'king-maker'. They quarrelled over Edward IV's marriage to Elizabeth Woodville, a middle-class widow with a large and avaricious family, and over foreign policy, the king preferring a Burgundian alliance, the king-maker a French one. So Warwick decided to unmake the king, whom he took a prisoner. After a brief incarceration Edward escaped to Burgundy. Warwick also made an alliance with Margaret, agreeing to marry his daughter Anne to Edward, Prince of Wales. With French support he restored to the throne Henry VI, by now such a gibbering idiot that his carefully staged progress through the streets of London embarrassed all who watched.

The following year, 1471, Edward returned to England with 2,000 men, paid for by the duke of Burgundy, landing at Ravenspur, at the mouth of the Humber. After winning considerable support in the north he moved south so quickly that he was able to face the Lancastrians, commanded by Warwick, at Barnet, nine miles north of London, on 14 April. Since Edward had drawn his forces up in the dark, they did not exactly face the enemy. A heavy morning mist quite literally added to the fog of battle, as each side slashed at each other. Mistaken identities which led to the earl of Oxford's division being attacked by their own side, and as a result fleeing the field shouting 'Treason! treason!', gave Edward a victory in which Warwick was killed, either in the heat of battle or in the ensuing rout. No one knew what would happen next. Sir John Paston wrote to his mother, 'The world I assure you is right queasy.'[36]

Two days later Edward heard that Margaret had landed with French troops on the south coast. Realising that her way to London was blocked she moved north to Bristol and then Gloucester. Edward caught up with her at Tewkesbury on 4 May, and although outnumbered, plunged into the attack. When it seemed that his left flank might break he committed his reserve of 200 spearmen whom he had concealed in a small wood. They were enough to decide the day. The Lancastrians broke, many being drowned as they tried to swim the rivers Avon and Severn in their heavy armour. Edward, Prince of Wales was killed. Those magnates who surrendered were executed on the spot, while Margaret was captured three days later, the Yorkists taking special pleasure in telling her of the death of her son. Three weeks afterwards Henry VI died, a few at the time said 'of pure displeasure and melancholy'. A recent exhumation, which revealed that the king's hair was matted with blood, supported the belief of most contemporaries that Edward had Henry VI murdered.

Edward had once again shown his abilities as a soldier. He was ruthless. He moved fast, forcing the enemy to give battle. He could win popular support by appealing to the interests of the nobility and merchants. Philip de Commynes, a contemporary historian, slyly noted that Edward, a renowned womaniser, gained control of London in 1471 because 'the wives of the rich citizens with whom he had been closely and secretly acquainted, won over their husbands and relatives to his cause'.[37] Whatever his prowess in the bedroom, his skill on the battlefield was not enough to earn him Colonel Burne's accolade, 'the greatest general of his age', except perhaps as a damning comment on the abysmally low standards of English leadership.[38]

As a royal warrior the achievements of his brother and successor, Richard III (1483–85), were as fatal as his ambitions were grandiose and his reputation vile. He had been dead but half a dozen years before John Rous, the Warwickshire priest and historian, alleged that Richard spent two years in his mother's womb before being born with a full set of teeth and hair down to his shoulder. 'Malicious, wrathful, envious' was the judgement of Sir Thomas More, 'little of stature, ill featured of limbs, crook back.' Shakespeare turned Richard (who had one shoulder slightly lower than the other), into the hunch-backed embodiment of evil [Plate 3.5].

In fact Richard was a far more complicated man. Not unusually villainous in an especially villainous age, his ultimate failings as a king were as a warrior. Such is surprising, for before he came to the throne Richard had fought bravely for his brother at the Battles of Tewkesbury and Barnet, and had campaigned effectively against the Scots. A letter of 1480 appointing him the King's Lieutenant-General of the North talks of 'his proven capacity in the arts of war', while two years later the House of Commons congratulated him on 'his princely courage' and 'memorable and laudable acts' performed 'in diverse battles'.[39]

Plate 3.5   Olivier as Richard III © Hulton-Deutsch Collection/Corbis

It could be argued that he made his fatal mistake in July 1483 when he deposed his nephew, Edward V, on the grounds that his father, Edward IV and mother, Elizabeth Woodville, had not been properly married, the ceremony having taken place in an unconsecrated building. Thus Edward and his brother, Richard, were bastards incapable of inheriting the throne. Whether Richard III had the princes murdered in the Tower has been a matter for debate amongst historians, although contemporaries had less doubt about the verdict. As a usurper and murderer Richard lost much public support, although at that time rebellions against kings, no matter how legally they wore the crown, were common. In late 1483 Richard managed to nip one such revolt in the bud.

What tipped the balance against him was yet another biological failure. In April 1484 his only son and heir, Edward, Prince of Wales, died suddenly at the age of nine. Both his parents went almost mad with grief. Since his mother, Anne, was beyond the age of child-bearing (and anyway died the following year), the lack of an heir opened the throne to anyone foolhardy enough to try and claim it.

The leading claimant was Henry Tudor, earl of Richmond. Little royal blood pulsed around his veins. His paternal great-grandfather was an outlawed Welsh brewer, his maternal great-grandfather was Edward III, while his grandmother Catherine, the widow of Henry V, had formed a liaison with Owen Tudor, her Clerk of the Wardrobe, who was executed after the Battle of Mortimer's Cross in 1461. But during the Wars of the Roses enough royal blood ran through Henry Tudor's veins to sign his death warrant. So in 1471 the last surviving member of the House of Lancaster went into exile in Brittany.

Henry Tudor's military record was mediocre: in 1483 he staged a landing at Poole Harbour but was driven back by the local militia. So when on 7 August 1485 he landed in Milford Haven with two thousand troops, recruited from the sweepings of France's jails – and a more evil lot, Philip de Commynes noted, one could not hope to find – Henry Tudor seemed likely to become yet one more victim of the Wars of the Roses. Contemporaries could not be blamed for thinking that the breakdown in English society would continue for perhaps another century or two, as God punished the realm for deposing His anointed.

This chaotic, confusing and sometimes tedious recitation of wars, battles, murder and deposition, had fundamental causes. As we have seen, the quality of kingship was poor. Monarchs went insane, inherited as children, and were incompetent. The longbow had ended the military dominance of the knight, being replaced by mercenaries who were both expensive and violent. The Black Death in the middle of the fourteenth century had killed off a third of England's population, producing a labour shortage that eroded the feudal system, ending serfdom. Even the church, once the bastion of stability, was in turmoil, with rival popes excommunicating each other from Avignon and Rome. No wonder England's future looked bleak in the summer of 1485.

For the first ten days after landing at Milford Haven Henry Tudor's future looked even bleaker. Few rallied to his standard, the red dragon of Wales. Richard made strenuous efforts to deal with the interloper. He learned of Henry's invasion within three days, and on 11 August ordered his friends and followers to rendezvous with him at Leicester 'in all haste'. There he assembled a formidable force, although there were questions about the loyalty of the earl of Northumberland and his men from the north. One of the few magnates to decline the king's summons was Thomas, Lord Stanley, who explained that he had the 'sweating sickness'. Since the plague was invariably fast and fatal, and Stanley remained alive and well, a suspicious Richard took his son, Lord Strange, hostage.

After an anxious night, which left Richard 'pale and deathlike' a contemporary noted, 'as if troubled by a host of demons', on 22 August he arrayed his forces on Ambion Hill, an oval-shaped feature, 400 feet above sea level that ran east to west, one and a half miles long and 350 feet wide. At first glance it would appear to have been a wise choice, for the sides of the hill were steep, making it a strong defensive position. But by drawing up his men, who numbered between nine and ten thousand, in a line, with the duke of Norfolk's division to the west, the earl of Northumberland's to the east and his own in the middle, he was unable to engage all his forces at the same time.

Henry Tudor's much smaller army, about 5,000 strong, approached from the west. Richard may have missed an opportunity by not attacking them as they were forming up. Instead he lost the initiative by allowing Henry's forces to attack Norfolk's division first, who after experiencing ineffective arrow and cannon fire, came down the hill to fight hand to hand. Here, in a remarkably confined area, a vicious encounter took place. When the duke of Norfolk was killed his division started to retreat. Richard ordered his reserves to relieve them. Northumberland refused saying that he best wait until he knew what Lord Stanley, who was poised with 5,000 men about a mile north of the battlefield, would do.

Richard had no doubt about what to do. After ordering the immediate execution of Stanley's son (a command which was not obeyed), Richard decided to personally lead some eighty of his most faithful followers in a sudden right hook around Norfolk's men to Henry Tudor, whose standard had been spotted a thousand yards or so away. Why he did so we cannot tell. He may have wanted to relieve Norfolk's broken division, to prevent Lord Stanley from intervening, to crush Northumberland's mutiny in the bud, or even out of an impetuous wish to punish those he regarded as traitors. Anyway it was a reasonable enough gamble. The rebellion would have collapsed had he slain Henry Tudor.

And he nearly did. With his battle axe Richard killed William Brandon, Henry's personal standard bearer. While dispatching Sir John Keyne, a knight renowned for his strength and courage, Richard himself was dismounted. Instead of cravenly begging, as Shakespeare would have us believe, for a horse, a horse, his kingdom for a horse, Richard continued to fight on foot, 'alone', wrote a contemporary historian, until 'he was killed fighting manfully in the press of his enemies'.

When his crown, which had fallen off his helmet, was found, it was handed to Henry Tudor, now by right of conquest the Seventh of England. Richard's body was pulled out of the pile of corpses, stripped naked, and with a felon's noose around the neck, thrown across the back of a pack-horse to be taken to Leicester, its blood-encrusted hair dragging across the ground. There it was exposed to public gaze for two days, to prove that Richard was well and truly dead, before the Franciscans buried him in an unmarked grave. A few years later Henry VII provided ten guineas for a coffin (an insultingly small sum for a king), so the friars could give it a Christian funeral. During the dissolution of the monasteries in the 1530s Richard's bones were dug up, and thrown into the River Soar, his stone coffin being used for several centuries as a horse trough by the patrons of the White Horse Inn.

Richard was the last English king to die in battle and the only one since 1066 with no known grave. Such is the fate of those who fail as royal warriors.

Notes

1. C. T. Allmand, *Henry V* (London: Methuen, 1997), 435.
2. T. Carlyle, *On Heroes, Hero-Worship and the Heroic in History* (London: Chapman and Hall, 1841), 110.
3. D. Seward, *Henry V as a Warlord* (London: Sedgewick and Jackson, 1987), xviii.
4. D. K. C. Todd, *Shakespeare's Agincourt* (Durham: New Center Press, 1985), 7.
5. J. Gillingham, 'Richard I and the Science of War', in J. Gillingham and J. Holt (eds), *War and Government in the Middle Ages* (Woodbridge: Boydell, 1984), 210–11.
6. C. D. Bowen, *The Lion and the Throne: the Life and Times of Sir Edward Coke, 1552–1634* (London: Hamish Hamilton, 1957), 391.
7. J. Bradbury, 'Philip Augustus and King John', in S. D. Church (ed.), *King John: New Interpretations* (Woodbridge: Boydell, 1999), 347–9.
8. Quoted by M. Ashley, *The Life and Times of King John* (London: Weidenfeld and Nicolson, 1977), 37–8.
9. Quoted ibid., 140.
10. Quoted by R. V. Turner, *King John* (London: Longmans, 1994), 254.

11. J. R. Green, *Short History of the English People* (London: Macmillan, 1874), I, 114.

12. Quoted by Turner, *op. cit.*, 14.

13. Bradbury, *op. cit.*, 347–9.

14. M. Prestwich, *The Three Edwards: War and State In England, 1272–1377* (London: Weidenfeld and Nicolson, 1980), 78–9.

15. Mary Saaler, *Edward III, 1307–27* (London: Robinson, 1997), 10–16.

16. Ibid., 32–5.

17. John Barbour, quoted by Caroline Bingham, *The Life and Times of Edward II* (London: Weidenfeld and Nicolson, 1973), 97.

18. Quoted by C. Bingham, *op. cit.*, 108.

19. Quoted by Saaler, *op. cit.*, 76.

20. For more on this see C. J. Rogers, 'The Military Revolution in the Hundred Years War', *Journal of Military History*, 57 (1993), 249–57, and M. Prestwich, *Armies and Warfare in the Middle Ages: the English Experience* (New Haven: Yale University Press, 1991), 236–46. The subject is discussed further in Chapter V.

21. Quoted by A. Ayton, *Knights and Warhorses: Military Service and the English Aristocracy under Edward III* (Woodbridge: Boydell, 1994), 12.

22. J. F. C. Fuller, *The Decisive Battles of the Western World*, quoted by J. Wintle, *The Dictionary of War Quotations* (New York: Macmillan, 1989), 216.

23. Quoted by Wintle, *op. cit.*, 217.

24. Quoted by M. Strickland, *Anglo-Norman Warfare* (Woodbridge: Boydell, 1992), 154.

25. Strickland, *op. cit.*, 284.

26. R. R. Vegetius, *Epitome of Military Science*, ed., N. P. Milner (Liverpool: Liverpool University Press, 1993), 108.

27. J. Falstolf, *Wars of the English in France*, II (ii), 596, quoted in Prestwich, *op. cit.*, 216.

28. Michael Drayton, 'To the Cambro-Britons, and their harp, his ballad of Agincourt', in John Stallworthy (ed.), *Oxford Book of War Poetry* (Oxford: Oxford University Press, 1988), 37.

29. Michael Bennett, *Agincourt, 1415: Triumph against the Odds* (London: Osprey, 1991), 50.

30. K. B. McFarlane, *Lancastrian Kings and Lollard Knights* (Oxford: Oxford University Press, 1972), 133. C. Hibbert, *Agincourt* (London: Batsford, 1978), 136.

31. Seward, *op. cit.*, 217.

32. *Richard II*, IV, i, 137.

33. *Richard III*, V, v, 23.

34. J. R. Lander, *The Wars of the Roses* (London: Secker and Warburg, 1985), 27.

35. Quoted by A. J. Slavin, *The Tudor Age and Beyond: England from the Black Death to the End of the Reign of Elizabeth* (Malibar, FL: Krieger, 1987), 74.

36. Quoted by G. Faulkes, *The Life and Times of Edward IV* (London: Wiedenfeld and Nicolson, 1981), 143.

37. Quoted D. Seward, *The Wars of the Roses* (London: Constable, 1995), 197.

38. A. Burne, *The Battlefields of England* (London: Greenhill, 1996), 114.

39. C. Ross, *Richard III* (London: Methuen, 1981), 142.

chapter 4

NO OTHER AIM OR
THOUGHT THAN WAR

'A Prince should have no other aim or thought, or take up any other thing for his study, but war, and its organization and discipline, for that is the only thing that is necessary to one who commands.'

Machiavelli, **The Prince**[1]

Today Henry VIII (1509–47) is best remembered as the larger than life figure of gross proportions and even grosser appetites who brawled, belched and bawdied his way through six wives, countless banquets, and one reformation. Instantly recognisable, the subject of several films and television series, Henry's waxen image, flanked by those of his six wives, dominates Madame Tussaud's, while his portrait is one of the best-selling postcards at London's National Portrait Gallery. He fascinated his contemporaries just as much as he has posterity. 'The King of England, this Henry, lies,' fulminated Martin Luther, 'and with his lies acts more the part of a comic jester than a king.' More diplomatically the French Ambassador called him 'a sly old fox'.[2]

While Henry, whose ego was as large as he was insecure, might have been gratified that during his lifetime and for centuries after his death he has been an eminently recognisable figure, he neither intended to be the much married man, nor start a reformation that was to be one of the most important events in English history. It established the Church of England, founded the roots of English hegemony, and, some would argue, produced a Tudor revolution in government. Instead Henry wanted to be remembered as a royal warrior.

And in this Henry was an utter failure.

The origins of his ambitions lie in the culture of his times, in his own complicated personality, and, perhaps, in the nature of human beings. If the biological drives to fight wars have not changed, the reasons men give for waging them have. In the last three hundred years or so Western societies have fought wars for territorial gains, or for economic advantages, such as the control of markets or raw materials, or to win support at home, or else for ideological reasons, such as spreading communism, liberty, a particular religious belief, or to make the world safer for democracy. As armies got bigger, being manned by conscripts, wars were often justified in moral terms, as good versus evil, or to protect the fatherland from some horrendous outside threat.

Neither Henry VIII nor his fellow princes, such as Francis I of France, or the Emperors Maximilian and Charles of Germany, fought wars for these objectives. Indeed they despised such goals as being unfit for gentlemen. 'Our king is not after gold, or gems or precious metals,' explained Lord Mountjoy soon after Henry VIII ascended the throne in 1509, 'but virtue, glory, immortality.'[3] In other words what Henry wanted more than anything else – more than his wives, more than the monastic lands, more even than a male heir – was honour. His biographer has concluded, 'Honour stood at the root of Henry Tudor's personality.'[4]

Honour is hard to define, and changes over time. Mainly a male concept, it has a lot to do with a man's self-worth as a man. Historically war has been an almost exclusively male activity. Being stronger and able to run faster than women, most men are better suited to survive the brutality of pre-modern war which, lacking complex weapon systems and chemical explosives, depended more on brawn than brains. So women were left behind in safety to look after the children, and be kept to breed replacements for those lost in battle.

In 1562 Gerald Legh defined honour as 'glory got by courage of manhood'.[5] Thus an excessive quest for honour and glory could be a means of compensating for private doubts about one's manhood. Henry certainly had such doubts. He did not get on well with his father, Henry VII who, according to Reginald Pole, a cousin who knew the family well, disliked his son greatly, 'having no affection, or fancy unto him'.[6] The Spanish Ambassador wrote home that the old king kept his heir 'as locked up as a woman', the only way to Prince Henry's bedroom being through his father's. So it is not surprising that when a dozen or so years later the Imperial ambassador hinted that Henry might not be physically capable of marrying Anne Boleyn, a woman sixteen years his junior, he furiously retorted, 'Am I not a man like other men? Am I not? Am I not?'[7] His Majesty protested too much. The colossal codpiece on Henry's suit of armour, now exhibited in the Tower of London, would suggest he linked both war and virility, and desperately needed to flaunt his masculinity [Plate 4.1].

Honour derived from the feudal concepts of knighthood and chivalry, which were becoming obsolete during Henry VIII's reign. At the same

Plate 4.1   Henry VIII's armour © The Board of Trustees of the Armouries

time as intellectuals known as the humanists were trying to civilise honour by making it less bellicose, monarchs attempted to control it by becoming the sole source of all honour.[8] In those pre-Freudian days honour was less connected with machismo, but more with birth and breeding, and the good opinion of one's fellows. Honour was gained from one's lineage. It was something one's family accumulated over generations, endowing its possessors with pride and potency. Maintaining the honour of one's dynasty was an overriding obligation. While a gentleman might not earn honour in the same way as a merchant could grub for money, he could lose it in a single act far more precipitously than a townsman could go bankrupt. As Iago pointed out:[9]

> *Who steals my purse steals trash – 'tis nothing . . .*
> *But he that filches from me my good name*
> *Robs me of that which not enriches him*
> *And makes me poor indeed.*

Throughout his life Henry valued his honour more than anything else. In 1544 he wrote to Francis I that he had 'always guarded inviolable' his honour, adding that 'I will never consent in my old age that it shall be anyway distrained.'[10] As a young man he was equally desperate to acquire honour which he believed could best be won in war. After inspecting the Venetian fleet on a courtesy visit to Southampton the young king insisted that their cannon fire repeated volleys. 'He is very curious about such matters,' reported the Venetian ambassador.[11] In addition to training for war by hurling javelins, shooting arrows in the butts, wrestling and taking part in tournaments, Henry read many of the books on chivalry, such as Mallory's *Morte D'Arthur*, romances about the Trojan Wars, and tales of Charlemagne and Roland that poured off the newly invented printing presses. He took a special delight in showing visitors to Winchester the round table around which Arthur and his knights supposedly sat. He encouraged Lord Berners to translate Froissart's *Chronicles* of the Hundred Years War, because of 'the great pleasure that my countrymen of England take in reading the worthy and knightly deeds of their valiant ancestors'.[12] His subjects agreed, being fixated with the longbow, which was 'God's instrument,' preached Bishop Hugh Latimer in 1540, 'a gift of God that he hath given us to excel over other nations.'[13]

Henry VIII, like many a king, was haunted by the achievements of his ancestors. As Edward III said about his own grandfather, Edward I, a most distinguished soldier, 'in a whole life of knightly deeds, no one was more illustrious or bold or prudent in leading armies.'[14] Henry VIII wanted the same to be said of himself. 'His ambition,' he admitted was 'not merely to equal, but to exceed the glorious deeds of his ancestors'.[15]

Henry would let nothing stand in the way of his military ambitions. After spending an hour walking with the king in his garden at Chelsea, Thomas Moore noted that Henry would cut off his head if it 'could win him a castle in France'.[16] (The King in fact did have Moore's head, but to win him a church in England.) Just before Henry invaded France in

1513 John Colet, the Dean of St Paul's and Moore's good friend, preached before the king and his court that an unjust peace was better than a just war. Afterwards Henry called the Doctor of Divinity in for a private chat. An hour later Colet emerged saying he had changed his mind, whether from the force of His Majesty's arguments or from the threat of physical force the good doctor did not say. He knew – as Moore was to fatally find out – that so long as you publicly agreed with him, Henry was your friend. 'Let everyone have his own doctor. This one is mine,' Henry announced as he embraced Dr John Colet.[17]

Henry had far less success with the French. In July of the previous year, 1512, he sent an expeditionary force under the Marquis of Dorset to Gascony. England's ally, Spain, reneged on its agreement to cooperate. Disease, mutiny, squabbling amongst the leaders, poor food, and over-indulgence in looted wine soon turned the army into a rabble, which the following month decamped for home in disgrace.

The next year Henry decided to lead an invasion in person. In part he may have done so to posthumously defy his father, whose advisers on the Privy Council urged peace, and whose two chief tax collectors, Richard Empson and Edmund Dudley, he had just hanged. But the main reason for Henry's invasion of France was to advance his honour. On landing at Calais, an English possession, on 30 June 1513 he imme-diately rode to St Nicholas Cathedral to dedicate himself to the service of God by fighting a Holy War. He certainly did not fight an uncom-fortable one. For three weeks the king and the three hundred members of the household he brought with him feasted and amused themselves. Eventually on 21 July they set out on campaign, with patrols scouting the countryside to make sure the enemy could not approach the king. Even if they had, a bodyguard plus a 60 lb suit of armour protected the royal personage, who spent every night in a warm feather bed, usually inside a portable wooden shed, complete with its own thunderbox.

The army's progress was nearly as comfortable. In the first eleven days they marched but forty miles. On 16 August they came across a strong French cavalry patrol, which after a brief skirmish bolted, leaving behind six standards, a duke, a marquis and a vice-admiral. Henry turned this incident, which was promptly dubbed the Battle of the Spurs, into a second Agincourt. The following day in a letter to Margaret of Savoy he described the altercation with all the dramatic detail one might expect from a participant. Significantly Henry failed to mention that he was a mile away from the action.

Henry was present at the Siege of Thérouanne, which fell on 24 August. A month later he captured Tournai, where he spent three weeks celebrat-ing, before returning home to London. Actually Henry had accomplished very little, particularly when compared to the earl of Surrey's victory at Flodden, where the Scots, who had taken advantage of Henry's involvement in France to invade England, lost ten thousand men, including their king, James IV, twelve earls, two bishops and two abbots.

Henry's marital problems, the break with Rome, as well as the prudence of his chief minister, Thomas Cromwell, postponed the king's next major military campaign for three decades. In the early 1540s Henry became seriously depressed. He was in constant pain from a leg injury, the result of a jousting accident. He realised he had made a serious mistake in 1540 by dismissing and executing Thomas Cromwell on a trumped-up charge of treason, and felt humiliated when Catherine Howard, his fifth wife, a trophy bride, apparently betrayed him with younger and presumably much more virile lovers. The king could not accept the blame for the failure of his marriages, which he attributed to 'ill luck in meeting such ill conditioned wives'. Rather he surrounded himself with a coterie of rip-roaring young blades who hankered for war, and despised anyone who was not a swashbuckling stud. Over their cups they sang:[18]

> *A Master of Art is not worth a fart,*
> *Except he be in schools,*
> *A Bachelor of Law is not worth a straw,*
> *Except he be among fools.*

Whatever his motives for invading France in the summer of 1544 may have been, Henry was extremely sensitive about being counted amongst the fools. In mid-June an advance party under the duke of Norfolk sailed for Calais, where for a month they devoted themselves to rest and recreation. 'Numbers of shameless prostitutes came at every tide from England,' wrote Elis Gruffudd, a disgusted Welsh captain, 'there was great rejoicing to sin without fear of retribution.'[19] The arrival of the king on 14 July gave his force of some 44,000 men, the largest ever to set sail from England until the end of the seventeenth century, a sense of purpose. Five days later they started to besiege Boulogne, a small port twenty miles south of Calais. Henry enjoyed himself greatly, supervising the fire of his cannon, urging his men into battle. On 18 September Boulogne surrendered, and the king entered the town in great triumph. Twelve days later he was back home, much happier, and far poorer [Plate 4.2].

Henry had hoped that his wars would demonstrate that he was as brave a soldier, and as glorious a commander as any of his ancestors. Instead they revealed him to be 'a rank amateur with money to burn'.[20] England's involvement with France, a throw-back to the Hundred Years War, may well have delayed its colonisation of America half a century.

THE SIEGE OF BOULOGNE BY KING HENRY VIII. MDXLIV.

Plate 4.2   Henry VIII's siege of Boulougne. The Royal Collection © 2003, HM Queen Elizabeth II

Certainly it cost a great deal of money. In the last five years of his life Henry spent roughly two million pounds on war. He raised this gigantic sum by debasing the coinage (which helped produce massive inflation), by selling a third of the land he had confiscated from the monasteries during the Reformation, and by resorting to forced loans and gifts, 'borrowing' church plate which he promptly melted down for silver coins. In return for being able to hold Boulogne for eight years, Henry left his successors a myriad of problems.

His son Edward VI, who reigned from 1547 to 1553, was too young to rule, power being exercised by regents who kept England out of foreign wars. Mary Tudor (1553–58), his eldest daughter, was more interested in returning England to the Catholic faith than fighting foreign enemies. In the last year of her reign England and France drifted into war, which resulted in the loss of Calais in 1558. At the time all thought it a desperate disgrace: in the long run it proved to be a blessing in disguise.

Up until 1558 England's external relations had mainly been with the continent. The island had been the target for foreign invaders: the Romans (whom Boadicea resisted), the Anglo-Saxons (whom Arthur fought), the Vikings (whom Alfred stopped), and the Normans (whom William led). During the Hundred Years War the English had become deeply involved in continental affairs. Henry VIII failed spectacularly to revive those glory days.

After 1588 England became a major naval power and shifted its military efforts internally to the conquest of Scotland and Ireland, and the formation of a British state, and then a British empire. After the loss of the first empire in 1783, with the independence of the United States, the British built a second empire, which ended in the generation after the Second World War. During the reign of the second Queen Elizabeth Britain's loss of empire and involvement with the European community was painful because it represented a shift as intense as that which took place during the reign of Queen Elizabeth the First [Plate 4.3].

Under Elizabeth I (1558–1603), war came increasingly to dominate the nation's affairs. Its origins lay in the reformation. The break-up of a united Christendom into feuding Protestant and Catholic factions gave war an ideological component, much like the world wars of the last century. It made war more total, and harder to confine. Thus the origins of Elizabeth's wars lie not in England, nor even in the new world, where pirates such as Sir Francis Drake and Sir Richard Hawkins were all too eager to capture Spanish gold and silver to swell the fame (and coffers) of their Virgin Queen, but in the Netherlands. After the Spanish refused in 1566 to abolish the Inquisition in the Low Countries, the Dutch,

Plate 4.3   Elizabeth I, 'The Armada Portrait' © By courtesy of the National Portrait Gallery, London

who had recently become Calvinists, rose in a revolt that dragged on for ninety years. When it appeared in 1585 that the Dutch were about to be beaten, Queen Elizabeth sent five thousand infantry and a thousand cavalry to help them, and provided a safe haven for their privateers, known as 'the Sea Beggars', in English ports. So Philip II of Spain determined on a massive invasion of England.

The Great Armada of 130 ships with 22,000 soldiers and sailors abroad, set sail in the summer of 1588. The smaller, yet faster, hardier and more powerful English ships intercepted them off Plymouth on 13 July, and for a week chased them up the Channel to their rendezvous off Dunkirk. The duke of Parma was supposed to meet them there with 30,000 troops, whom they were to transport to England. But Parma and his men failed to turn up. So after being harassed by fireships, the Spanish decided to take the long way back around Scotland and Ireland. Only half of them made it home.

While history has rightly judged the Armada a decisive victory, it did not appear to be so at the time. Large numbers of English troops continued to fight on the continent, some in France, many more in the Netherlands. After England became Protestant and Ireland remained Catholic ideological conflict between the two was inevitable. The Queen's enemies were only too happy to widen the fracture. 'He that England will win, let him in Ireland begin', a Jesuit once advised Philip II. So when the Irish revolted in 1595 the king of Spain sent 100 ships and 10,000 men to help them. Luckily for England a gale decimated the Spanish fleet. On land the English were not so fortunate. Hugh O'Neil, the earl of Tyrone, equipped his rebel army with modern muskets, and thus beat the English at Clontribet and Yellow Ford, forcing Elizabeth's commander (and spoilt favourite) the earl of Essex into making an ignominious truce. Victory eluded the English until 1603 when Lord Mountjoy, who fought the Irish without pity and through the cold wet winter, destroying their food supplies, forced Tyrone to surrender.

Elizabeth's wars were expensive in both men and material. They cost approximately four million pounds, half of which the queen raised by taxes, and much of the rest by selling the church lands her father had confiscated. Nearly forty thousand English and Welsh troops served in Ireland in the last decade of Elizabeth's reign, and probably as many served at sea or on the continent – about as high a proportion of the population as went overseas in the Second World War. So unpopular was foreign service that a proverb declared that it was 'better to be hanged at home than die like dogs in Ireland'.[21]

Elizabeth regretted the price in men far less than the cost in money. War was uncertain, and expensive. Moreover it was – as they made perfectly clear to her – a male sport, in which men, like spoiled boys, indulged themselves at Her Majesty's expense, heedless of her pleas to be cautious and thrifty.

Elizabeth recognised the limits gender placed on her as a royal warrior in the summer of 1588 when she went to address the troops at Tilbury who were waiting to repulse a Spanish invasion. The earl of Leicester invited the queen to inspect his 23,000 men encamped at the mouth of the Thames to protect London. 'You shall (dear lady), behold as goodly, as loyal and as able men as any Prince Christian can show you,' he promised. Despite the Privy Council's objections that it was not safe to visit an area where the Spanish might land at any moment, the queen insisted. After being rowed from St James Place to Tilbury on 8 August, she rode around the camp on a white gelding, led by Leicester, looking like 'some Amazonian empress' in a white dress, wearing a silver breast plate and a silver helmet, with the sword of state born before her. As drummers and pipes played, and standards flapped in the breeze, she inspected the troops, saying 'God bless you all', as many soldiers fell to their knees crying 'Lord Preserve our Queen'. The next morning she returned to the camp, where she was welcomed so tumultuously that her chaplain recalled that 'the earth and air did sound like thunder', and the queen remarked she felt as if she was 'in the midst and heat of battle'. Then mounting her horse, wearing her silver breast plate and carrying a general's baton, she gave the most famous speech of her life:[22]

> Let tyrants fear, I have always persuaded myself that, under God, I have placed my chiefest strength and safeguard under the loyal hearts and good will of my subjects, and therefore I am come amongst you, as you see at this time, nor for my recreating or disport, but being resolved in the midst and heat of battle to live and die amongst you all, to lay down for my God and my kingdom, and for my people, my honour and my blood, even in the dust.
>
> I know that I have the body of a weak and feeble woman, but I have the heart and stomach of a king, and a king of England too, and think it foul scorn that Parma or Spain, or any prince of Europe should dare to invade the borders of my realm: to the which, rather than any dishonour grow by me, I will take up arms.

At the end of 'this most excellent oration' the troops 'all at once a mighty shout or cry did give'. Leicester thought that the Queen's speech 'had so inflamed the hearts of her good subjects, as I think the weakest among them is able to match the proudest Spaniard that dares land in England'.

In many ways Elizabeth's oration at Tilbury was typical of pep talks that generals give their troops going into battle. A bit like Montgomery atop his jeep she got the soldiers to surround her. Like Henry V she claimed to be sharing their danger, and declared a willingness if needs be to die among them. She expressed an esteem for honour of which her father would have approved. Her appeal to patriotism, her contempt for foreign enemies, mirrored a growing sense of English nationalism that has since become a commonplace in motivating soldiers. Indeed she used it to overcome her major weakness as a royal warrior; even if she had a woman's weak and feeble body, she had the heart and stomach of an English king.

Not having been born a boy was the most important thing in Elizabeth's life. Her father had disowned her, divorced and executed her mother when she was three just because he wanted a son. As the second daughter, she was shunted from household to household, and constantly felt she was being bullied by men. Less than two years after the earl of Essex, the spoiled son she never had, turned against her in 1601, and had to be executed for treason, Elizabeth died. Refusing food or drink she curled up in a foetal position and passed away deeply depressed, perhaps because she felt guilty at not being the son her father wanted.[23]

Posterity has judged Elizabeth kindly. Had she been a male she might well have got involved in wars as costly and wasteful as her father's futile search for ephemeral glory. Instead her wars against Spain saved Protestantism, ensured the independence of the Netherlands, and in Ireland laid the foundations of a united kingdom, which paradoxically led to the civil wars that bedevilled her successors.

James the Sixth of Scotland and First of England (1603–25), was not a martial figure. 'He was infinitely inclined to peace,' wrote Sir Anthony Weldon in a thumbnail sketch of the king he served.[24] Sir John Oglander, a gentleman from the Isle of Wight, was less charitable. 'King James was the most cowardly man I ever knew,' he recalled, 'He could not endure a soldier or to see men drilled, to hear of war was death to him.'[25] Both attributed the king's gutlessness to a dread of assassination. James trembled at the thought of violence, wearing a stiletto-proof padded jerkin. 'The King is in terror,' the Venetian Ambassador reported after the Guy Fawkes Plot.[26] In 1610 he posted guards on the *Prince Royal* to stop saboteurs creeping aboard at night with augurs to bore holes in the hull so that when the next day the ship was launched with the royal family aboard it would not sink. James once called body armour an excellent invention: it not only saved the life of the wearer but was so cumbersome that it prevented him from hurting anyone else.

To be fair James worked hard for peace. The sobriquet he most treasured was *Rex Pacificus*. 'I am a king who loves peace,' he declared in 1621. 'I do not delight in the shedding of blood, and therefore strain every nerve to avert it if possible.'[27]

The only battles King James enjoyed were mock ones to celebrate some grand family occasion, such as the investiture of his son, Henry, as Prince of Wales in June 1606. A sea fight was staged between two English ships and a Turkish vessel on the Thames opposite Whitehall Palace, which ended with the rout of the enemy, the storming of a Turkish fort on the opposite bank, and a magnificent fireworks display. For the marriage of his eldest daughter, Elizabeth, in 1614, the king decided on an encore. This time the battle was a fiasco. No one bothered to storm the Turkish fort, and the general confusion of cannon and fireworks did more harm to the re-enactors than it did to the 'infidels'. One man lost his eyes, another both arms. 'I ran more danger than if it had been a sea service in good earnest,' recalled a veteran sailor.[28]

Yet for a nation which had seen a generation go to Elizabeth's wars there was something to be said for mock battles, no matter how chaotic. Immediately on becoming king James made peace with Spain, his reign being untroubled by war until the very end when his son, Charles, and his favourite, the duke of Buckingham, took over the reins of power from the increasingly senile sovereign.[29]

Between 1624 and 1628 Charles and Buckingham waged four military campaigns, all of which failed.

In 1624 they sent an expedition under the German mercenary, Count Ernest von Mansfeld, to the Low Countries, where the hapless conscripts perished from poor food, scanty clothing, rudimentary shelter and disease. The following year Charles and Buckingham sent a squadron to attack the Spanish port of Cadiz hoping to capture the treasure fleet from the Americas which by law had to make landfall there. They arrived a few days too early. After a desultory bombardment of the fort guarding Cadiz, the English landed troops on the dunes to the south. Having forgotten to fill their water bottles, they were extremely thirsty after a long hot trudge along the beach, so when they came across the main wine warehouse for the Spanish navy they refreshed themselves with prodigious enthusiasm. 'They became so drunk that in my life I never saw such beastliness,' a colonel admitted.[30] The Spanish attacked. Inebriated, the English died.

In 1627 Buckingham personally led an expedition against the island of Ré, just off the French port of La Rochelle, which rebellious Protestants, known as the Huguenots, were holding against King Louis XIII. Initially the landing went well, but after the English assault on the main French fort at St Martin failed because the scaling ladders were a few feet too short, Buckingham had to order a withdrawal. Due to his incompetent posting of the rear guard at the wrong end of a bridge across a creek which led to the embarkation point, the retreat became a rout. Only three of the eight thousand who left England returned home. In September 1628 the English once again tried to relieve the Huguenots at La Rochelle, but failed to blow up the boom across the harbour mouth.

While militarily insignificant, these four bungled expeditions had a profound political effect. Buckingham became increasingly unpopular as the scapegoat for the failure of British arms, and was assassinated by a deranged army officer in August 1628. Relations between the king and parliament deteriorated so precipitously that in March 1629 Charles decided to rule on his own. During the eleven years of the so-called Personal Rule, Charles was unable to raise parliamentary taxes to fight a major land war, so he made the best of a bad job by using propagandists, such as the court painter Rubens, to show the virtues of peace. In *Landscape with St George* Rubens represents Charles as England's patron saint, who has just slain the dragon of war, and rescued the fair maid (who looks just like his wife Henrietta Maria). In the painting England enjoys the benefits of peace, as compared to the horrors of the Thirty Years War which raged on the continent, as represented by the corpses and ravaged women.

Charles I (1625–49) was not a particularly warlike man. To be sure he delighted in having himself painted wearing full armour, riding a pugnacious stallion. But in his portraits the king adopted a number of poses: the family man surrounded by his children and a dog or two, the country gentleman about to go out hunting, the statesman dressed in the robes of state. While the causes of the civil war are many and complicated, having been debated with much ferocity by historians ever since, they owe little to the king's bellicosity. 'We have insensible slid into the beginnings of a civil war, by one unexpected accident after another, as waves of the sea,' Bulstrode Whitelock wrote to his wife in July 1642.[31] Two months later, after Charles raised the Royal Standard at Nottingham, formally declaring war against his rebellious subjects, he was still hesitant to fight. Three days later, under intense pressure from his council, the king spent a tearful, sleepless night before sending parliament an appeal for peace. It was promptly rejected.

Charles was a reluctant royal warrior. He did not fight for economic gain or personal glory. Neither did he relish combat as a means of proving his manhood. For him war was a matter of loyalty. 'The time is now come for my faithful friends to show themselves,' he wrote to the earl of Traquair a few days after raising the standard.[32] War was also a highly personal matter. 'I am going to fight for my crown and dignity,' he explained to Richard Shuckburgh, a country gentleman who asked him why he was marching at the head of his army toward Edgehill, the site of the war's first major battle.[33] Charles personalised the civil war. Whether its causes were religious (as the Victorians believed), or deep-rooted and economic (as Marxist historians have argued), or random and short-term (as revisionists have recently maintained), as far as Charles was concerned he was fighting to preserve his God-given prerogatives. The claim to rule by divine rights was a great psychological comfort to a man as insecure as Charles.

If God was on his side then He could not possibly be on that of the king's enemies. As bad men they deserved to be chastised, if necessary by the sword. Such an explanation had all the power of simplicity. If the king was to blame – and Charles occasionally admitted to such a remote possibility – then it was for bowing to parliamentary pressure by signing the death warrant of the earl of Stafford, his trusted adviser, in May 1642. Such a failure, like St Peter's denial of Christ thrice before the cock crowed twice, spurred a basically pacific king to fight.

No one could question Charles's energy. He was constantly campaigning. For instance, between 9 April and 23 November 1644 he moved on 92 days, or 40 per cent of the time. On these days he rode 949 miles, the longest he stayed in one place being at Boconnoc, Cornwall, during the Lostwithiel campaign. Between 7 May and 5 November 1645 the king moved an average of 16 miles at day on 76 occasions (again 40 per cent of the days). In 1644 Charles was involved in three major battles, Lostwithiel, Cropredy and Second Newbury, while the following year he was at Naseby and Rowton Heath.

Neither could the king's physical courage be doubted. When in June 1644 it seemed that the parliamentary army might capture him, Charles declared that 'possibly he might be found in the hand of the earl of Essex, but that he would be dead first'. The following August during a reconnaissance near Beacon Hill the king came under cannon fire that smashed a sergeant near him to pulp. He did not flinch.[34] Towards the end of the Battle of Naseby, sensing that his cavalry were about to break, the first of the fear-stricken men having already galloped past him, Charles wanted to lead his reserves into the affray in one last do-or-die charge. The war, however, was not to have a Hollywood ending, with Charles and Cromwell fighting it out hand to hand. Grabbing his sovereign's bridle the earl of Carnwath shouted, 'will you go unto your death?' The gesture, plus a nebulous order, panicked the reserves who rode hell for leather back to Leicester, leaving the infantry to their fate.

Charles also tried to identify with his common soldiers. He stayed all night on the field after Edgehill, listening to the cries and sobs of the wounded and dying. He was, alas, too restrained to go and dress their wounds, or order medical attention for them. The only sign of emotion he displayed was in a letter written four days later. 'You cannot be more sensible,' he consoled the earl of Lindsey 'of your father's loss than myself, his death confirming the estimation I ever had of him.'[35]

Such self-control, joined with a painful stutter, hampered the king's ability to communicate with the rank and file. After the victory of Cropredy in 1644 when the royalists were in hot pursuit of the foe, the king's carriage broke down during a thunderstorm. His bodyguard offered to cut a gap in a hedge so he could shelter in an adjacent cottage. He told them not to bother. They congratulated him on his fortitude. Charles replied 'that as God had given him afflictions to exercise his patience, so he had given him patience to bear his afflictions'.[36] What a wonderful reply for a martyr! What a miserable rejoinder for a warrior! Leaders are not supposed to be passive but active. Rather than enduring suffering their job is to inflict pain on other side.

To do so they require a killer instinct, a ruthless craving to achieve their goals. Wars, as General Patton observed, are not won by dying for one's country but by making the other poor fellow die for his. Before the Battle of Edgehill the king performed the ceremonial duties of leadership by riding up and down before his men dressed in an ermine-lined cape to inspire them. But he failed to exercise command by resolving the bitter dispute between his generals as to what formation they should use. After the battle the king was too stunned to do anything for nearly twenty-four hours. The carnage he confessed had 'left him exceedingly and deeply grieved'.[37] For over three weeks he rejected the advice of his leading general and nephew, Prince Rupert, to advance on London. When he did so the city's defences had become so strong that he lost all chance of capturing the capital and winning the civil war.

Observers all agree on the king's equanimity as a soldier. 'He showed a very great and exemplary temperance,' recalled Sir Philip Warwick. 'I never observed any great severity in the king,' added Sir Henry Slingsby.[38] The only time Slingsby remembered Charles losing his temper was at Wing, near Uppingham, where he ordered a soldier hanged on a signpost for stealing a chalice from a church.

Such severity was unusual. Charles failed to follow the advice that Sir Ralph Hopton, the King's General in the West, laid down in *Maxims for the Management of an Army* (1643): 'pay well, command well, hang well.' Apart from the looter at Wing, whose theft of a chalice used in Holy Communion disturbed the pious king, the only other execution Charles personally ordered was at Lostwithiel of some soldiers who stripped and murdered a woman who had given birth but three days before. Charles usually pardoned deserters, especially after it became clear that he was losing the war and desperately needed all the men he could find. His soldiers were consistently paid late – if at all – and as the war went on relied increasingly on plunder to keep body and soul together.

Although the king's men continued to fight long after his cause was lost, few of them displayed any direct personal affection for him. After being presented to Charles in 1643, Henry Verney, a cavalry major, whose father had died for the crown at Edgehill, wrote to his wife, 'The king's hand I have kissed. He looked earnestly upon me, but spoke not to me. In time, if the war goes on, I hope to be known to him . . .'.[39]

Charles was not without his military achievements. He handled his forces well, particularly during the 1644 campaign. On 28 June at Cropredy he trounced Sir William Waller's roundheads so badly that many mutinied and went home. His coordination of forces at Lostwithiel where he trapped the earl of Essex's army in Cornwall was masterful. With great skill he operated in bocage-like terrain, where communications were extremely difficult. And then he threw his victory away by allowing the surrendered parliamentarians to march back towards London. Some thirty miles west of the capital they turned the tide, ambushing Charles's forces at the Second Battle of Newbury, from which the king was barely able to escape by a well-conducted night march to Oxford.

In spite of his cold nature, and occasional flashes of brilliance, the king had one great advantage – one that he squandered. As the earl of Manchester observed 'If we beat the king nine & ninety times, he is king still. But if the king beats us but once we shall be hanged, and our posterity made slaves'.[40] As monarch Charles had an aura of legitimacy: subjects were accustomed to obeying him. He was the undoubted leader of the royalist forces who tried to give the impression of being in total command. A portrait shows the king, baton in hand, serene and commanding, dictating commands to Sir Edward Walker, the secretary of his council of war, who uses a drum for a desk – a surface which presumably would render any order nigh illegible [Plate 4.4]. In fact the four volumes of Walker's papers show very little input from the king, only one letter being in Charles's own hand.

As king Charles never exercised complete control over his high-spirited subordinates, especially his nephew, Prince Rupert, the dashing cavalry commander. The vague orders he gave Rupert on 14 June 1644 led to the royalist defeat two weeks later at Marston Moor, the war's bloodiest battle. Rupert never forgave his uncle, carrying the ambiguous letter on him for the rest of his life. Charles failed to devise an effective intelligence service, and had little interest in the crucial area of logistics. Only once, in June 1645 did he ever have clear-cut options set before him, and then chose the one that led to his decisive defeat at Naseby. Even then he refused to recognise reality. He told Rupert that while as a 'mere soldier or statesman' he could not hope to win the war, as a Christian he knew God would not permit him to lose. But Charles's problem was that he never really defined his goals. Even during the negotiations with parliament and the army after his surrender in 1646 his objectives kept on changing, making any negotiated solution impossible. His refusal to bargain in good faith brought about a second civil

Plate 4.4 Charles I dictating to his secretary Edward Walker © By courtesy of the National Portrait Gallery, London

war in 1648, which was fought with far greater ferocity than the first. Prisoners were executed in cold blood: at Preston Cromwell decimated the Scots army which invaded England.

Charles did not go to war for the normal reasons – gold, glory, aggression, even ambition. He was not just an ineffective warrior, but a reluctant one. And for this he paid with the soldier's ultimate coin, with his life, though not on the field of battle, but on the scaffold at Whitehall on 30 January 1649. His enemies believed he deserved to die because they saw him as a 'man of blood': he was no longer a legitimate royal warrior.

Charles II (1660–85) never forgot his father's execution. Two years later, intent on revenge, he tried to regain his patrimony by landing in Scotland. After swearing to become a Presbyterian, he lead an army of 16,000 troops across the Border. At Worcester on 3 September with 28,000 roundheads Oliver Cromwell routed him in yet another brilliant victory. Charles managed to escape back to the continent, unlike his troops, very few of whom made it home. Cromwell's problem was not that he was a mediocre warrior. Far from it: he was one of England's greatest English military commanders. His problem was that he was not royal. So the republic he helped establish largely by force of arms lacked legitimacy, and collapsed two years after his death with the restoration of Charles II in 1660.

Charles II was a peace-loving rake with a bevy of beautiful mistresses and sixteen acknowledged bastards, who wanted to die quietly in his own bed – or, better still, someone else's. His brother James II (1685–88), was very different.

Born in 1633, James was barely eight when he first encountered rebellion. On 22 April 1642, as both king and parliament were preparing for war, Charles I sent James with fifty retainers commanded by his nephew, Prince Charles Louis, the Elector Palatine, into Hull, an important arsenal whose governor, Sir John Hotham, inclined toward parliament. Lest he offend the king, the next day Hotham entertained Prince James's party with a sumptuous feast, in the midst of which he learned that the king was outside with three hundred cavalry demanding admittance. So Hotham shut the gate and hauled up the drawbridge in Charles's face, preventing the king from seizing the large stocks of weapons and ammunition inside. Humiliated, Charles had difficulty in persuading Hotham to release his son.

Six months later, barely nine, James saw his first battle, at Edgehill in October 1642. According to one story, which is as delightful as it is dubious, the king asked his physician, Dr William Harvey (the discoverer of the circulation of blood), to guard his sons during the battle. So engrossed was the doctor with a book he was reading while sitting

Plate 2.2 Richard I and Saladin (Add. 42130. Folio No: 82. Min. (L)) © By permission of the British Library

Plate 3.4   Henry V – The Royal Collection © 2003, HM Queen Elizabeth II

Plate 6.3 The Duke of Cumberland at Culloden © Christie's Images Ltd

Plate 6.5 The Presentation of Crimean Medals by Queen Victoria. The Royal Collection © 2003, HM Queen Elizabeth II

under a hedge that only the sound of a cannonball landing near him reminded Harvey to withdraw with his royal charges. Most likely the king asked Sir William Howard and his fifty gentlemen pensioners, a group whose blood was as blue as their bodies were aged, to look after his boys. They advanced with the rest of the royal army down the slope of Edgehill, into enemy musket range. After some close hand-to-hand fighting, in which Sir Ralph Verney was killed carrying the king's standard, Howard and his charges withdrew up Edgehill scarp to a small barn which was being used as a field dressing station. Even so they were not out of danger. Recognising them, a group of roundhead cavalry charged. Sir John Hinton shot one with his pistol, while Miles Matthews killed another with a poleaxe. For the young prince it was an impressionable experience.

James spent the rest of the war in Oxford, a most exciting place, where he and his brother Charles, three years his senior, ran almost wild. Their tutor, Bishop Brian Duppa, was barely able to control, let alone teach them. Raucous sergeants replaced contemplative dons. The handful of students left lived in 'a dark nasty room' in New College. When the scholars complained about their conditions hardly anyone listened, for most of the undergraduates had joined up. Cavalry patrols jangled through the streets trying to catch the eye of those pretty girls who seemed to flock wherever the court met. Women waved, and children skipped alongside the columns of infantry as they marched through the streets, their step light as they set out, their pace heavy if they returned. The colleges were used as barracks or warehouses. Magdalen became an artillery park, the Great Quad at Christ Church was a cattle pen. In the Music and Astronomy Schools tailors stitched uniforms. The Schools of Law and Logic were granaries, that of Rhetoric a workshop for portable bridges. A powder mill was set up at Osney Abbey, and a sword factory at Wolvercote. At New Inn Hall a mint turned college plate into coins, as well as striking medals for brave soldiers. All over town printing presses churned out propaganda that carters smuggled throughout the land.

In May 1646 Charles I slipped out of Oxford disguised as a groom, and after nine days on the run surrendered to the Scots whose invading army was camped at Newark. Two months later Oxford capitulated to the parliamentary forces commanded by General Fairfax. The roundheads treated James with the respect due the king's son, who had just been created duke of York: Fairfax and Oliver Cromwell knelt to kiss his hand. The following month he was sent to London to be lodged with his brother, Henry, duke of Gloucester, and sister, Princess Elizabeth, in St James's Palace. They were under the tutelage of Algenon Percy, earl of Northumberland, a kindly man, whose service as Lord High Admiral may have kindled James's interest in naval warfare. Their confinement was comfortable. Parliament allocated £10,500 to maintain the royal children, and let them visit their father when he was held prisoner in Hampton Court.

During one such visit they could have discussed plans for James's escape, which seemed to become more necessary by the day. In the winter of 1647, after a coded letter was intercepted and deciphered, a parliamentary committee interrogated the duke, and threatened to incarcerate him in the Tower. To save his son Charles gave Colonel Joseph Bampfield and his mistress, Anne Murray, money to arrange the breakout. James provided Bampfield with his measurements, so he could arrange for women's clothing to be made – the tailor remarked that he had never stitched a dress for so short a girl with so large a body.

Northumberland allowed James, Henry and Elizabeth to play hide and seek in the walled gardens of St James's Palace. James was particularly good at the game, often staying hidden for up to half an hour before he was discovered. On 20 April 1648, taking advantage of Northumberland's leniency, and making sure that their dog was safely inside, James slipped out through a wicket gate, for which he had secretly been given a key. He met Bampfield, who took him by hackney to a house near London Bridge, where he put on the newly tailored clothes. They went by barge to Tilbury to board a Dutch merchantman. After James scratched his leg in a most unladylike fashion the Dutch captain became suspicious and had to be told his passenger's real identity. Fortunately the man was a confirmed royalist, and was happy to slip past Tilbury Blockhouse with his ship's running lights unlit, and land James at Middleburg, Holland.

James hated exile. His mother wanted to control him. His father's execution came as a shock, convincing him of the folly of compromise. His brother, having being defeated at Worcester, seemed to have lost all hope of regaining the crown, and sought consolation in the beds of numerous women. Demoralised hangers-on at Louis XIV's court, the royalist emigrés were broke and bickered amongst themselves with the zest of desperate men who had nothing else to lose.

So it was with profound relief that on 24 April 1652 James rode off to enlist in the French army as a gentleman volunteer. He was so destitute that he had to borrow 300 pistoles to pay his retinue, which consisted of Sir John Berkeley, Colonel Sir John Werden, half a dozen servants, six horses, and two mules for their baggage. Even before he joined the French army under Henri, Vicomte de Turenne, James displayed his military prowess. Just outside Corbeil he came across several companies of the King's Guards who had been denied access to the town, the inhabitants wanting to stay out of the civil war, known as the Fronde, that engulfed France. James strolled up to the gate, and started talking to the watchman whom he persuaded to let him in. Then he convinced the city authorities to admit the Royal Guard. Surely he had learned the lesson of his father's failure at Hull?

Less than ten days after joining the French Army James fought his first battle. With great daring Turenne moved five thousand troops in a thirty-mile night march (always a difficult operation), to Etaples, where he surprised the rebel forces. Even though outnumbered, for three out of his five thousand men had got lost on the march, Turenne ordered an immediate attack. James fought bravely, turning up wherever the fighting was hottest. The French royalists won, killing a thousand enemy for the loss of five hundred men. Emboldened James won even more distinction five weeks later at the Siege of Etaples where he personally led several cavalry attacks. According to Edward Hyde, earl of Clarendon (the contemporary historian who became James's father-in-law), the duke of York 'behaved himself with exemplary courage and gallantry'. During Turenne's ill-fated attack on Paris, James conducted himself with equal distinction, and the following year barely avoided being killed or captured when he mistook an enemy cavalry patrol for one of his own. In September 1653 he fought at the Siege of Mouzin, where he had a couple of narrow escapes: a musket round ricocheted off a helmet, went through a pioneer's leg, 'and lastly stroke the toe of my boot, without doing me any harm'; a cannon-ball hit three barrels of gunpowder, just beside him, but did not set them off. 'But the danger came so suddenly and was so soon over, that none of us had time to be concerned for it.'[41]

Such *sang-froid* was characteristic of James's military service. In his memoirs he writes coolly about the summer of 1654 when, promoted lieutenant general, he commanded five battalions of infantry and forty squadrons of cavalry in a diversionary raid against the Spanish Netherlands. At the Siege of Arras he fought without stint: he captured enemy cavalry, was nearly taken prisoner, led raids in which each side showered the other with grenades, and survived an explosion in the cellars of the house where he and Turenne were having dinner. Turenne, who was the outstanding field marshal of his day, thought highly of James, whom he believed was 'like to be the best general of his time'.[42]

So James was bitterly disappointed the following year when Louis XIV made an alliance with Oliver Cromwell's Commonwealth in which he agreed to dismiss the duke of York from French service. He had to join the Spanish army, which he quickly discovered to be a lackadaisical bunch, no match for Turenne's disciplined troops. His commander Don Juan (Philip IV's illegitimate son), was as incompetent as he was idle. He

spent most days in bed in his tent, taking special pride in being inaccess-
ible. So it is not surprising that when on 14 June 1658, Philip stirred
himself to attack the French forces, reinforced by some six thousand
British Ironsides, at Dunkirk, he was thrashed. At the Battle of the
Dunes James personally led a cavalry charge against the enemy, his horse
stumbling in the soft sand. It was 'to no purpose,' he confessed, 'I was
beaten off and all who were at the head of my own Troop were either
killed or wounded.'[43] A second charge against some Ironsides was more
successful. They refused quarter, James recalled with admiration for the
courage of his compatriots: one even dismounted him.

James's valour could not make up for Don Juan's incompetence. The
Spanish were routed, losing a thousand killed and three to four times as
many taken prisoner. The duke was lucky to escape with his reputation
intact. Indeed he was negotiating with the Portuguese to command
their fleet when Charles was restored to the throne in May 1660, and
the royal family's exile ended.

The duke who returned to England was very different from the boy who
had fled to France disguised as a girl fourteen years earlier. At twenty-
six James was a self-confident soldier who had proven himself in combat, having earned, the count of Gramont noted, 'a reputation for his
undaunted courage'.[44]

Even though he had held the office of Lord High Admiral since
childhood, after the Restoration James became an active and effective
incumbent. Under Oliver Cromwell the Navy had become a formidable
force of 156 ships carrying 4,642 guns. Building on this substantial
foundation, and with the help of competent administrators, such as
Sir William Penn, Peter Pett and Samuel Pepys, James did more to
improve the Royal Navy than any other English sovereign. After paying
the sailors their arrears, some up to four years late, they set up the Naval
Board. They resolved the conflict between the high-born gentlemen
captains and the 'tarpaulins', those professional seamen whose claim to
command lay more in their competence than their lineage, by establishing
a system of exams for promotion. James wrote standing orders which
defined everything from tactics to petty discipline – 'those who pisseth
on the deck' were to receive ten lashes.[45] All this they did to defeat the
Dutch, for as Samuel Pepys told his diary, 'The trade of the world is too
little for us two, therefore one must stand down.'[46]

So James encouraged trade in both the East and West Indies, Africa
and North America, sending Colonel Richard Nicholas with three hundred men to the Dutch colony of New Amsterdam, which they captured
in 1664 and renamed New York in the duke's honour.

On the formal outbreak of hostilities, known as the Second Dutch War, James took personal command of the fleet, spending much of April 1665 at Chatham aboard his flagship, *The Royal Charles*, discussing tactics with his captains. In early May they weighed anchor for the Dutch naval base at Texel. After they captured an enemy supply convoy a gale (plus the fact that they had run out of beer), drove the English back to port. At the end of May they set sail again, anchoring at Southwold Bay, just south of Lowestoft on 1 June. That afternoon a Dutch fleet of 113 ships under Admiral Jacob Opdam appeared above the horizon, and for the next two days the two forces manoeuvred to get upwind of the other. The Battle of Lowestoft started at about three in the morning of 3 June, about forty minutes before sunrise. Since the wind had dropped considerably it took the fleets six hours to come into contact. James ordered his ships to close on the Dutch on a starboard tack, which resulted in the loss of the *Charity*. At about ten, the weather being ideal – the day fine, the seas calm, and the wind steady from the southwest – James and Opdam's ships engaged each other. The duke became dangerously vulnerable after cannon fire and a leak respectively forced his consorts, the *Saint George* and the *Old James*, to withdraw. Aboard the flagship a cannon-ball killed Charles Berkeley (the earl of Falmouth), Lord Donough Muskerry and Richard Boyle, showering James with their brains and blood. The duke was deeply upset: Berkeley and Muskerry were comrades with whom he had fought in France and Flanders. Yet he continued to direct the fighting. By about two in the afternoon the tide of battle began to turn. As the Dutch started to edge back to their ports, James used a technique he had learned from Turenne. He ordered his guns to cease firing so the black gunpowder smoke, which reduced visibility to a pea-souper, could clear. Then he told his master gunner to fire the cannon in sequence, aiming them in person. The third shot hit the magazine on Opdam's ship, which in an instant blew up, routing the rest of the enemy fleet except for the *Orange*, which, staying to fight, was set alight and abandoned. 'We all ran away,' confessed Admiral Cornelius van Tromp.

James ordered his fleet to hotly pursue the enemy, four of whom they sunk by nightfall. But after the duke retired for a few hours of much-needed sleep at about eleven, his instructions to press on post haste were countermanded by Henry Brounker, who as a Groom of the Bedchamber, a mere courtier, had no business telling sailors what to do. Brounker's motivations for doing so have never been properly explained. Some thought he was a Dutch agent (and he was lucky to escape being court-martialled as such). Others suggested that from London James's mother, Henrietta Maria, or his wife, Anne Hyde, persuaded him to do so to save the duke from further harm. Whatever Brounker's reasons, the results of his actions were disastrous. Although the public greeted James as the hero of the hour on his return to London, where Parliament voted him £120,000, it was plain that notwithstanding the loss of five to six thousand Dutch sailors at Lowestoft for only nine hundred dead, the British victory was far from complete.

Its partiality was demonstrated exactly a year later when the Dutch, using chain shot for the first time, routed the English off the Nore during the Four Days Fight. John Evelyn, the diarist, 'beheld the sad spectacle. . . . Hardly a vessel entire, but appearing so many wrecks and hulls, so cruelly had the Dutch mangled us.'[47]

There was worse to come. Expecting peace the English started to demobilise leaving their fleet woefully vulnerable. In June 1667 a Dutch fleet under Admiral Michael de Ruyter sailed into Chatham, burned seven vessels, and towed away *The Royal Charles*, James's flagship at Lowestoft, as a prize. For a few weeks they blockaded the Thames, terrifying Londoners. 'I think the Devil shits Dutchmen,' one told Pepys.[48] Evelyn was so scared that he removed 'my best goods, plate, etc., from my house to another place in the country'.[49]

Even though a month later at Breda the English made peace with the Dutch (on surprisingly favourable terms), James was blamed for the fiasco at Chatham. Relations with his brother, who also reproached the earl of Clarendon, deteriorated so badly that they could well have pushed James into doing what he had been contemplating for well over a dozen years, becoming a Roman Catholic – the most disastrous decision of a prince whose life was fraught with calamitous choices.

In late April 1672, six weeks after the Third Dutch War broke out, James set sail from Chatham aboard the *Prince*, a brand new 100-gun vessel, with 62 ships. After failing to make contact with the Dutch his fleet, by now ninety strong, returned to Southwold Bay for replenishment. Here, on a lee shore, the Dutch under De Ruyter surprised them on 28 May. Even though the *Prince* managed to escape two fireships, by noon she was so badly damaged, having lost two hundred crew, that James had to transfer his flag to the *Saint Michael*. For five hours Dutch ships pounded her from both port and starboard until she had lost so many men and had taken on so much water, her captain told the duke he must leave before she sunk. So for the third time James transferred his flag, moving to the *London* which was disabled within a few more hours. 'He is everything a man can be,' wrote Captain John Narborough, his second in command, 'and most pleasant when the great shot are thundering about his ears.'[50]

The Battle of Southwold Bay had been long and brutal, 2,500 being killed on each side. The *Royal James* burned to the waterline with the loss of 600 of her 1,000 crew, and would have exploded had not all her ammunition been expended. James, who had lost five ships to the enemy's four, wanted to pursue them the following day, but could not do so since his vessels were too badly damaged, and were out of gunpowder.

For the next sixteen years James's battles were to be political ones against his fellow countrymen, who were determined to do all they could to exclude a Catholic from inheriting the throne. Their efforts failed, so when in February 1685 his brother died without a legitimate heir (although with sixteen acknowledged bastards), King James became the Second of England and Seventh of Scotland, and, within three years, the last of both.

Initially the new king was welcomed warmly. 'I cannot but predict much happiness to the Nation,' John Evelyn wrote in his diary. 'Well may our monarchy triumphant stand,' rhymed the poet John Dryden in one of his less memorable verses, 'While warlike JAMES protects both sea and land.'[51]

James easily protected England from its first threat, an invasion led by the duke of Monmouth, Charles II's eldest illegitimate son, who claimed that his father had actually married his mother making him the rightful monarch. The rebels were readily routed at the Battle of Sedgemoor on 6 July 1685, the survivors being harshly punished, their leader having his head cut off before a huge crowd on Tower Hill by an incompetent axeman who took five blows to complete the job.

Emboldened by the lack of support for Monmouth, James summoned a parliament. Although he had packed its membership by changing the franchise in many boroughs, he could not work with parliament, which he soon dismissed. Turning on his friends, the universities which were bastions of High Church Anglicans who believed in the divine right of monarchs, he appointed Catholics as heads of colleges. He also commissioned Catholics in the army, waiving the requirement laid down by the Test Act that they swear an oath abjuring the pope. When Colonel John Bates's coachman brought a suit against his master's appointment to command a regiment in order to collect the five hundred pounds paid to successful plaintiffs, Lord Chief Justice Sir Edward Herbert ruled that 'there was nothing whatever with which the King, as supreme lawgiver, could not dispense.'[52]

So the king issued a Declaration of Indulgence that dispensed with all the laws which discriminated against those, both Catholics and Non-Conformists, who were not members of the Church of England. To ensure that everyone knew of his determination the king instructed every bishop and priest to read the Declaration from their pulpits during divine service. Seven bishops refused. So in a fit of pique James had them tried for seditious libel, an outrageously exaggerated charge, on which a London jury acquitted them on 30 June 1688. The public was ecstatic. The bishops were rowed up the Thames to the cheers of crowds on both sides of the river. When the news reached the army camp at Hounslow, ten miles to the west, the troops joined in the celebration. James, who was there dining with Lord Louis Feversham, an old comrade from the Battle of Southwold Bay, in his tent, asked why the men were cheering. 'It was nothing but the joy of the soldiers at the acquittal of the Bishops,' came a reply. 'And you call that nothing?' answered a disheartened monarch.

It was a bitter pill to swallow so soon after the birth of a son three weeks before, the first by his second wife, Mary of Modena. After fourteen years of a barren marriage James and Mary decided to go on a pilgrimage in 1687 to the springs at Holywell, Clwyd, where Winfride, the Welsh saint, had been martyred in the seventh century. Catholics thought the result miraculous. Protestants believed it to be fraudulent, claiming the child was a warming-pan baby, a foundling smuggled into the queen's bed to prevent the accession of James's eldest daughter, Mary, a sound Protestant, married to William, the ruler of Holland.

The birth of an heir, who was bound to be brought up as adamant a papist as his mother and father, was the final straw for Lords Devonshire, Danby, Shrewsbury and Lumley, and Bishop Compton of London, and Henry Sidney, who on 30 June secretly wrote to William inviting him to England.

He arrived on 5 November 1688, a propitious day for Protestants who were convinced that exactly eighty-three years earlier the Almighty had saved England from another papist conspiracy led by Guy Fawkes. William landed with some ten thousand men, a mixed force of Dutch, English and mercenary troops, at Torbay, to find little public support. The Mayor of Exeter refused to open the city gates. William talked about going home, having no wish to share Monmouth's bloody fate on Tower Hill. But slowly people came over to him. The first royalist desertions, few in number though great in significance, were sixty horsemen from a reconnaissance patrol which included their commander, Lord Henry Cornbury, the eldest son of James's first father-in-law, the earl of Clarendon, who was doubtless upset by the king's refusal to let the earl return from exile.

On 16 November James left London to join the bulk of his forces at Salisbury which he reached three days later. Lord Charles Middleton, the secretary of state, reported him 'in perfect health', confident that reinforcements from Scotland and Ireland would bring him victory. The day after learning of Cornbury's treachery the king had a copious nosebleed which lasted for at least forty-eight hours. In effect he suffered both a nervous and physical breakdown, the latter most likely caused by high blood pressure. The 'prodigious bleeding' observed the duke of Berwick, the king's illegitimate son by Arabella Churchill, made him lethargic and incapable of taking decisions, a condition which his doctors worsened by medical bleeding, the cure-all of the day. On 22 November a council of war, dominated by Lord Feversham, urged the king to withdraw to London. Early the next morning his leading general, John Churchill, who opposed the retreat and owed his meteoric rise to the king's favours – as well as his sister Arabella's to James – deserted taking the bulk of the royal army with him. For the next two days James ran hither and thither like some demented corporal ordering, counter-ordering and disordering, until he withdrew to London. He fled the capital on 19 December, throwing the Great Seal of England into the Thames as he was being rowed across the river. Although James was detained at Faversham, William let him escape to France, which he reached on Christmas Day. Protestants construed James's dropping the Great Seal into the Thames as an irrevocable act of abdication.

James did not interpret it as such. Twelve weeks later he was back in his realm, landing in Kinsale, Ireland with some French volunteers and 20,000 muskets sent by Louis XIV. On arriving in Dublin, James discovered that the Irish were not very interested in returning him to his throne in London, being more concerned with their own independence. Having failed in August to capture Londonderry he tried to engage the 10,000 troops commanded by the duke of Schomberg, who refused to fight, waiting instead for William to arrive with reinforcements. He did so the following summer, bringing some 45,000 men.

The two kings met on 1 July 1690 at the Boyne [Plate 4.5]. Though fordable, narrow and sluggish, the river was the best defensive position north of Dublin. James drew his men up on the south bank at Oldenbridge to prevent William's forces, who equalled his in size, from taking the Irish capital. When William dispatched some of his men to Rosenaree Ford, four miles to the west, to cross the river and cut off James's retreat, he countered by sending two thirds of his troops to stop them. It was a mistake, for William had retained the bulk of his strength at Oldenbridge, allowing him to cross the river and rout James's divided army. They ran, a veteran recalled 'like sheep flying before the wolf'. James arrived in Dublin breathless at ten that night, and after a brief meeting of the Privy Council decided to return to France.

THE REVOLUTION.

Plate 4.5 The Battle of the Boyne © Mary Evans Picture Library

He lost the last and faintest chance of regaining the throne in 1692 when Admiral Edward Russell's fleet destroyed the French ships tasked for an invasion of England at Cap de la Hague, near Cherbourg. From the cliffs James watched his hopes drown. Yet he could not help but applaud his countrymen who had rejected him and his religion, exclaiming with pride, 'Ah! None but my brave English could do so brave an action.'[53]

Why then did so brave an Englishman as James do so many stupid things in his brief, but disastrous reign? Why did he advance Catholicism in a country which was overwhelmingly, even fanatically, Protestant? Why did he try to build up a standing army in a land which still smarted from the memory of Oliver Cromwell, and of the 'tyrannical' rule of the Major Generals who abolished Christmas and made adultery a capital offence? Why did this proven brave warrior, who in more recent times would have surely won medals for courage above and beyond the call of duty, panic in November 1688, and behave so cravenly at the Boyne two years later?

According to John Miller the answer is simple. 'James's downfall, therefore, owes much to his inability to cope with the complex demands of kingship, and more to his Catholicism. In the last resort, however, it stemmed above all, from a lack of human understanding.' Another biographer, Peter Earle, put it more pithily: 'Piety makes people outrageously stupid.'[54]

To be sure James was tolerant of other religions, becoming a close friend of William Penn, the Quaker who founded Pennsylvania. James did not, as his enemies later maintained, intend restoring England to Rome. While he might have wanted to do so, even he knew that was impossible. But why then did he tempt the impossible by offending the Protestant hegemony, arousing their easily aroused paranoia that the Bishop of Rome, his cardinals, Jesuits and the Inquisition were hell bent on undoing the Reformation? It could be a matter of faith, which, by definition, is unfathomable.

James's faith was rooted in his military experiences. The piety of his French Catholic comrades profoundly impressed the duke. He recalled how just prior to the final assault on Arras in August 1654 there 'were public prayers at the head of each Battalion and Squadron for several days before, and as many as could confessed and received the Blessed Sacrament. So that I am confident that no Army ever shown more mark of true devotion than ours.'[55] In the French army his brother officers were not the stereotypical papist zealots his Protestant upbringing had led him to expect. Neither was his first wife, Anne Hyde, a highly intelligent woman, who converted him to Catholicism. James became a different man. His new faith made him so certain, dour and obdurate, that Charles's cockney mistress, Nell Gwynn, dubbed him 'Dismal Jimmy'.

James was convinced that had his father stood firm there would have been no civil war. Recalling the time when he was nine and Governor Hotham had held him prisoner in Hull, while denying Charles I access to the royal arsenal, James wrote, 'Some vigorous bold man should have secured him or knocked him on the head. Either would have done the work.'[56] On his first day in French service he had been the vigorous bold man who had persuaded Corbeil to open the town gates. The ease with which the standing army crushed Monmouth's revolt in 1685 convinced the king – if further conviction was necessary – of its potency.

The country gentry were sure that England did not need a standing army: its militia (which they commanded) was protection enough from foreign invasion. In September of that year James confirmed their suspicions that the army, now forty thousand strong, was a threat to Protestant liberties, by bringing three and a half thousand Catholic troops over from Ireland and by court-martialling English officers, such as Colonel John Beaumont, who refused to accept the interlopers into their regiments.

James's defeat in the Glorious Revolution was by no means inevitable. The turning point came in mid-November 1688, when stricken by a nosebleed he broke down for two or three crucial days. Rather than charging gallantly when something was to be done, he retreated to London and then ran away to the continent. Even his comeback in Ireland was half-hearted. Afterwards back again in exile he blamed the Irish for his defeat.

He also blamed himself. As a devout Catholic and a believer in divine right he had to explain why God had let him loose. Perhaps James did not want to win, and by courting failure was punishing himself for his sins. And, he was sure, he had committed sins enough, particularly those of the flesh. His sexual appetites were voracious. Bishop Gilbert Burnet, the contemporary historian, sniffed that 'James was perpetually in one amour or another without being very nice about his choice.' His brother cruelly remarked that James's confessors must have prescribed his mistresses as a penance for they were so ugly! Even Charles II – no mean stud himself – admitted that his brother's libido was stronger than his own.

In exile James mended his ways, ascribing his fate to his fornications. He warned his son that 'Nothing has been more fatal to men, and to great men, that the letting themselves go to the forbidden love of Women. Of all the vices it is the most bewitching, and harder to be mastered if it not be crushed in the very bud.'[57] James tried to crush it through obsessive piety. He spent more and more time with the monks of La Trappe, an order silent except for their greeting to each other, 'We must die, brother, we must die.'[58] They spent their days contemplating open graves and their nights sleeping in winding sheets. As James lay dying of a stroke in August 1701 he told his wife, 'I am going to be happy.'

No early modern prince followed Machiavelli's advice to study and practise war more than James II. It brought him little happiness, and less success, although it did help change the course of British history.

Notes

1. T. Royles, *A Dictionary of Military Quotations* (London: Routledge, 1990), 90: 3.
2. F. A. Mumby, *The Youth of Henry VIII* (Boston: Constable, 1913), 127. N. S. Tjernegal, *Henry VIII and the Lutherans* (St Louis: Concordia, 1965), 19.
3. Quoted by J. Scarisbrick, *Henry VIII* (London: Methuen, 1981), 12.
4. Ibid., 156.
5. M. James, *English Politics and the Concept of Honour* (Durham, NC: Duke University Press, 1978), 4–12, 73.
6. J. Gardiner and R. H. Brodie, *Letters and Papers, Foreign and Domestic, of the Reign of Henry VIII* (London, 1862–1910), XIII, ii, 804.
7. E. W. Ives, *Anne Boleyn* (Oxford: Oxford University Press, 1986), 238.
8. J. Bampfield, *Apologia* (The Hague, 1685), 4.
9. *Othello*, Act III, iii, 158–64.
10. M. St. C. Byrne, *The Letters of Henry VIII* (New York: Funk and Wagnall, 1968), 364.
11. L. B. Smith, *Henry VIII: the Mask of Royalty* (Boston: Houghton Mifflin, 1973), 35.
12. Steve Gunn, 'The French Wars of Henry VIII', in Jeremy Black (ed.), *The Origins of War in Early Modern Europe* (Edinburgh: Donald, 1987), 34.
13. Quoted by D. Eltis, *The Military Revolution in Sixteenth Century Europe* (London: Tauria, 1995), 101.
14. Quoted by Scott C. Waugh, *England in the Reign of Edward III* (Cambridge: Cambridge University Press, 1991), 237.
15. Gardiner and Brodie, *op. cit.*, 2555.
16. Scarisbrick, *op. cit.*, 157.
17. Ibid., 3, 17.
18. Smith, *op. cit.*, 173.
19. Elis Gruffudd, 'Boulogne and Calais from 1545 to 1550', *Bulletin of the Faculty of Arts, Fauad University*, XII (1950), 13.
20. C. Cruickshank, *Henry VIII and the Invasion of France* (Stroud: Sutton, 1994), 78.
21. H. Davis, 'The Military Career of Sir Thomas North', *Huntington Library Quarterly*, XII (1949), 317.
22. Alison Weir, *The Life of Elizabeth I* (New York: Ballantine, 1998), 392–3.
23. C. Carlton, *Royal Childhoods* (London: Routledge and Keegan Paul, 1986), 78–99. Anne Somerset, *Elizabeth I* (New York: Knopf, 1991), 566–7.
24. R. Ashton (ed.), *James I by his Contemporaries* (London: Hutchinson, 1969), 16.

25. Sir John Oglander, *A Royalist Notebook. The Commonplace Book of Sir John Oglander* (London: Constable, 1936), 193.

26. Quoted by D. H. Willson, *King James VI and I* (New York: Oxford University Press, 1967), 227.

27. Ibid., 419.

28. P. Pett, *The Autobiography of Phineas Pett* (London: Naval Records Society, 1918), 103.

29. The material for Charles I is based on C. Carlton, *Charles I: the Personal Monarch* (London: Routledge, 1995), and C. Carlton, *Going to the Wars: the Experience of the British Civil Wars, 1638–53* (London: Routledge, 1992).

30. Quoted by C. Barnett, *Britain and Her Army* (London: Cassel, 1970), 62.

31. W. A. Day, *The Pythouse Papers* (London: Bickers, 1879), xvii.

32. Historical Manuscripts Commission, *Ninth Report* (London, 1884), appendix 2, 243.

33. S. R. Gardiner, *History of the Great Civil War, 1642–49* (London: Windrush, 1987), I, 41.

34. Edward Hyde, Earl of Clarendon, *The History of the Rebellion and Civil Wars in England* (Oxford: Clarendon, 1889), III, 353.

35. W. D. Fellowes, *Historical Sketches of Charles I, Cromwell, Charles II and the principal persons of that period, including the King's Trial and Execution* (London, 1824), 321.

36. Peter Heylyn, *Short View of the Life and Reign of King Charles* (London, 1658), 63–4.

37. E. Warburton, *Memoirs of Prince Rupert and the Cavaliers* (London: R. Bentley, 1849), II, 167–8.

38. P. Warwick, *Memoirs of the Reign of King Charles I* (London: 1815), 262. H. Slingsby, *Original Memoirs written during the Great Civil War* (London: 1806), 66–7.

39. J. Adair, *By the Sword Divided: Eye Witness Accounts of the English Civil War* (London: Century, 1983), 63.

40. Public Record Office: SP 16/503/56, IX.

41. James II, *The Memoirs of James II: his Campaigns as Duke of York, 1652–1660* translated by A. Lytton Sells (London: Chatto and Windus, 1962), 145, 150.

42. Quoted by M. Ashley, *James II* (Minneapolis: University of Minnesota Press, 1977), 10.

43. James, *op. cit.*, 265.

44. Quoted by Ashley, *op. cit.*, 49.

45. Ibid., 77.

46. Earle, *The Life and Times of James II* (London: Weidenfeld and Nicolson, 1972), 72.

47. Quoted by J. Haswell, *James II: Soldier and Sailor* (London: History Book Club, 1972), 171.

48. Earle, *op. cit.*, 79–81.

49. E. S. de Beer, *The Diary of John Evelyn* (London: Oxford University Press, 1959), 516.

50. John Narborough, *Journal and Narrative of the Third Dutch War* (London: Naval Record Society, 1917), 97.

51. J. Dryden, 'To my Friend Mr. J. Northleigh', J. Kinsley, *The Poetical Works of John Dryden* (Oxford: Clarendon, 1958), I, 459.
52. Quoted by Haswell, *op. cit.*, 255.
53. Ibid., 304.
54. Miller, *op. cit.*, 242. Earle, *op. cit.*, 217.
55. James, *op. cit.*, 170.
56. Quoted by Earle, *op. cit.*, 26.
57. Quoted by Haswell, *op. cit.*, 24.
58. Earle, *op. cit.*, 214.

chapter 5

TO THREATEN BOLD PRESUMPTUOUS KINGS WITH WAR

'Tis Britain's care to watch o'er Europe's fate
And hold in balance each contending state
To Threaten bold presumptuous king with war
And answer her afflicted neighbour's prayer.
                    Joseph Addison (1672–1719)

When George II, king of Great Britain and Ireland, and Elector of Hanover, set out to campaign in the War of Austrian Succession in early June 1743 he did so in grand style. His Majesty's entourage included 662 horses, 15 Berlin carriages, 55 wagons and 54 carts, which carried a huge amount of baggage, including nearly 12,000 table napkins, to ensure that the 60-year-old monarch did not lack the slightest comfort. He was accompanied by his son, the 22-year-old duke of Cumberland. They joined the allied army at Aschaffenburg, on the banks of the River Main in Germany. Having spent an unpleasant winter in the Netherlands the troops were fed up. 'I am heartily sick of this place,' Second Lieutenant Richard Davenport of the Horse Guards wrote home, 'the people are disagreeable, and cheat us in everything: as for the women, I have not seen one that is as handsome as my laundress's sister.'[1] Lord Stair commanded the allied forces; over seventy, his 'military genius,' a brother aristocrat remarked, 'never very bright, was rusted with age'.[2]

For their first week in camp the royal party amused themselves by going out hunting, while the common soldiery had fun by committing 'great disorders' as they foraged and plundered. After the king severely punished a few miscreants, the allied troops marched off to war. Promptly the French forces trapped them just east of the village of Dettingen, on the north bank of the Main. Once they started to bombard the allies with artillery located on the south bank of the river, George II led his army into battle, the last reigning monarch ever to do so [Plate 5.1].

Plate 5.1   George II © Topham Picturepoint

Since James II and William III had both led armies into battle at the Boyne half a century earlier, changes in British political, financial and military affairs had taken place which were so profound that they can only be described as revolutionary. Of course, the origins of these shifts can be traced back to the civil wars, if not before: yet the rate of change peaked after 1688.

The political revolution consisted of the creation of a British state dominated by parliament. It was preceded by the emergence of an English state, which Shakespeare boasted was, 'This royal throne of kings, this scepter'd isle, this earth of majesty, this seat of Mars', in a process that can best be described as nation building.[3] It was a consensual bottom-up accomplishment, being completed gradually with little coercion, and was based on a common culture. The Welsh, who spoke a different language, accepted this process because they saw Henry Tudor, later Henry VII, as one of their own, and because their élite rapidly became anglicised.

In contrast the making of the British state and then the Empire was a process of state formation. It was a top-down conquest by the English, to which few Irish and Scots consented. Indeed one can view the 195 years from Bosworth Field (1485) to the Boyne (1690) as ones of isolationism, similar to those experienced by the United States from 1783 to 1917 or even 1941. There were moments of violent overkill, such as the British and American Civil Wars. Henry VIII's French expeditions were attempts to regain the glory of the Hundred Years War, as quixotic as, say, the War of 1812. While the three Dutch Wars of 1652–54, 1665–67 and 1672–74 may have anticipated the future, being basically over the issues of trade, most of England's military energies were internally directed, intent on establishing a British state.

Much of this was the legacy of Oliver Cromwell and the New Model Army. Founded in 1645 the New Model Army was England's first standing military force. By the measure of the time it was well paid and supplied, particularly when it fought the Scots and Irish. Known as 'the Ironsides' for their prowess in combat, they decimated the Scots in three devastating battles at Preston (1648), Dunbar (1650) and Worcester (1651), inflicting perhaps as many as 60,000 casualties on that small nation. Afterward Scotland became an English satrap.

During the Revolution of 1688 many Scots, especially in the Highlands, championed James II and afterwards his son, James, the Old Pretender, who landed in Scotland in 1715 and invaded England to regain the throne. They did not support the Act of Union passed in 1707 uniting Scotland and England, giving the former parliamentary representation in Westminster. Indeed it took at least a generation for most Scots to be reconciled with this change, which happened largely because they found jobs in the army, navy and empire which were, ironically, the result of the formation of a powerful British state.

A similar, although less successful process can be seen with Ireland. The conquest of Ireland which began under the Tudors was brutally completed by Oliver Cromwell. In 1649 he invaded the island, massacring the garrisons at Drogheda and Wexford. During the 1650s the British confiscated over half of Ireland, transferring it from the native inhabitants to the English and Scots. Any Irishman remotely connected with the rebellion was forced on pain of death to move to the barren west. 'To hell or Connaugh' were the alternatives the English offered Irish Catholics whom they could not imagine going anywhere but down in the next life. Cromwell's army left such a lasting impression on Ireland that three centuries later in 1972 as the British army returned to the streets of Belfast at the start of the latest troubles, the chorus of Ireland's best-selling pop record announced 'Cromwell's men are here again'.[4]

William III's victory at the Boyne in 1690 brought Ireland firmly under English rule, giving the Protestants domination over the island's politics, society and economy. Penal laws were passed turning Catholics into second-class citizens. Protestant hegenomy was as complete and cruel as apartheid, lasting without effective challenge for over a century.

The formation of a British state was only part of the political revolution that centred on 1688. As a result of the Glorious Revolution parliament became the dominant constitutional power. Of course, tension is bound to occur between the legislative and executive branches – as the writers of the American Constitution recognised. But with a monarch sitting for life such conflicts were hard to resolve. On the continent kings, such as Louis XIV in 1618, did so by getting rid of the legislature and concentrating all power in an absolute monarchy. In the first four decades of the seventeenth century these developments sorely worried many members of parliament who, unable to work out some compromise with Charles I, fought a civil war against the king, cut off his head and declared a republic. But the republic did not work; monarchy had to be restored in 1660. As we have seen, James II upset the uneasy balance between crown and parliament so badly that he provoked the revolution of 1688 that made parliament the dominant power. Kings had to call parliaments every year to vote new taxes and pass for another twelve months the Mutiny Act, without which the armed forces could not enforce discipline. The revolutionary settlement did not abolish the executive, which during the 1720s and 1730s under Sir Robert Walpole moved to the office of the prime minister. Because the prime minister needed the support of the king, and (more important), that of the majority of members of parliament, who were in turn elected, the new system was remarkably stable. To a large degree the Revolution of 1688 brought about taxation with representation by giving those who paid the most taxes – the aristocracy, gentry and large merchants – the lion's share of power.

These political changes made possible a financial revolution. Confident of its newly won powers the legislature introduced new taxes and extended excise duties, which had been proven so efficacious during the civil wars, to new commodities such as salt and alcohol. The land tax was increased to four shillings in the pound, producing nearly half of the crown's income. In all taxes raised some £54 million during the Nine Years War (1688–97), the overwhelming majority of which went to the armed forces. Most people felt that they got good value for the money. After the great victory at Blenheim in 1704, one Tory squire remarked that taxpayers had got 'more for the four shillings in the pound than they had ever seen before.'[5]

Taxes had risen to unprecedented heights. Not only did war expenditure go up sixfold over the previous decade, but the government's share of the national income increased by almost as much. Before and after the British Civil Wars it remained at around 2 per cent. For the century after 1688 it averaged 11 per cent.[6] So confident were people in the government's ability to raise revenue that they were willing to lend to it at increasingly lower rates of return. When the National Debt started in 1693 the government paid 19 per cent interest which fell to 8 per cent within a few years. Within half a century it was a mere 2 per cent. Lenders felt their money was being spent wisely by first rate administrators, such as William Lowndes, the Secretary of the Treasury from 1695 to 1724, who coined the adage 'take care of the pence and the pounds will take care of themselves'. The Bank of England was founded in 1694 to provide loans for the Nine Year's War. Its first governor, Michael Godfrey, was killed in the trenches at the Siege of Namur the following year while discussing finances with William III, an indication of the bank's key role in making Britain a major military power. In short, an effective credit system permitted Britain at the outbreak of a war to raise money, enlist men and outfit ships far faster than anyone else, giving her 'the decisive margin' over any enemy.[7] So within a generation Britain had become 'a fiscal military state' that remained a major world power for over two and a half centuries.

Unlike the financial and political revolutions, the military revolution was a European-wide phenomena.

Professor Michael Roberts first suggested the concept of a military revolution in 1956.[8] He argued that between 1560 and 1660 a significant shift took place in the way that European states waged war. For one thing armies became much larger, increasing tenfold in size. They grew more professional, with a defined and better trained officer corps, and other ranks who enlisted for as long as twenty years. Soldiers wore uniforms and lived apart from civilians in barracks. The introduction of gunpowder changed weapons. Muskets replaced the longbow and crossbow, enabling ranks of infantry to fire volley after volley at each other at point blank range. With the introduction of the bayonet, at the end of the seventeenth century, the pike man became obsolete, while the demands on foot soldiers grew so great that it could take up to a year to drill them into the stoic obedience demanded on the new, far more lethal, battlefield.

Artillery added to the carnage the infantry had to face. It transformed siege warfare. Initially it gave the attackers an advantage, for gunpowder-propelled cast iron shot could readily knock down the vertical stone walls of medieval castles. But after military engineers, like the great French general, Sébastien Vauban, built star-shaped fortresses with sloping earthen covered walls, the advantage returned to the defender. Wars ceased to be fought for ideological reasons such as religion, about which it was hard to compromise, becoming instead dynastic contests over territory or trade, over which concessions could more readily be negotiated. States were recognised as the only parties legitimately authorised to wage war – once the pursuit of rebellious feudal nobles – while the demands of war greatly enhanced the power of governments. As Professor Charles Tilly succinctly put it, 'the state made war, and war made the state'.

War also made armies, and armies were liable to take over governments. Such had been the case in the British Civil Wars. Oliver Cromwell once asserted, 'I would rather have a plain russet coated captain who knows what he fights for and loves what he knows than that you would call a gentleman and is nothing else.'[9] The trouble was that having fought for and won what they loved, the plain russet coated captains would not return to civilian life. During the 1650s a large standing army remained in place – the only time in British history when the end of a war has not been followed by a precipitous demobilisation. Unable to govern through parliament Cromwell became a military dictator, who used his major generals to administer the land. Although their rule was not as despotic as posterity came to believe, it left an enduring scar on British memories. 'No standing armies!' became the watchword for nearly a century.

The fear of a standing army was so strong that when Charles II was restored to the throne in 1660 efforts were made to disband it. Soon it was realised a standing army was a necessary evil, so three regiments were retained. The question then became, who would control the officer corps. Obviously plain russet coated captains were not acceptable lest they turn upon the establishment. Thus the system of purchasing commissions was developed in order to ensure that the officer corps was recruited from the élite, mainly the younger sons of the nobility and gentry, whose loyalty was as sure as their abilities might be dubious.

The Royal Navy did not use the system of purchasing commissions for two simple reasons. First, being at sea or confined to bases on the coast, sailors were geographically incapable of taking over the government. Second, while it required little intelligence to be an infantry or cavalry officer – indeed a lack of imagination was a distinct advantage in withstanding musket or cannon fire – sailing a ship was a highly skilled craft with disastrous consequences for failure. No infantry officer is known to have marched his company off the edge of a cliff: many a naval captain has wrecked his sailing ship on the rocks below. To lessen the chances of that happening midshipmen had to serve a set number of years at sea before being allowed to take an examination for promotion to lieutenant.

After the revolution of 1688 the political, financial and military revolutions came together to produce a much strengthened British state that had a permanently enhanced military system with a standing army whose officers lacked political ambitions, a proficient navy led by skilled sailors, an Ordnance Office which supplied the armed forces reasonably well. All this was paid for by an effective system of taxation and credit, supported by a parliament that dominated the political system, at the expense of the crown. The story of the monarch's loss of military power can be seen in the reigns of William III, Queen Anne and the first two Georges.

There was nothing inevitable about that change. It greatly depended on one man, the Protestant ruler of the Netherlands, for whom saving his native land from the ambitions of King Louis XIV of France was, wrote Bishop Burnet, the contemporary historian, 'the governing passion of his life'.[10] This passion governed Britain's foreign policy for over a century, bringing about what some have called the Second Hundred Years War with France that ended at Waterloo in 1815.

William of Orange's first efforts to thwart the French began badly. When it appeared likely in 1672 that Louis XIV would attack the Netherlands the Dutch parliament, the States, made him their Captain General for a year. They trusted neither his military abilities nor his ambitions, fearing that he itched to become an absolute monarch. The small Dutch army of some 9,000 men was 'in a miserable condition, with sickness & want of pay,' English intelligence reported, 'they desert in great numbers.'[11] When the French invaded in April with orders to 'plunder, murder and destroy', the Dutch collapsed. So desperate were the States that they made William Captain General for life and cut the dykes to stem the French invasion.

The following year, after William had purged the Dutch forces of their most cowardly and disobedient officers, Louis once again invaded, capturing Maastricht in June. After the Dutch navy thwarted a landing by an Anglo-French fleet in August, William made alliances with Spain, the German Empire and Lorraine. On 6 September he captured Naarden, an important fortress that guarded Amsterdam. It was his first major victory. Two months later he took Bochum, personally leading the assault on its star-shaped bastion, forcing the French to withdraw. On his return to The Hague William was welcomed as a conquering hero.

The war was far from over. On 11 August 1674, William confronted a large French army under the command of Prince Louis Condé at Seneffe. It was a long brutal battle, starting at midday and ending at midnight in a draw. Even William's enemies had to admit he had acquitted himself well. 'The prince of Orange has acted in all respects like an old captain, except in venturing his life too much, like a young one,' observed Condé.[12] William's capture of Grave in October persuaded the French to withdraw and the Dutch to make him their Stadtholder, or ruler, for life.

Three years later in 1677 the Stadtholder was once more called out to defend his native land from Louis XIV. This time he took the war into French territory by marching some thirty thousand men towards St Omer. At Mont Cassel they met a much larger French force, which defeated them. William had two horses killed under him, and a bullet tore away a sleeve. He tried to stem the panic, slashing one of his own running troopers across the face, shouting, 'I'll mark you, so that I will be able to hang you later.'[13] That there was a later for William and the Dutch Army, the duke of Monmouth, who took part in the battle, attributed to William's personal bravery.

No one could doubt the Prince of Orange's courage. But before 1688 many could question his skill as a strategic commander, especially when faced with the immensely difficult challenge of invading England.

When William set out to do so in the autumn of 1688 he was helped by an act of God – an unusual east wind – and the decision of one who regarded himself almost on a par with the Almighty. By dispatching his army into central Europe, Louis XIV freed the Netherlands from the threat of a French invasion, thus permitting William to move his troops to England. They landed at Torbay on 5 November 1688 as liberators with strict orders not to plunder but to pay for all they needed. William hung two of his soldiers at Exeter for stealing a chicken. His army was first rate, much better than the English they easily overcame.

By early 1690, after the Convention parliament had offered William and his wife Mary (James II's eldest daughter) the crown, the English army was in even worse shape. Those soldiers who had not been disbanded for lack of pay after Henry Shales, the Commissioner General, embezzled £70,000, mutinied. After returning to their duty in late 1689, they were sent to Ireland under the command of the Dutch general, the duke of Schomberg, where they spent the winter at Lisburn. Neglecting to build themselves adequate shelter, three quarters of them 'died like rotten sheep'.

The following summer William landed in Ireland to complete his conquest in person. He brought some 45,000 men, a siege train, ample supplies, and £200,000 in cash. As we have seen he defeated James II easily at the Boyne on 1 July 1690, showing his usual courage under fire. The official account downplayed the shoulder wound he received from a two-pound cannon-ball while reconnoitring the field the previous day by reporting that 'His Majesty had lost near half a spoonful of blood'.[14] There was nothing understated about William's daring in leading the Enniskilling Horse across the river in the battle's decisive charge. But he failed to follow up his victory, and his conquest of Ireland was not complete until the Treaty of Limerick was signed in October 1691. The treaty allowed some twelve thousand Irish, the so-called 'Wild Geese', to leave their native land to enlist in Louis XIV's service, and thus hampered William's lifelong goal, the confusion of the French.

The Nine Years War (1688–97) was essentially one of attrition. After being beaten at Steenkirk in 1692 and Landen the following year, William, who was still Stadtholder of the Netherlands, as well as king of Britain, captured the heavily defended fortress of Namur in 1695, enhancing his military reputation. By now all sides were war-weary. France was especially exhausted. The bad weather of 1693 produced the worst famine for centuries. Although the Treaty of Ryswick, which ended hostilities in 1697, only gave the allies modest gains, the public were delighted. 'It is impossible to conceive what joy the peace brings here,' William noted on his return to London.

Three years later he died. While William was a brave man, although less than a stellar commander, no reign was of greater military importance than his. He was the first monarch to effectively build and maintain alliances against Britain's enemies, the secret to her success in wars ever since. In doing so he contributed to the military decline of the Netherlands. Even though he built an effective Dutch army, introducing howitzers and heavy mortars, training grenadiers, and introducing night fighting techniques, he overtaxed Dutch resources, while liberating those of Britain, potentially a far more powerful nation.

By accepting in February 1689 the principle that 'the raising or keeping of a standing army within the kingdom in time of war, unless it be with the consent of parliament, is against the law', William made possible a standing army, since it (like the enhanced navy), came under parliamentary control. The purchase system ensured that the army officers were loyal to the established order. The allegiance of the aristocracy, who in feudal times had rebelled against the crown, was now guaranteed because the purchase system allowed them to dominate the officer corps, particularly its senior ranks. Younger sons, debarred by primogeniture from inheriting the family estates, found a rewarding career in the armed forces. A growing professionalisation and the need for increased military training meant that there were also greater opportunities for officers. While a civil war regiment had approximately one officer for every sixty men, by the eighteenth century this figure had risen to one in nineteen.[15]

Notwithstanding all of these contributions neither William nor the English particularly liked each other. After trying and failing to win the friendship of the nobility at Newmarket races, William ruefully remarked to a Dutch confidant, 'I see I am not made for these people, nor they for me.'[16]

Some of Britain's greatest feats of arms came not during the reign of William III, a veteran campaigner, but during that of his successor, Queen Anne (1702–14), who as a woman was precluded from any active military role. Custom confined women to the petticoat politics of the court, which made possible the continued rise of Britain as a major world power.

Anne was born in 1665, the second daughter of James, duke of York, by his first wife, Anne Hyde. Her mother died when she was only six, her father remarrying two years later. For much of her childhood she was overshadowed by her elder sister Mary, who wed William of Orange in 1677.

While Anne may have played with Sarah Jennings when she was five or six, their friendship really started eight years later after Sarah joined the duke of York's household as a maid of honour. Both girls had lost mothers when they were young. Sarah and Anne formed an intense friendship which lasted over thirty years. It began as an adolescent crush, between the plain Jane of the lower fourth and the games mistress. It was an attraction of opposites. Anne, fourteen, chubby, awkward and uncertain; Sarah a confident, beautiful, self-assured nineteen-year-old. While Anne waffled, Sarah was decisive and insightful. She promised to always be frank with her royal friend, who despised the flattery so often laid upon royalty by the trowelful, particularly in the Restoration court where back-stabbing and deceit were as common as cuckoldry. So Anne told Sarah not to call her 'Highness' or 'Majesty' since these titles got in the way of honest intercourse. Instead they were to use the aliases of Mrs Morely and Mrs Freeman, as if they were merchants' wives gossiping over a dish of tea while their husbands were away at the Exchange seeking the family fortunes. At times Anne could become cloying. 'I hope that next to Lord Churchill,' she wrote to Sarah in 1684, 'I may claim the first place in your heart.'[17]

Marriage did not diminish their friendship. Anne and George's marriage in July 1683 was a brilliant union between two basically dull people. 'I have tried him drunk and I have tried him sober, and there is nothing in him,' was Charles II's verdict on the Danish prince, whose main interests in life were food, drink and his wife. He indulged himself so assiduously in these appetites that he became fat, and his wife got pregnant eighteen times.

In 1676 Sarah Jennings married John Churchill, the son of a Devonshire gentleman who had suffered sorely for his loyalty to Charles I. 'Of all the men I ever knew in my life,' recalled Lord Chesterfield, 'his manner was irresistible, by either man or woman.'[18] Initially she rebuffed his advances since John was a rake. 'But on my faith,' he maintained, 'I do only now love you.'[19]

Although both families opposed the union on the familiar grounds that the other partner was not good enough for their child, it was an extremely happy and satisfying one which profoundly affected the monarchy and Britain's military development. Time and time again they proclaimed their love. In 1684 John wrote to Sarah that he would gladly ride 'a 100 miles for the happiness of one night' with her.[20] 'God Almighty hath pleased to give us a victory,' he wrote to her on 24 May 1706, the day after Ramillies, 'I love you more than I can express.'[21] In old age Sarah fondly recalled how on returning from his campaigns John would 'pleasure me with his boots on'. No wonder as a widow she turned down a proposal from Lord Somerset. 'If I were young and handsome as I was instead of old and faded as I am, and you could lay the empire of the world at my feet, you should not share the heart and hand of one that had once belonged to John, duke of Marlborough.'[22]

Sarah's love for John and her friendship with Anne much enhanced his military career. While William had never fully trusted him since he had betrayed James in 1688 by defecting to the Dutch invaders at the critical moment, Anne had no such reservations. On coming to the throne she gave Marlborough the Order of the Garter and made Sarah Lady of the Bedchamber. So generous was the queen that within twelve months the Churchills were making some £60,000 a year, a more than prodigious reward for the man who was leading the allied armies in the War of Spanish Succession (1701–14).

For the first two years of the war Marlborough built the Anglo-Dutch-Imperial alliance, but could do little with his forces because the Dutch were reluctant to risk their contingent. In 1704, having concentrated his troops at Koblenz, he marched south-east towards the Danube, neglecting to inform the Dutch of his plans. His army was superbly prepared, supply depots having been established along the route of the march enabling them to move fast without having to live off the land. On 13 August he met the French army at Blenheim, on the north bank of the Danube. 'The victory we obtained,' he wrote home that night, 'is greater than has been known in the memories of men.' Twenty thousand French lay dead, as compared to twelve thousand allied troops. Louis's hopes of dominating Europe were equally moribund: Marlborough's reputation and that of the British army were made.

But the war was far from over. After being beaten at Ramillies in 1706 Louis offered peace, which the allies refused. Two years later, after a third great victory at Oudenarde, the war degenerated into a series of sieges in the Low Countries, the so-called cockpit of Europe, which became a charnel house as bloody as it was to be from 1914 to 1918. Marlborough's last great victory, Malplaquet in 1709, was a Pyrrhic one. The duke admitted it had been 'a very murdering battle' in which the allies lost twice as many men as the French. But Malborough had not lost his skills, for his turning the *Ne Plus Ultra* lines in Northern France in the summer of 1711 was a masterpiece of military genius.

What made Marlborough such a great general, the greatest perhaps in British history? He was, it goes without saying, very brave, his presence on the battlefield always reassured his men. 'It is quite impossible for me to express the joy which the sight of this man gave me at this critical moment', remembered Captain Robert Parker of the Battle of Bouchain (1711), when Marlborough posted himself next to his company. He did not order Parker's men to advance against overwhelming odds, for as the captain recalled, 'it was the sense of the whole army, both officers and soldiers' that their general would never squander their lives in hopeless ventures.[23] 'Corporal John', as they called him, was a decent man, who would give tired soldiers a ride in his coach. He rarely punished, and with his attention to detail kept his armies well fed and supplied – after the 250-mile march to the Danube in 1704 there were new shoes waiting for the men before they fought at Blenheim. 'The known world could not produce a man of more humanity', raved Matthew Bishop, who served under him as a corporal.[24]

As a battlefield commander Marlborough was highly energetic, even in his sixties, galloping from place to place to spot the enemy's weak points. He had a good eye for the lay of the land, being able to take advantage of dead ground to manoeuvre his forces. He coordinated artillery, infantry and cavalry into effective combat groups, relying on first-rate intelligence for their depositions. He always seized the initiative. He would attack the enemy to force them to concentrate their troops to hold his, and then shift his assault to the weakened place from which their soldiers had been withdrawn, thus breaking his adversary's lines.

What made Marlborough unique among other great British commanders was his charm, tact and diplomacy, qualities that say, Cromwell, Wellington and Montgomery lacked, and which held together the grand alliance of the Holy Roman Empire, Holland and Britain, plus a host of other smaller nations. He combined the battlefield skills of a Montgomery with the coalition-building genius of an Eisenhower. Like Ike everyone liked 'Corporal John', some 67,000 lines of verse being written in his praise during his lifetime. The reason was simple. As Captain Parker wrote, 'he never fought a battle which he did not gain, nor laid siege to town which he did not take.'[25]

Malborough's ability to do so depended on his wife's friendship with the queen, and when that ended he lost the last battle of his career.

As early as 1704, the year of Blenheim, rifts could be discerned in Sarah and Anne's friendship. 'It was exceedingly tedious,' Sarah recalled, 'to be so much where there could be no manner of conversation.'[26] Two years later, after her husband's great victory at Oudenarde, Sarah and Anne had a bitter fight over the appointment of Charles Spencer, earl of Sunderland, a leading Whig, and her son-in-law, to be secretary of state. Their nemesis was Abigail Hill, a distant cousin whom she had taken into her own household, to stand in for her as the queen's companion. Abigail was all Sarah was not – eager to please, comfortable and comforting. She played the harpsichord well, was a hilarious mimic, and, above all, a solid Tory. Meek, she inherited the earth. Realising that she had introduced a cuckoo into her own nest, in 1708 Sarah got Arthur Maynwaring, her secretary, to pen some scurrilous verse:

> *When as Queen Anne of great Renown*
> *Great Britain's Sceptre sway'd*
> *Beside the Church she deeply loved*
> *A Dirty Chamber-Maid.*

Sarah told Anne that Abigail had 'no inclination for any but of one's own sex'. The queen never forgave this baseless allegation of lesbianism.[27] The two finally broke on 6 April 1710 at Kensington Palace. When Sarah demanded time and time again why Anne was no longer her friend, Anne insisted she could not answer and that Sarah must submit questions in writing. Three decades of friendship crashed in vain upon a stonewall. Sarah left in tears. The following year both she and John were dismissed from all their offices. He died in 1722: she outlived him by twenty-two years.

It is tempting to assume – as Sarah maintained afterwards – that the dismissal of England's greatest general was basically due to the machinations of Abigail Hill. In fact Anne treated Sarah with exemplary patience. She, like many of her subjects, especially the Tories, was getting fed up with the war, which Marlborough and the Whigs wanted to prolong even though Britain had achieved most of its gains, and Louis was eager to make terms. Marlborough, like many a great commander, did not know when to stop. Perhaps in old age he recognised this fault, for it was said that when he came across a portrait of himself painted long before by Sir Geoffrey Kneller, he sighed, 'That was once a man.'[28]

As a royal warrior Anne's problem was that she was not a man. She had neither the energy, health, nor the charisma to rally her troops as Elizabeth I had done at Tilbury. But then she had not the need: the monarchy had lost much of its powers. However, Anne did have the fortitude to stick to her principles, which mainly consisted of a firm support of the Church of England, and the sense to recognise that direction of affairs had passed to parliament. She had sufficient sense to support Marlborough at the start of the War of Spanish Succession, when her support was needed, and judgement enough to dismiss him at the end, when his removal was called for. Anne was much more than 'a weak irresolute woman beset by Bedchamber quarrels'. Rather, by succeeding as 'an anomaly, a woman ruler in an age of war', she set the pattern for the long-term future military role of the crown.[29]

Ironically Anne's successors, George I (1714–27) and George II (1727–60), men brought up as soldiers, were reluctant to follow this path.

George I first saw action at the age of fifteen in 1675 when he went campaigning with his father, Ernst Augustus, the ruler of Hanover. The following year he took part in the Siege of Maastricht, and in 1677–78 commanded Hanoverian troops with distinction against the Turks. In 1679 he succeeded his father as ruler of Hanover. On the outbreak of the War of Spanish Succession George wanted to be a senior commander in the anti-French alliance, but neither his abilities nor Hanover's military contribution warranted the appointment. In 1707 he commanded the Hanoverian forces protecting the electorate from a French invasion, which never took place because Louis shifted his forces south to Toulon. Nonetheless George proudly accepted the accolade 'saviour of the fatherland'. It was enough to win him the command of an army, but not sufficient to prevent Marlborough from sidelining him for lack of confidence in his abilities. The duke's judgement was proven right the next year, when the French thrashed George at Rumersheim.[30]

As king of England George I played little role in its military history – or for that matter in its history in general. Like his son, George II, he was interested in promoting Hanover, a place both preferred to Britain. They were only too happy to have their kingdom pay to protect their electorate. As with William III, having a foreign monarch meant that Great Britain got far more involved militarily in continental affairs.

George II was twenty-five when he first saw action in 1708 at the Battle of Oudenarde where he commanded eight cavalry squadrons under Prince Eugene of Savoy. He led them in a charge against the French horse, having his own mount killed under him. An English ballad celebrated his courage.[31]

> When his war horse was shot
> He valued it not,
> But fought on foot like a king.

Nineteen years later he became king of England. He meddled so much in the British Army that Lord Chesterfield suggested that it would be far less expensive and hazardous if he were be given a box of lead clockwork soldiers to play with instead of the real thing. He took his pleasure like a soldier. If he arrived early at the apartments of Henrietta Howard, his mistress, he would march up and down outside, watch in hand, until the stroke of 9pm so as not to be early on parade.

Some of George's military contributions were useful. He insisted that a new standardised drill manual be issued in 1727, replacing the old system by which each foot regiment exercised in its own fashion. He opposed the purchase system, which lessened his own patronage and promoted incompetents. 'His Majesty keeps an exact account of all the officers,' wrote Hugh Walpole, 'knows their characters and long services, and generally nominates at his own time the colonels to the vacant regiments.'[32] Hugh's father, Sir Robert Walpole, would have agreed that the monarch was obsessed with military trivia. Whenever the prime minister went to see the king with some twenty or so agenda items to discuss, George would harangue him for so long about the need to fight the French that there was no time left for the nation's business. Fortunately for the nation its business was in the hands of Sir Robert Walpole and, as everyone knew, Queen Caroline. A broadsheet published before her untimely death in 1737 mocked:[33]

> You may strut, dapper George, but 'twill all be in vain.
> We know 'tis Queen Caroline, not you, that reign.

George's memories of Oudenarde made him increasingly bellicose. He pushed for Britain's entry into the War of Austrian Succession (1740– 47), because 'age was coming on fast,' he explained, and he 'could not bear the thought of growing old in peace'.[34]

Impatience, nostalgia and a plain lack of military common sense prompted George II to lead an allied army of some 40,000 into a French ambush at Dettingen on 27 June 1743. Outnumbered by the 60,000 enemy commanded by the Duc de Noallies, George desperately tried to bring eight cannon from the rear of the baggage train forward so they could begin a counter fire. In spite of the king's exhortations, and much waving of his sword, a traffic jam prevented the artillery from moving into position. The French fired at his majesty from a battery of twelve cannon but aimed too high. 'I saw the balls go with half a yard of his head,' recalled Mr Kendall a member of Lord Albermarle's troop, 'He is certainly the boldest man I ever saw.'[35] He was not, however, the most effective, for it took four hours to sort out the confusion.[36]

When the French crossed the river in force, taking cover in a wood, George drew his sword and ordered his Hanoverian and British Infantry to advance. They did not do so until a battery of six-pounders moved into place to provide covering fire. The infantry fired devastating vollies at each other at a hundred yards range. 'The shot flew as thick as hail,' an observer recalled, as the king, ignoring the maelstrom, continued to wave his sword urging his men into battle. 'Now boys!' he cried, 'Now for the honour of England! Fire and the French will run.' Frederick the Great of Prussia found the king's antics amusing, sneering that he behaved 'like a fencing master'. His men did not agree. They cheered him as they charged the French.

Unfortunately the king's horse was not as courageous as John Wooton's portrait would suggest [Plate 5.2]. It bolted, galloping to the rear. The 60-year-old monarch leapt off, and, remarking that he trusted his own two feet far more than his charger's four, ran back to the front line. He ordered his men to advance to within sixty paces of the enemy, and fire volley after volley. The effects were murderous. 'The smoke blew off a little,' a British soldier remembered, 'Instead of being among the living we found the dead in heaps about us.' The French retreated. Lord Stair urged hot pursuit, but George II vetoed the idea saying that they had done enough for one day. Thus the king snatched stalemate from the jaws of victory.

George failed at Dettingen because he could not act like a general – although he might have made a tolerably good battalion commander. 'A lot of noise about very little, and a lot of men killed uselessly', was Frederick the Great's verdict on George's generalship.

After the battle George adjourned to a nearby cottage for a supper of cold mutton, having ordered two oxen per battalion killed and roasted to feast his men. He inspected the troops, bantering with them. He teased Colonel Sir Andrew Agnew that his Royal Scots Fusiliers had let some French cavalry get in amongst them. 'Oh aye, your Majesty,' Agnew

Plate 5.2   George II at the Battle of Dettingen © Courtesy of the Director, National Army Museum, London

replied, 'but they dinna get oot again.' The king knighted several officers, including Lord Stair, as well as Trooper Brown, who managed to recapture his regimental standard after three quarters of his comrades had been killed or wounded, suffering several wounds and losing two fingers in the process. In addition the king gave Brown a pension of £30 per annum, sufficient for the trooper to drink himself to death within three years.

The next day, George and his Secretary of State, Lord Carteret (who had spent the battle huddled petrified in the baggage train) composed a dispatch home. 'His Majesty (God be praised) has this day gained a very great considerable Battle,' they wrote, 'This is a very good beginning of the Campaign.'[37]

They were far too optimistic. The campaign quickly fizzled. In November the king returned to England. William Pitt sneered that he had been in no more hazard at Dettingen than he would have been at home from an overturned coach or bucking horse. Others were upset that George had fought at Dettingen wearing the brown-orange sash of Hanover: one pamphlet even suggested that during the battle the petrified monarch stained his breeches a similar hue. But most of the public was more generous. London was brilliantly illuminated to receive the king whom the citizens carried shoulder high to the palace. For the thanksgiving service at the Chapel Royal Handel composed a *Te Deum* so bombastic that it required the services of practically every kettle drum in the land.

Far from deserving a *Te Deum* a *Nunc Dimittis* would have been more appropriate. From both political and military leadership the monarchy had departed in peace. Dettingen was a throwback. By now the monarch, who once claimed to be the Lord's servant by divine right, was a figurehead whose role in war, as in politics, was to become increasingly symbolic. Because the monarch had lost his role as a royal warrior, Great Britain could become great – a world power sufficiently strong to win an empire and maintain the balance of power in Europe. Now she was, as the poet Joseph Addison noted, mighty enough 'To threaten bold presumptive kings with war'.

Notes

1. M. Orr, *Dettingen* (London: Knight, 1972), 27.
2. Sir John Fortescue, *History of the British Army* (London: Macmillan, 1920), II, 92.
3. *Richard II*, I, i, 41.
4. 'The Men behind the Wire', in C. Carlton, *Bigotry and Blood: Documents on the Ulster Troubles* (Chicago: Nelson Hall, 1976), 111.
5. Quoted by G. Curtis, *Life and Times of Queen Anne* (London: Weidenfeld and Nicolson, 1972), 133.
6. P. K. O'Brien and P. A. Hunt, 'The Rise of the Fiscal State in England, 1485–1815', *Historical Research*, LXVI (1983), 174–5.
7. P. G. M. Dickson, *The Financial Revolution in England* (London: Macmillan, 1967), 9.
8. M. Roberts, *The Military Revolution* (Belfast: Queen's University, 1956). G. Parker, *The Military Revolution: Military Innovation and the Rise of the West, 1500–1800* (Cambridge: Cambridge University Press, 1988). J. Black, *A Military Revolution?: Military Change and European Society, 1550–1800* (London: Macmillan, 1991), 1–5.
9. T. Carlyle, *Oliver Cromwell's Letters and Speeches* (London: Methuen, 1904), II, 154.
10. Quoted by J. Miller, *The Life and Times of William and Mary* (London: Weidenfeld and Nicolson, 1974), 199.
11. Quoted by S. Baxter, *William III* (London: Longmans, 1966), 65.
12. Miller, *op. cit.*, 40.
13. Quoted by H. and B. Van der Zee, *William and Mary* (London: Macmillan, 1973), 110.
14. Baxter, *op. cit.*, 265.

15. C. Carlton, *Going to the Wars: the Experience of the British Civil Wars* (London: Routledge, 1992), 185. R. O'Connell, *Of Arms and Men: a History of War, Weapons and Aggression* (Oxford: Oxford University Press, 1990), 155.
16. Ibid., 255.
17. Quoted by E. Gregg, *Queen Anne* (London: Routledge and Kegan Paul, 1980), 30.
18. Correlli Barnett, *Marlborough* (London: Eyre Methuen, 1974), 12.
19. Ibid., 32.
20. Ibid., 81.
21. Curtis, *op. cit.*, 148.
22. Ibid., 34.
23. Robert Parker, *Memoirs of the Most Remarkable Military Transactions* (London, 1741), 107–9.
24. M. Bishop, *Life and Adventures of Matthew Bishop* (London, 1744), 267.
25. Parker, *op. cit.* (1968), 125.
26. Curtis, *op. cit.*, 133.
27. Gregg, *op. cit.*, 27.
28. Barnett, *op. cit.*, 270.
29. Gregg, *op. cit.*, 401–2.
30. R. Hatton, *George I: Elector and King* (Cambridge, MA: Harvard University Press, 1978), 34–35, 100–4.
31. Charles Chenevix-Trench, *George II* (London: Allen Lane, 1973), 18–19.
32. J. B. Owen, 'George II reconsidered', in W. Whiteman, J. Bromley and P. G. M. Dickson, *Statesmen, Scholars and Merchants* (Oxford: Oxford University Press, 1973), 120.
33. J. Van de Kiste, *King George and Queen Caroline* (Stroud: Sutton, 1997), 103.
34. John, Baron Hervey, *Lord Hervey's Memoirs*, ed. R. Sedgewick (Harmondsworth: Penguin, 1984), 61.
35. Chenevix-Trench, *op. cit.*, 218–19.
36. Orr, *op. cit.*, 5, 50–7.
37. Ibid., 59, 67.

chapter 6

AND HE MARCHED THEM
DOWN AGAIN

The Brave old duke of York,
He had ten thousand men.
He marched them up to the top of a hill
And he marched them down again.

I. and P. Opie *(eds)*, **The Oxford Dictionary of**
Nursery Rhymes *(Oxford: Clarendon, 1957), 442.*

In many ways George II's personal leadership of his army into battle at Dettingen in 1743 was an anachronism, for the crown had long since lost most of its political powers. To be sure his grandson George III (1760–1820) was later charged with interfering in politics: the Declaration of Independence accused him of depriving his loyal American subjects of their unalienable rights. In the nineteenth century Queen Victoria (1837–1901) was constantly telling her ministers what to do, yet they took little heed, since after the Great Reform Bill of 1832 Britain was becoming increasingly democratic.

The monarchy adjusted to democracy reasonably well. It became a symbol of national identity, particularly in times of war when subjects tend to rally around the flag. George III became an icon of a Britishness with which the Scots and Irish identified. Queen Victoria made the empire glamorous, giving her subjects of every race and creed, both at home and overseas, someone with whom they could identify and pledge allegiance. Since war always raises national passions, it is not surprising that the monarch, the focus of such feelings, became a symbolic hero leading his or her subjects into battle.

The battles which their peoples faced changed drastically after Dettingen, when a few, highly trained and ferociously disciplined professional soldiers stood side by side to fire volley after volley at the enemy at point-blank range. In the next two centuries technology made war far

Plate 6.1   Sir Thomas Lawrence's painting of the Prince Regent as one of the 'Liberators of Europe', 1814 © By courtesy of the National Portrait Gallery, London

more devastating. The 'Brown Bess' musket was replaced by the rifle and machine gun, cannon by rifled breach-loading artillery that fired exploding shells, horses by tanks, sailing ships by powered vessels. As war became more real to more people, the monarch became a symbolic warrior.

Members of the royal family projected themselves as symbolic warriors in portraits and public appearances. George IV, the Prince Regent, and perhaps the most unmartial man to sit on the British throne, had Sir David Wilkie paint him as a kilt Highland warrior, claymore in hand, and Sir Thomas Lawrence depict him as a British general [Plate 6.1]. In more recent times when photography, film and television portray the state occasions of royalty, they invariably wear uniforms. They get married in uniform, they wear uniforms for the opening of parliament and speeches from the throne: they even attend funerals wearing military dress. Edward VII's (1901–10) first official portrait shows him gripping a baton and wearing the regalia of a field marshal [Plate 6.2]. Even intimate portrayals can have martial overtones. In Sir John Lavery's 1913 royal family group George V (1910–36) wore an admiral's uniform, and his son (later Edward VIII) a midshipman's. A 1930s newsreel showed the duke of Kent in the full rig of a field marshal, taking tea on the lawn of his country house with his infant children, as the narrator praises the informality of the king's younger brother!

As sovereigns lost their direct military roles, the armed forces provided employment for their children. The army and navy were convenient places to park an heir as he waited to become king, and acceptable occupations for younger sons with little expectation of inheriting the throne. The armed forces were above the hurly burly of business, and did not demand the energy or brains required in academia, medicine, the law or even the church. In the army a dull prince could do little damage, especially when assigned a particularly competent second in command. If he did mess up, a harsh military discipline mitigated complaints, which a brotherhood of incompetence was all too happy to squelch.

Of course when a prince served with distinction, or even mediocrity, his achievements were well publicised, sometimes to the point of exaggeration. Having sons in the military had advantages. It strengthened the links between crown and the armed forces, especially if they served in combat – as did Prince William at Cape St Vincent, Prince George at Jutland, or Prince Andrew in the Falklands. Younger sons might also be appointed as senior administrative commanders where they could protect the conservative military from reforming politicians.

William, duke of Cumberland, George II's second son, performed both these roles. His military career began in 1740 when he was barely nineteen and his father, George II, made him colonel of the Coldstream Guards. Wishing to serve afloat, in August he was assigned to HMS *Victory* at Portsmouth, which was tasked to attack Ferrol. After HMS *Victory* collided with HMS *Lion* the raid on Spain was called off, and Cumberland's naval career ended.

Plate 6.2   Edward VII dressed as a field marshall © By courtesy of the National
Portrait Gallery, London

In early 1741 he returned to the Coldstream Guards and spent the next couple of years trying to improve the regiment's three battalions. In late 1742 his father promoted him Lieutenant General, even though he was only twenty-one, and in April 1743 the king took him to Germany where he served as an ADC to General Clayton during the Battle of Dettingen. 'He gave his orders with a great deal of calmness, and seemed quite unconcerned,' recalled James Wolfe, adding that 'the soldiers were in high delight having him so near.' The king was even more delighted at his courage, telling him, 'William, I'm glad you behaved yourself so well – you acted like my son.'

George II was also relieved that his son did not die from the two wounds he sustained during the battle. The most serious, a bullet hole in his calf the size of a hen's egg, broke several tendons. Although he had lost a lot of blood, the military surgeon John Ranby bled the prince, who was in considerable pain, before applying a dressing. Ranby bled him twice more as he changed the dressing and, fearing the prince would die from gangrene, considered amputation. Luckily Cumberland survived, allowing Ranby to feature the injury in his text *The Treatment of Gunshot Wounds* (1744), and Cumberland to modestly shrug off his ordeal at Dettingen. 'The part I have in the success was cheaply bought at the expense of a little pain.'[1]

The wound, which hurt him for the rest of his life, did not affect his military career. After returning home in November to share his father's glory, Cumberland was appointed commander of the allied forces fighting the French. On 11 May 1744 he failed his first test. At Fontenoy he immediately 'lost control of his army' by marching it straight at the enemy, without regard for his – and their – lives.[2] Only his courage prevented a rout. 'The Duke was everywhere,' reported Richard Lyttleton, an ADC, 'He rallied his troops when broken, and made a stand which saved his army from being utterly cut to pieces.'[3] Even though he lost 1,500 of his men, the survivors did not hold it against him. There was something most attractive about the king's second son. The troopers liked his good nature, they admired his courage, they laughed at his coarse jokes. Whilst he might be the king's son, the fat, red-faced young man had the common touch, sharing his food and – more important – his drink with them. Anyway as the king's son he could always blame someone else for the débâcle at Fontenoy. Had the Dutch not collapsed, the French, who were about to run, would have been routed; had Brigadier Ingoldsby obeyed orders, Cumberland told the court martial, we would have won. Although Ingoldsby was acquitted of the more serious charge of disobedience, being found guilty of an error of judgement, Cumberland's fame did not suffer. As Horace Walpole noted, 'He will be as popular with the lower orders as he has been for three or four years with the low women.'[4]

The man who did more than anyone else to enhance the duke of Cumberland's popularity with all orders and sexes, both high and low, was Charles, James II's grandson. Born in 1720, he had served with credit in the French army at the siege of Gaeta in 1734. Soon afterwards Louis-Gabriel Blanchet painted him as a confident young officer, wearing the cross of Saint Andrew on his armoured breast plate. It was an omen. On 22 June 1745, having borrowed 180,000 livres and pawned his jewels, he set sail aboard the French frigate *Doutelle* from St Nazaire for Scotland. On 1 July he rendezvoused with the *Elizabeth*, which was carrying 1,500 muskets, 1,800 swords and 800 Irish volunteers. Nine days later they encountered HMS *Lion*, 100 miles off The Lizard. After a fierce fight the *Elizabeth* and *Lion* were so badly damaged that they had to limp back to port, leaving the *Doutelle* to sail alone to Scotland without the *Elizabeth*'s weapons and troops. On 23 July Charles landed at Eriskay, and two days later at Arisaig on the mainland. He waited until 19 August before raising his standard at Glenfinnan. With a small army of about 900 he entered Perth on 4 September, to proclaim his father, James III, the true king of Great Britain.

At first many Englishmen took the whole thing as a joke. 'I'm sorry the young squire has gone a-grouse shooting in Scotland,' sneered Robert Trevor.[5] Obviously Trevor had forgotten the 1715 Rebellion when James, the Old Pretender, landed in Scotland, rallied 9,000 men to his cause, and marched with 3,000 of them across the border to Preston, where after terrifying the government in London half out of their wits, they surrendered. Afterwards the British government built some 260 miles of roads across the Highlands, which it dotted with fortresses. This policy actually made things worse, for by cultivating the Lowlanders, the British alienated the Highlanders, whom they forbade to carry weapons, making them more sympathetic to the Jacobite cause.

Equally serious was the decline in British military leadership. Field Marshal George Wade, who had built many of the Highland roads, had become so feeble that it took him a couple of days' rest to get over a four-hour ride. 'The poor old man does the best he can,' explained Henry Pelham.[6] Sir John Cope demonstrated his incompetence at the Battle of Prestonpans. In ten – some said four – minutes on 21 September 1745 Charles's army routed the government's forces, killing 300 and taking 1,500 enemy, at the cost of 25 of their own. 'Never deer ran faster before hounds than these betrayed men ran before the rabble,' gloated an observer.[7] Even though the court of enquiry whitewashed Cope, blaming the defeat on 'the shameful behaviour of the private men', the government was deeply worried.[8] They administered a loyalty oath to identify Jacobite sympathisers in England, and recalled Cumberland and his English forces from the continent.

Charles failed to follow up his advantage. Lacking sufficient men to take Berwick, which guarded the eastern road to England, he returned to Edinburgh where he could not even capture the castle. After his Council of War decided by a single vote to invade England, Charles ordered his army to cross the border. They reached Carlisle on 9 November. The town surrendered on the 15th, enabling the Jacobites to continue their march south through Manchester to Derby, where they arrived on 4 December. They made a bad impression on the locals, only three of whom volunteered to join the Scots, who were 'so many fiends from hell,' wrote Mr Bateman, Derby's town clerk, that 'babble like a band of Hottentots'.

Charles hoped that recruits would flock to join his army, particularly in Lancashire, a heavily Catholic county. Few did do. While happy to drink the health of 'the King over the water', English Tories found the prospect of fighting for him after he sailed across the seas to claim their allegiance distinctly unhealthy – hanging, castration, drawing and quartering being the punishment for treason. So on 6 December, with his command in disarray, and hearing no word of a possible French landing on the south coast, Charles ordered a retreat.

Perhaps he could have gone for broke, and marched on London, staking everything on a desperate victory. After all, the English were terrified of the Scottish invaders, whom they vilified as 'filthy, farting, pissing, shiting . . . vermin'. In retreat the Jacobites remained a formidable force, as General Henry Hawley discovered at Falkirk on 17 January 1746. 'Hangman Hawley', a ferocious disciplinarian nicknamed for his penchant for the gallows, lost 450 men. 'Such scandalous cowardice I never saw before,' he justified himself in a letter to Cumberland, blaming 'the whole second line of foot' who 'ran away without firing a shot.'[9]

Far from taking advantage of his victory, which had cost him only 25 men, Charles surrendered the initiative, preferring the comfort of his mistress, Clementina Walkinshaw, to the hardship of visiting the troops. Many Highlanders drifted back home, as Charles came to rely more and more on the advice of Thomas Sheridan, a tired old man, who had last seen combat at the Boyne, 56 years before.

When the duke of Cumberland returned from Flanders in October 1745 he was determined that 'Great Britain is not to be conquered by 3,000 rabble'. With him he brought 25 infantry battalions, 23 squadrons of cavalry and 40 artillery companies. These formed the core of the army that shadowed Charles's advance to Derby, and dogged his retreat back to Edinburgh. Cumberland was resolute that the rebels must not escape unpunished by drifting back to the Highlands.

In January 1746, after a brief visit to London, Cumberland was ready to take the initiative. Having studied General Wade's reports on the clans, he trained his men to fire by ranks, giving them plenty of practice ammunition. He had at least learned something from his defeat at Fontenoy – the devastating effect of volley musket fire at close range against charging infantry. He also instructed his troops to use their bayonets not to stab the man to their front, but the one to their left, thus penetrating that man's armpit as he raised his sword, unprotected by his shield. Having fought professional soldiers in Europe, Cumberland reassured his men, 'you will find it an easy matter . . . to crush the insolencies of a set of thieves and plunderers . . . remember you are the free soldiers of a free people.'[10]

Confident of victory, and sure of the justness of their cause, Cumberland's men marched out of Edinburgh on 31 January singing the old Highland melody, 'Will you play me fair, Highland Laddie?'

They moved up the east coast, supplied by the Royal Navy, stopping at Aberdeen, with Inverness, Charles's last bastion, their objective. They crossed the River Spey on 12 April, reaching Nairn sixteen miles east of Inverness on the 14th, where they rested for a day to celebrate the duke's twenty-fifth birthday with brandy he issued at his own expense. But their cheers of 'Good old Billy' were genuine: morale was high.

In contrast Charles's troops were dispirited. Many had deserted back home, leaving their comrades weak and hungry. Determined to protect his last stronghold their leader disregarded advice to fight north of the Moray Firth, where the rougher land negated Cumberland's advantage in cavalry. Instead he marched his men east to Culloden Moor.

It was a bleak, treeless place, some 500 feet above sea level. Cumberland drew his men up to the north, with a stone wall protecting his left flank. After a brief and ineffective bombardment, Charles's Highlanders charged. The massacre lasted but half an hour. 'In their rage they could not make any impressions upon the battalions, they threw stones at them for at least a minute of time before the total rout began', Cumberland reported. 'I never saw such dreadful slaughter as we had made,' George Stanhope wrote to his brother, 'and our men gave no quarter.' For 200 killed and wounded, Cumberland's army of English and Lowland Scots killed 1,500 rebels and took several hundred prisoner, many of whom they murdered in cold blood. Of some 3,400 prisoners taken after they had fled the battlefield, 120 were tried and executed (40 as deserters from the royal army), while 1,142 were transported to the New World [Plate 6.3 – colour].

Soon after Culloden stories about atrocities began to emerge, and within weeks Cumberland became known as 'The Butcher'. It was reported that after congratulating his men on their victory – 'Well done, my brave boys!' – Cumberland told them to treat 'all prisoners born subjects of His Majesty as traitors and rebels'. The punitive expeditions across the Highlands that followed the battle ruthlessly enforced this policy. After torching some 7,000 crofts, 'Hangman Hawley' reported 'There's still so many houses to burn, and I hope still more to be put to death.'

When Cumberland first returned to London he was welcomed with prodigious enthusiasm.

> *Britons, behold the Royal Youth, 'tis he*
> *Who fights your battles, sets your country free.*
> *The rebels heard and tremble at his Name*
> *And Charles with envy, eyes his rising Fame.*

Thus gloated *The Highlander's Medley or the Duke Triumphant* (1746). The government ordered gold medals struck and presented to the troops who had fought at Culloden, and – more appreciated – paid them all a special bounty. Handel's 'Conquering Hero' was first performed and dedicated to the duke at a special service of thanksgiving held in St Paul's Cathedral.

Did Cumberland deserve these accolades? After all at Culloden he outnumbered the rebels three to one. His men were well fed and equipped: the enemy were starving. His men were well drilled and trained to handle the Highland charge: the rebels were a brave but disorderly mob. Culloden anticipated the battles of imperial warfare, such as Omdurman or Rorke's Drift, where tribesmen, no matter how courageous, could not prevail against the superior organisation and technology of the west.

When Cumberland fought enemies of similar strength, such as the French, the results were very different. As we have seen, he was routed at Fontenoy. In 1747 at Lauffeld Marshall Maurice Saxe defeated the allied army Cumberland led. A decade later, at the outbreak of the Seven Years War, in command of another allied army he was beaten at Hastenbeck. More serious, on his own initiative Cumberland signed the convention of Kloster-Zeven in 1757, a humiliating surrender which his father and the British Government repudiated, prompting his recall home in disgrace.

Prince Charles's career after escaping from Culloden was even more negligible. After eluding the government's forces he reached to France. In exile, he consoled himself with drink and Clementina Walkinshaw. Following years of physical and verbal abuse from her increasingly alcoholic lover, Clementina entered a nunnery. Nursed by their illegitimate daughter, Charlotte, Charles died in Rome in 1788. He left behind a romantic legend, and tens of thousands of shattered Highland lives.

Was it all in vain? Did his invasion have a chance of success? At the time many Englishmen thought so. When they sang 'God Save the King', the national anthem being first performed in public in the autumn of 1745, they took the words quite literally, afraid that the House of Hanover could well be overthrown. General Wade thought all was lost; Horace Walpole was convinced he would be driven into exile and forced to earn his bread tutoring Latin in Copenhagen. England was, after all, dominated by a narrowly based aristocracy. Bribery and corruption fuelled its politics. Crime was rampant and social disorder greatly feared, both being ferociously punished. But there was something anachronistic about Charles's belief that what mattered was changing the king. His attempted conquest was more like that of William I, Henry IV or Henry Tudor, imposed from outside, with little domestic support. But they won and he lost. An autocrat, the Young Pretender took loyal opposition for dissatisfaction, and disloyal toasts to the king over the water as pledges of firm support. No cabal of aristocrats invited him over; only a few thousand, poor illiterate Highlanders, all too often coerced by their clan chiefs on pain of having their crofts burned, mutely rallied around his standard.

They were the folk who ultimately paid the price. To be sure Highlanders such as Flora Macdonald helped the Pretender's getaway, turning the man who cared as little for them as much as he did for himself into the legendary 'Bonnie Prince Charlie,' whose escape from the redcoats was glorified by poets, pipers and novelists. Reality was less romantic: thousands of Highlanders died for their loyalty and many thousands more were cleared from their lands, often by the same lairds who forced them into rebellion. Exiled rebels never forgot the price of rebellion. During the American Revolution the Highlanders who settled in North Carolina fought for King George III, finding another Culloden at the Battle of Moores Creek.

Over the next two and a half centuries many Scots fought for King and Country as part of the British armed forces. In 1760 a quarter of Scots males of military age were serving in the Royal Navy or Army. Culloden was the last gasp for Highland independence. After 1746 the English had come to dominate the whole of Britain, the Lowlanders having been subdued a generation before. In several ways modern Britain, with its emphasis on empire and technological superiority, was born at Culloden. So Cumberland, the last royal warrior to command an army in battle, deserves some credit for this major change. The irony is that unlike other modern decisive battles, such as Blenheim, Waterloo or El Alamein, none of the British regiments who fought there have 'Culloden' embroidered on their colours. It was a battle without honours.

Over the next two generations, until the end of the Napoleonic Wars in 1815, British regiments had many an opportunity to win battle honours as the nation became increasingly militarised. During the American Revolution (the only war Britain has lost), the regular armed forces reached a peak of 164,678 men. During the Napoleonic Wars they crested at 463,949. Over half of them were in the militia, the balance being in the regular forces. Between 1793 and 1815 at least three quarters of a million Britons served full- or part-time in the armed forces. Of the 2,000 members of parliament to sit between 1790 and 1820 nearly half served in the militia or volunteers, 400 in the regular army, and 100 in the Royal Navy. Military uniforms became splendid and expensive. One might cost a militia officer ten to fifty pounds, twenty to a hundred weeks' wages for a farm labourer. If not in the forefront of battle, members of the royal family led this movement of martial elegance, having themselves painted as field marshals or admirals of the fleet. George III designed special uniforms for staff officers in 1784, for generals in 1793, and for naval officers in 1799. By 1815 uniforms had been prescribed for all court officers and lord lieutenants.[11]

As the nation became more militarised it is not surprising that members of the royal family served in the armed forces. George III had fifteen children, six girls and nine boys, five of whom entered the armed forces. His second son, Frederick, duke of York, joined the army, while his third boy, William, duke of Clarence (and later William IV), served in the Navy. His fourth son, Edward, duke of Kent, his fifth son, Ernest August, duke of Cumberland, and his seventh boy, Adolphus Frederick, duke of Cambridge, were all soldiers of varying degrees of distinction.

The first of the king's sons, George, Prince of Wales, later the Prince Regent (1811–20) and then George IV (1820–30), did not serve in the armed forces. As the heir his life was too precious to hazard in war, and anyway he was too indolent and obsessed with inheriting to serve his country. But he did like to project the image of himself as a royal warrior. He admired William Beechey's painting of him in full uniform, reviewing his troops as if he were about to lead them into battle so much that he knighted the artist [Plate 6.4]. George came to believe his own image. He once reminisced with the duke of Wellington how they had both led soldiers up a hill in a battle against Napoleon. 'Steep, very steep,' the duke replied, presumably referring not to the terrain, but to his sovereign's veracity.

Plate 6.4 George III Reviewing his troops by Sir William Beechey. In the background is the Prince of Wales in Light Dragoon uniform. The Royal Collection © 2003, HM Queen Elizabeth II

In popular imagination at least, George III's second son Frederick was 'The Brave old duke of York', who marched his troops to the top of the hill and marched them down again. The nursery rhyme is not wholly fair; even though Frederick's career as a soldier was at best undistinguished, he was a more than competent military administrator. Born in 1763 Frederick was only seventeen when he left England to join the Hanoverian army. He met Frederick the Great of Prussia (who was not impressed). Lord Charles Cornwallis (the British general whom Washington had just defeated) was equally underwhelmed, writing that Frederick 'does not give much hope, further than a great deal of good nature and a very good heart. His military ideas are of a wild boy of the Guards.' Nonetheless he was allowed home to England in 1787, where soon afterwards he displayed the foolhardy courage of a guards subaltern by fighting a duel on Wimbledon Common with Colonel Charles Lennox. When his opponent missed, Frederick stood his ground, refusing to fire.

It was his royal birth, not bravery nor magnanimity, that won him the command of the British expedition sent to the Low Countries in 1793 to fight the French, who having just executed their king, Louis XVI, declared war on 1 February. George III insisted that his 29-year-old second son be appointed a major-general, arguing that the Republican Dutch would less mind serving under a prince than a commoner, no matter how able. After taking two months to capture Valenciennes, the allied forces failed to take Dunkirk, and by September were in full and fervent retreat back to the Netherlands. The following year Frederick, now the duke of York, was given command of 20,000 British troops under the Prince of Coburg-Saalfeld, commander-in-chief of the Austrian Army. 'We are the most ignorant, the worst provided army that ever took to the field,' Frederick's adjutant general confided to a friend, explaining that 21 of their 46 regiments were commanded by 'boys or idiots'.

In May, as this motley crew advanced on Lille, the French ambushed them at Tourcoing, where they were badly mauled, losing 1,000 men and 19 of their 25 cannon. Frederick could not handle the French skirmishers, whom a British officer complained were 'as far-sighted as ferrets, and as active as squirrels'. As Sir John Fortescue, the great historian of the British Army put it with studied understatement, 'The Duke did not shine in the field.'[12]

No wonder Frederick was recalled home, where surprisingly he shone. Being the king's son got him the job of Commander-in-Chief; it also brought him sufficient prestige to help put through a number of badly needed reforms. Frederick laboured diligently from nine in the morning to seven at night, answering as many as three hundred letters a day.

Once or twice a week he held an open house, to which any officer could come and see him. Hard work, and the Teutonic stubbornness for which the Hanoverians were famous, enabled him to modify the purchase system, insisting that officers remain a certain time in rank before buying a promotion. Thus a lieutenant had to serve two years before becoming a captain. The reforms worked. 'We no longer hear,' reported *The British Military Journal* in 1801, 'of beardless lieutenant colonels lording it over veterans.'[13] Frederick started a system of annual confidential performance reports on officers, and insisted on keeping records such as war diaries and casualty statistics. To educate officers he founded the Woolwich Academy, and a school in Buckinghamshire which eventually became the Royal Military College, Sandhurst. He greatly enhanced the quality of the troops by increasing the pay of private soldiers by 80 per cent, abolishing pigtails, improving food, and providing greatcoats. He improved medical facilities, introducing smallpox vaccinations. Frederick revised the infantry training manual, and even got the cavalry to accept a common drill book. Between 1801 and 1803 he built up the defences of the south coast using Martello towers to thwart a French invasion.

The only blot on his record came in 1809 when Colonel Wardle alleged in the House of Commons that Mrs Clarke, Frederick's mistress, had been taking bribes to influence promotions. After a seven-week investigation the Commons exonerated him by 278 votes to 196: the majority was insufficient. Conservatives were upset that he had supposedly tried to commission Samuel Carter, Mrs Clarke's footman; radicals simply wanted to embarrass the government. So Frederick resigned.

Two years later he was reinstated, and in 1814, after Napoleon's abdication, received a vote of thanks from the whole House of Commons. He deserved it. Off the field of battle no man did more than Frederick to make possible the victories Wellington won in the Spanish Peninsula and at Waterloo. The duke admitted as much, telling parliament that thanks to Frederick's efforts, 'the staff of the army is better than it was, officers better educated and discipline much improved'.[14] Sir John Fortescue was equally laudatory, writing that in 1795 Frederick 'took over a number of undisciplined and disorganised regiments, filled for the most part with worthless stumps of men or officers, and in less than seven years, he converted these unpromising elements into an army'.[15]

Frederick became a genuinely popular figure: in Staffordshire alone there were twelve pubs named after him – as compared to ten for Wellington. William Thackeray remembered him as, 'big, burly, loud, jolly, cursing and courageous'.[16] Frederick died in 1827, widely and genuinely mourned. 'The Joy of our heart is ceased', wrote William Crotch in the anthem he specially composed.[17] Seven years later a column was raised in his honour near Horse Guard's Parade: it is an honour he shares with only one other military hero – Horatio Nelson.

Nelson thought highly of the king's third son, William, duke of Clarence. 'As an individual I love him,' the admiral declared, 'as a Prince I honour and revere him.'[18] Born in 1765 William was brought up by a governess, Lady Charlotte French, a sensible and kindly woman who treated him well. At the age of seven he was handed over to a governor, General J. Budé, a peculiar man with a passion for eating anchovies. Sarcastic and haughty he alternately fawned upon and scolded his royal charge, utterly confusing the poor boy. Dr John Majendie, William's tutor (who had a pass degree from Cambridge in classics), was a more positive influence. William's upbringing was fairly simple: lessons in the morning followed by physical work on the king's model farm in the afternoon. His diet was equally plain: milk, a glass of wine, ungarnished meats. Although William chaffed against the restrictions, he was a cheerful boisterous child.

In 1778 George III decided to send his third son into the navy. The story that he did so after two of the queen's maids of honour had seduced him is improbable, for at thirteen William was too young to start an amorous career, and too old to begin a naval one. In truth the king sent him to sea to remove him from the malign influence of his elder brother, the Prince of Wales. The decision was not without its dangers, for Britain was involved in the American War of Independence, fighting not just the colonists, but also the French and Spanish.

On 15 July 1779 Midshipman Prince William and his tutor, Dr Majendie, reported for duty aboard the *Prince George*. 'I flatter myself you will be pleased with the appearance of the boy, who neither wants resolution nor cheerfulness,' the king wrote to Rear Admiral Robert Digby, his son's new commanding officer. Apart from occasionally dining with the admiral, he received few privileges. According to an almost certainly apocryphal story, on coming aboard someone once asked him what he should be called. The prince replied, 'My father's name is Guelph and therefore, if you please, you may call me William Guelph, for I am nothing more than a sailor like yourselves.'[19]

During his first summer the new sailor cruised with the fleet off Torbay and learned to swim – an unusual skill, for most matelots believed that if their ship sank, being able to do so only postponed the inevitable. After a short furlough to see his family William returned to his ship for a six-month cruise. Almost immediately the *Prince George* intercepted a Spanish convoy, capturing its flagship, a 68-gun first rate, which they renamed *The Prince William* in his honour. On 16 January 1780 he took part in the Battle of Cape St Vincent, and saw the *Santo Domingo* blow up. It was 'a most shocking sight,' he wrote to his father, 'I felt horror all over me.' The captured Spanish admiral, Don Juan de Langara, was presented to the prince. Afterwards, recognising the midshipman in charge of the admiral's barge, the Spaniard observed, 'Well does Great Britain merit the empire of the sea, when the humblest stations in its navy are filled by princes of the blood.'[20]

The fleet returned to Gibraltar to celebrate their victory. William and his friend, Augustus Beauclerk, did so with such inebriated enthusiasm that they got into a fight with some sailors, and their admiral had to spring the two midshipmen from prison. In February on the way back home the fleet intercepted a French convoy, capturing its flagship which was carrying £100,000. 'Everything has been successful on our side,' the prince reported to the king.

William arrived in London in March 1781 to present his parents with flags captured from enemy ships. King George and Queen Charlotte were openly (and with good cause) proud of the boy, whom Henry Pye, the poet laureate, called 'a budding rose beneath the morning dew'.[21] They took their son to see 'The Tempest' at Drury Lane Theatre, where a standing ovation delayed the start of the play for fifteen minutes.

If these plaudits went to the lad's head, they were knocked out of him the following year when his father sent him aboard *The Prince George*, once more under Admiral Digby, to sail to New York in the hope that having a royal prince on their soil might encourage the Loyalists. He made a good impression on John Peebles, an army officer, who thought him 'a very fine young man, smart and sensible for his years'.[22] Although he was warmly welcomed, being introduced to Benedict Arnold and being praised from the pulpit by the local Episcopal rector, William did not like New York. It was dirty; the women were ugly. So he used to go off on long walks into the countryside of upper Manhattan or Brooklyn by himself. When Colonel Matthias Ogden suggested that the rebel forces capture the prince to hold him hostage, George Washington replied that the plan 'merits applause, and you have my authority to make the attempt in any manner, and at such time, as your judgment may direct'.

Fortunately for Washington's reputation, the Continental Army did not have time to perpetrate this act of terrorism, Prince William being sent to sea aboard HMS *Warwick*. Injured, perhaps by a fall from the rigging, he returned to New York, and after three weeks' rest moved to Lord Howe's flagship. By now the fighting was well and truly over, Cornwallis having surrendered at Yorktown in October 1781. 'Prince William is in the dumps about the peace,' Admiral Hood told General

Budé, 'as his heart was set upon seeing service.'[23] He did manage to see the Caribbean, spending some time in Jamaica where he supposedly fell in love with Dona Maria Solena, a Spanish admiral's daughter. Here he met Horatio Nelson, then captain of HMS *Albemarle*. After some hesitation the two became good friends. The prince had wit enough to spot Nelson's potential, succumbing, like most officers and men, to his charisma. He wrote that, 'there is something irresistibly pleasing in his manner and conversation, and an enthusiasm, when speaking on professional subjects, that showed he was no common being'. Nelson responded with equal warmth, venturing the opinion that the prince 'will be, I am certain, an ornament to our profession'.

Nelson was no sycophant. The following year, Horace Walpole (an iconoclast if ever there was one), found William 'lively, cheerful, talkative, manly, well bred, sensible . . .'. Without doubt four years in the navy had done the prince a world of good.

With his chronic poor judgement as far as the education of his children was concerned, George III decided in 1783 to remove William from the navy to send him to Hanover to learn German. Accompanied by Captain William Merrick, a cheerful rake, William gambled so wantonly that Baron Hardenberg, a notorious card sharp, challenged him to a duel. In Hanover William discovered fornication, an activity that would occupy much his energy for the next decade. He caught the pox, he told his eldest brother, 'with a woman of the town against a wall'. Distraught he longed 'for England and the pretty girls of Westminster: at least to such as would not clap or pox me every time I fucked'.[24] Forbidden to return home, William travelled to Prague, which he found equally dissolute. After one ball he ended up with cards from 47 women seeking assignations – which he thought quite an achievement until he discovered that the local bishop had collected 53.

After many appeals the king eventually allowed William to return home, where on 17 January 1785 he passed his examinations to be promoted lieutenant. Lord Howe, who chaired the examining board told George III that his son 'was every inch a sailor'. Almost immediately he was posted to HMS *Hebé*, a frigate captured from the French, which sailed right around the British Isles. William did not think much of the Highlanders, who 'are in a more miserable state than the Negroes of the West Indies'.

In April 1786, after the king had turned down several requests for a command, William was appointed captain of his own ship, HMS *Pegasus*, a 28-gun frigate, with orders to proceed to Canada. On 21 August, as they sailed across the Atlantic, the prince invited his officers to a lunch celebrating his 21st birthday. They did so with great enthusiasm. The whole crew got so drunk that they carried their captain shoulder high around the deck. 'It was altogether a strange scene,' a midshipman recorded in his diary, 'one that would have astonished the members of a temperance society.'[25]

The following year HMS *Pegasus* cruised in the Caribbean before returning to Quebec, where William ran up large gambling debts and had an affair with Frances Wentworth, the 25-year-old wife of a 50-year-old surgeon. His ship returned to Plymouth on 27 December, where William immediately incurred his father's displeasure by hosting the Prince of Wales in a dissolute homecoming. After a liaison with Sally Winne, the daughter of an ambitious merchant who encouraged the affair hoping that it would get him appointed Agent Victualler to the Fleet, William was transferred to HMS *Andromeda*, and in February 1788 ordered back to Canada. He found Halifax disappointing. Frances Wentworth had shifted her affections elsewhere. His squadron commander, Captain Charles Sandys, was an even greater drunkard than he. At one party 20 officers consumed 66 bottles of wine, the prince being the only one left on his feet. His parties aboard the HMS *Andromeda* became shamelessly dissolute – one included a performance of lesbian sex. During one debauch at Bridgeton, Barbados, he and his brother officers did some £700 worth of damage to Mrs Pringle's high-class bordello. At about this time William started the first of at least three mercury treatments for syphilis. 'I am sorry to say that I have been living a terribly debauched life,' he admitted.[26]

In late 1788 HMS *Andromeda* sailed to Jamaica, where the prince attended debates in the legislature, voicing a strong support for slavery and an ambition to become the colony's next governor. But his brother, George, the Prince of Wales, ordered him home, needing his support after their father had once again lost his wits. On his return George made William the duke of Clarence, an honour he sorely wanted since with it came an extra £12,000 a year pension from the civil list.

William had made a serious mistake, for as a duke he could no longer command a mere frigate – a battleship, if not a squadron or even a fleet, being more appropriate to the dignity of a duke. Having an aristocrat of the highest rank serving under captains and admirals who might not be knights, let alone lords, would create an intolerable conflict between the order of noble hierarchy and naval rank.

William was a reasonably good small ship captain. His vessels were well turned out. Perhaps he went in for too much spit and polish. He forbade the hanging of washing to dry between decks because it was untidy, even if that meant sailors had to go on watch wearing wet clothes. He prohibited officers wearing jackets in port, even in places as frigid as Quebec or Halifax. He was a firm, sometimes brutal disciplinarian, but had great energy, and looked after his men. If he sometimes found it hard to get on with his more experienced lieutenants, he was at least kind to his midshipmen.

Ending William's naval career was a shame. Bored, deprived of the one job he enjoyed, William began an affair with Mrs Dorothy Jordan, by whom he had ten children. When England went to war with revolutionary France, William felt guilty at shirking his duty. 'All I require is active service,' he wrote to the Admiralty in March 1794, requesting a ship so 'that I may not have the imputation thrown upon me of living a life of inglorious ease, when I ought to be in the front of danger.'[27] He had to wait twenty years before hearing a shot fired in anger. In 1814 during a visit to the British expeditionary forces in the Low Countries he watched the bombardment of Antwerp from a church steeple, which came under fire, a bullet piercing the prince's coat. The incident enhanced his reputation amongst the allied soldiers who exuberantly welcomed him to Brussels. 'The game is up with Bonaparte' the prince exulted, 'and I shall be in at the kill.'[28]

Apart from being in charge of *The Royal Sovereign*, which conveyed the Bourbons back across the Channel to France to reclaim the throne after Napoleon's abdication, William did very little until February 1827 when the prime minister revived the office of lord high admiral, appointing the prince to this ancient position. He did so less to use William's talents, and more to placate one of his ministers, Lord Melville, a reactionary Tory, and a crashing snob who once refused to serve under another prime minister on the grounds that the fellow's mother had been an actress. When William quarrelled with the politicoes his brother refused to support him. 'You are in error from beginning to end,' wrote George IV, 'this is not a matter of opinion, but of positive fact.' In a huff the new lord high admiral took the fleet to sea for ten days without telling anyone where they were going. Although he made some reforms, limiting flogging, overhauling the promotion system, insisting on six-monthly reports from all ships, and commissioning HMS *Lightning*, the navy's first steamship, he did not last for long.

And yet as William IV (1834–37), he was a fairly good king. Service in the Royal Navy enabled 'The Sailor King', as he was popularly known, to have sown his wild oats as a young man out of the sight and mind of the growing middle classes who insisted on high moral standards. Had he indulged his gross appetites for drink and dissolution in public and at home instead of overseas and aboard ship, he might have become as loathed as George IV, whose obituary in *The Times* noted, 'There never was an individual less regretted by his fellow-creatures than the deceased king.'[29]

Many regarded George III's third son, Edward, duke of Kent, in a similar fashion. Born in 1767 he was sent to Hanover at the age of seventeen to be trained as a soldier. Instead all he did was waste other people's time and (by borrowing it) their money. In 1790 he returned home without permission. After a ten-minute interview his father packed him off to Gibraltar to command the Royal Fusiliers. Edward was so ferocious a disciplinarian that he flogged the regiment almost to mutiny. Within a year he was sent to Canada, where he both flogged and borrowed without restraint. After awarding several sentences of 999 lashes (about 900 more than the strongest fellow could hope to survive), the garrison plotted to murder him. The mutiny discovered, he sentenced their ring leader, one Private Draper, to death, commuting the sentence at the last moment.

Clemency did not endear him to the troops. Edward was such a vicious man that nothing – not even his service during the capture of the Leeward and Windward Isles the following year – could win their loyalty. The troops were delighted when he fell from his horse in 1798 and had to be invalided home to take the waters at Bath. Eventually he returned to Canada as Commander-in-Chief, North America. The following year he was appointed governor of Gibraltar with express orders to restore discipline. Here he broke his previous record for driving a garrison into mutiny by issuing standing orders that ran to 300 closely printed pages which, *inter alia*, forbade carrying umbrellas, regulated haircuts, and closed down 50 of the Rock's 90 wine shops. 'Drunkenness is the bane of soldiers,' the duke of Kent fulminated, as he prohibited the consumption of alcohol on Christmas Day. 'He was a bad man,' a veteran recalled, 'he would not let us drink.' In protest the wine shop owners issued free grog to any soldier. On Boxing Day fighting broke out, several of the garrison being killed. William executed the ring leaders, and flogged the rest. His second-in-command, Major General Barnett, looked on the bright side. 'It is for the best thing that could happen: now we shall be rid of him.'[30]

They were the following March, when Edward was recalled. He spent the rest of his life in banal idleness, first with Madame De St Laurent, the mistress whom he had met in Canada, and then with Princess Victoria of Leiningen, a widow, whom he married solely to increase his civil list pension.

George III's fifth son, Ernest, duke of Cumberland was only 19 when he joined the Ninth Hanoverian Hussars in 1790 as a lieutenant, being promoted colonel in 1793, and major general the following year. He soon won a reputation for ferocious bravery. Even though his sword broke during a hand to hand fight with a French dragoon in 1794, he managed to capture the fellow. The forbidding face wound he received at the Battle of Tournai in May of that year made him look all the more ferocious, adding to his reputation as a brutal disciplinarian. On his return to England in 1796 Ernest became the most hated figure in the land after Napoleon. Nurses were said to threaten their charges that he would come and get them if they did not behave. In 1810 the officers of the Fifteenth Light Dragoons petitioned parliament for Ernest's removal as their commanding officer. So when his valet, Joseph Sellis, attacked him in a fit of madness, slashing his skull badly enough to reveal his brains, before slitting his own throat, many believed that Ernest had murdered his valet who found him in bed with Mrs Sellis. Three years later Ernest left England to serve with the Hanoverian army at the Battle of Leipzig.

After the war Ernest spent most of his time overseas, rarely returning to his native land, where he was so loathed as an ultra-tory, papist-hating, anti-semitic, bigoted reactionary that he was booed in the streets. When he inherited the throne of Hanover in 1837 he asked Wellington how long he should stay in England before taking up his new throne. The duke advised, 'Go before you are pelted out.' In fact Ernest was a popular monarch. His German subjects found his reactionary authoritarianism more palatable than *The Times* which noted in his 1851 obituary that 'the good that can be said of the Royal Dead is little or none'.[31]

About the same could be said about Adolphus Frederick, duke of Cambridge, George III's seventh son. Like Ernest he served in the Hanoverian army in the Low Countries, being wounded in the shoulder. When it appeared likely that Napoleon would invade Hanover, George III made Adolphus commander of the Hanoverian army. He was determined to die for the kingdom. 'Rest assured that I will sacrifice my blood and life for a country to which I am much attached,' he vowed to a friend. The Hanoverians were less bellicose: on their borders they erected large placards stating in French, 'Neutral Territory'.[32] So Adolphus returned to England to command the Home District.

At best George III's sons were mediocrities: at worst they were thoroughly nasty human beings. The duke of Wellington called them 'the damnedest millstones about the neck of any government that can be imagined'.[33] They were an embarrassment, particularly to the new middle classes of the industrial revolution (many of whom were Methodists), who demanded decorum from men in public life. Service in the armed forces got them out of the way, hidden in a place where they could not do too much damage; and if they did, it could be readily hushed up.

Under Queen Victoria (1837–1901), this changed. Although she was less than a year old when her father, Edward, the duke of Kent, died,

Victoria was proud to be a soldier's daughter. Her chronic seasickness may have enhanced an innate distrust of the navy. 'A most distasteful profession,' she called it, 'the worst for morals or anything that can be imagined', adding, 'I have always had a special feeling about the army.'[34] In August 1837, having been on the throne for less than three months, she insisted on reviewing the troops at Windsor wearing a form of uniform with a field marshal's badges of rank. Spurning Prime Minister Melbourne's entreaties to use a carriage, it being more ladylike and civilian, she insisted on doing so on horseback like a soldier. A ballad commented:[35]

> *You may wonder and blunder and argue and stare*
> *But remember I am your Queen*
> *And learn that it is not a trifling affair*
> *To please a young girl of eighteen.*

During the Crimean War the queen fully demonstrated her commitment to the army, ardently supporting Britain and France's efforts to prevent Russia from taking over the Turkish Empire. 'You never saw anyone so taken up with military affairs as she is,' noted Lord Panmure, her minister for war.[36] Although as a woman she could not fight, she supported the efforts of Florence Nightingale, a member of her own sex, to improve medical conditions for the troops. 'I envy her for being able to do so much good & look after the noble brave heroes whose behaviour is so admirable,' wrote the Queen, who gave Panmure and Lord Aberdeen, the prime minister, merry hell whenever they opposed Miss Nightingale. After inspecting Chatham Hospital, she sent Panmure a blistering rebuke complaining that the wards were more like prison cells, and that there were no recreation facilities or separate mess halls for the wounded veterans. She wrote personal letters of condolence to soldiers' widows, and instituted the Victoria Cross for bravery. After awarding the first batch in May 1855, she wrote in her diary, 'all touched my hand, the first time a simple Private would touch the hand of the Sovereign. . . . I am so proud of it – proud of the tie which links the lowly brave soldier to his Sovereign' [Plate 6.5 – colour].

Big burly troopers turned the queen on. They were, she confessed to her diary, 'strikingly handsome', adding that talking to them 'is one of the *few* agreeable privileges of our position'. Her feelings were heartfelt and sincere. 'I thank God all your dangers are over,' she told the returned servicemen at the victory parade held in Aldershot in July 1856. That evening she wrote in her dairy: 'Surrounded by troops & I found it so exciting.' The next day she took the salute from Buckingham Palace balcony as the queen's men marched past.[37]

Half a century later, during the Boer War, Victoria showed a similar personal concern for the soldiers who fought in South Africa to put down a revolt by the Dutch settlers against English expansion into the goldfields of the Transvaal. For Christmas 1899, the year the war started, she dispatched a metal chocolate box engraved with her head to every man serving in South Africa. Many refused to eat the chocolate, preferring to keep the gift from their sovereign intact, some turning down offers of five pounds (two months pay). On 18 December 1899, after a run of trouncings so serious that it became known as Black Week, the queen informed Arthur Balfour, 'we are not interested in the possibilities of defeat'. The following November she inspected the Life Guards, among the first troops to return from the war, and the next day some 240 Canadian veterans who had volunteered to fight for Queen and Empire. As he left their adjutant vowed, 'I could die for her.'[38] It was the pledge of a medieval vassal to his feudal lord.

But that time was long gone. The growth of democracy during Victoria's long reign changed the monarch's constitutional role as much as it altered its military one. The Queen/Empress became the symbol for national and imperial loyalties. A remote figure, concerned like a mother for her sons, she was also the unobtainable female to whom men could pledge their troth. 'The Widow's uniform is not the soldier-man's disgrace,' wrote Rudyard Kipling.[39] Victoria delighted in the title Empress of India. She enjoyed becoming a national symbol. Yet she was hesitant, especially as far as her beloved army was concerned, about the growth of democracy, which she once called 'a great calamity for the country'.[40]

While admiring the enlisted men – particularly as men – she believed that the officer corps should remain an aristocratic bastion, protecting her own place at the apex of the pyramid of hereditary privilege. Thus she successfully opposed the appointment of Frederick Lugard as minister for war in 1855 because of his humble origins, preferring instead the more aristocratic Panmure, later the Earl of Dalhousie.

More serious she supported her cousin, George, second duke of Cambridge, an unmitigated reactionary who, for 38 years from 1857 to 1895 as Commander in Chief of the Army, opposed nearly every reform. Admittedly he expanded the Royal Military College, Sandhurst, and encouraged the study of military history, but most of the time he remained true to his belief, 'I don't see any good in changing everything. We have done well as we are.'[41]

As a soldier Cambridge had done rather badly. During the Crimean War the sight of piled mutilated corpses at Inkerman unnerved him so badly that he fled for Malta. As long as the Royal Navy remained efficient, adapting to the introduction of steam power, and the army continued to fight imperial wars in which human waves of natives bravely but futilely charged Gatling guns, the management of a man who was as resolute in the face of change as he had been craven at the sight of carnage, would not have mattered too much. But in 1870 Edward Cardwell, William Gladstone's Secretary of State for War, proposed reforms to deal with the growing threat from Germany, which had just defeated France and become a united nation. Germany had a huge conscript army, equipped with bolt-action rifles and breech-loading artillery, coordinated by professionally trained staff officers. Cardwell proposed that soldiers serve a six-year enlistment, followed by six years in the reserves. Locally based regiments, able to recruit from militia units, would have two battalions: the one at home acting as a training support for the other overseas. Cardwell wanted to abolish flogging and the purchase of commissions, introduce breech-loading Martin-Henry rifles, subordinate the commander in chief to the minister for war, increase the pay of private soldiers to a shilling a day, and provide them with food without charge. The duke of Cambridge opposed these changes because they were changes. The queen supported the duke because he was her cousin. 'Mr. C. is much disliked by the Army, who know he understands nothing of military affairs,' wrote Victoria.[42] Initially their opposition made no difference, for the Cardwell reforms were all implemented by 1872. Yet they were able to thwart further reforms, such as the development of an effective army staff officer system, the malign effects of which would be felt during the Boer and First World Wars.

Notes

1. R. Whitworth, *William Augustus, Duke of Cumberland: a Life* (London: Leo Cooper, 1992), 32, 34.
2. C. Barnett, *Britain and Her Army* (London: Cassel, 1970), 192.
3. Whitworth, *op. cit.*, 50–1.
4. Ibid., 51.
5. Ibid., 56–7.
6. J. Black, *Culloden and the Suppression of the 45* (Stroud: Sutton, 1990), 145–6.
7. W. Speck, *The Butcher: the Duke of Cumberland and the Suppression of the 45* (Caernafon: Welsh Academic, 1995), 51.
8. Black, *op. cit.*, 82.
9. Barnett, *op. cit.*, 194.
10. Speck, *op. cit.*, 111.
11. L. Colley, *Britons: Forging a Nation, 1707–1837* (New Haven: Yale University Press, 1994), 185, 288.
12. A. H. Burne, *The Noble Duke: the Military Life of Frederick Duke of York and Albany* (London: Staples, 1948), 13.
13. Burne, *op. cit.*, 239.

14. Barnett, *op. cit.*, 246.
15. Sir John Fortescue, *History of the British Army* (London: Macmillan, 1920), IV, 929.
16. Burne, *op. cit.*, 235.
17. Cambridge University Library, Anderson Room, MR230.A.80.30.
18. P. Ziegler, *King William IV* (London: Collins, 1971), 55.
19. R. Fulford, *Royal Dukes: the Father and Uncles of Queen Victoria* (London: Collins, 1973), 100.
20. Ibid., 31–3.
21. Ibid., 105.
22. R. Holmes, *Redcoat: the British Soldier in the Age of Horse and Musket* (London: Harper Collins, 2001), 82.
23. Ziegler, *op. cit.*, 43.
24. Ibid., 49–53.
25. Fulford, *op. cit.*, 104.
26. Ziegler, *op. cit.*, 69.
27. W. G. Allen, *King William IV* (London: Cresset Press, 1960), 40–1.
28. Ziegler, *op. cit.*, 114–15.
29. C. Hibbert, *George IV* (Harmondsworth: Penguin, 1973), II, 432.
30. Fulford, *op. cit.*, 180–89.
31. Ibid., 212, 247–50.
32. Fulford, *op. cit.*, 286.
33. J. H. Plumb, *The First Four Georges* (London: Collins, 1969), 148.
34. F. Hardie, *The Political Influence of the British Monarchy, 1868–1952* (London: Batsford, 1970), 19–20.
35. E. Longford, *Victoria, R. I.* (London: Weidenfeld and Nicolson, 1964), 70.
36. S. Weintraub, *Victoria: Biography of a Queen* (London: Unwin Hyman, 1987), 249.
37. Ibid., 235–57.
38. Ibid., 609, 629–30.
39. Rudyard Kipling, 'Tommy', Jon Stallworthy (ed.), *The Oxford Book of War Poetry* (Oxford: Oxford University Press, 1988), 144.
40. Hardie, *op. cit.*, 33.
41. G. St Aubyn, *Royal George, 1819–1904: the Life of HRH Prince George, Duke of Cambridge* (London: Constable, 1963), 330.
42. Hardie, *op. cit.*, 20.

chapter 7

LOOKING THEM IN THE FACE

⸻ ❧ ⸻

'I'm glad that we have been bombed. It made me feel that we can look the East End in the face.' Queen Elizabeth, consort of George VI, September, 1940

In 1985 in a poem celebrating the 85th birthday of Elizabeth, the Queen Mother, Ted Hughes, the Poet Laureate, described her as the 'Lion' who 'our longship Island bore/through the night-sea of war'.[1] If there is an image which the royal family would like to endure it is, I suspect, that of King George VI and Queen Elizabeth inspecting the blitzed cities of Britain during the Second World War. He wore his uniform as a field marshal or admiral of the fleet: she was dressed for a Buckingham Palace garden party, as if to say Britain's business would continue as usual in spite of Hitler and his lackeys. It was their finest hour, a time when they epitomised a resistance to foreign invaders as stalwart as Elizabeth I's at Tilbury. They showed a deep concern for the suffering of the bombed, as well as a stoic commitment to duty, confident that in the end all will come right. Even though posterity has exaggerated their popularity during the Second World War, there is no doubt that George VI's courage was genuine, and that war brought certainty to a deeply insecure man.

If the growth of democracy and empire can be seen as the defining themes of Victorian Britain, then the two world wars and the consequent loss of empire may be viewed as those of the twentieth century. Not surprisingly the world wars did much to shape the monarchy, allowing it to grow in prestige as it lost power. For instance no monarch died more respected than George V, largely because of his role in the Great War of 1914–18.

Prince George, Edward VII's second son, was only twelve when he and his older brother, Prince Albert, duke of Clarence, joined HMS

Britannia, the Royal Navy's preparatory school. Conditions aboard this hulk moored on the River Dart were arduous. 'It never did me any good to be a prince, I can tell you,' he recalled, 'It was a pretty tough place.' He only got a shilling a week pocket money. He had to fag for the elder boys, being so small that he was known as 'the sprat', a pun on Wales, his father being its prince. He showed no intellectual distinction. One tutor wrote to his father about 'the abnormally dormant condition of his mental powers' [Plate 7.1].

Two years later George and Albert went to sea on HMS *Bacchante*. When Queen Victoria expressed a concern that the vessel might sink with her grandchildren aboard, the Admiralty – less worried about the crew – sent it out in a gale to prove it would not. For three years the two midshipmen sailed around the world in HMS *Bacchante*, enjoying themselves, visiting foreign ports, being entertained across the empire in the style befitting the queen's grandsons. George even got tattooed. The two young men got on so well that they shared mistresses at Southsea and St John's Wood. 'She is a ripper,' George raved about the latter.[2]

In 1883 after being posted to HMS *Canada*, George was promoted Sub-Lieutenant, and sent to attend the gunnery school at the Royal Naval College, Greenwich. From 1886 to 1889 he served as a lieutenant aboard HMS *Thunderer*, mainly in the Mediterranean, before getting his first command, HMS Torpedo Boat *79*. Victoria was worried, noting that 'Torpedo boats are dangerous'. She was right. George had to rescue his sister ship as it floundered in a gale off the Irish coast. The following year he took command of HMS *Thrush*, a corvette, which he sailed to Gibraltar and the West Indies.

The prince's naval career ended in 1892, when Albert, his eldest brother, died, and he was recalled home as heir apparent. For the nation it was a blessing in disguise. Albert was a dissolute wastrel, as stupid as he was idle, who would have been a terrible monarch. For George it was a personal tragedy. He loved the navy, and like William IV could have become an ornament to his profession. The navy affected him profoundly, reinforcing existing traits. For instance, separation from home enhanced the influence of his family, to whom he was deeply committed. From every port he would send them long letters saying how much he missed them and their house at Sandringham: at Christmas time he became particularly homesick. He once described Edward VII as 'my best friend, and the best of fathers' – which is a bit of an irony since unlike the uxorious George his father was a serial philanderer.

Extensive naval travel did not broaden George's outlook. 'The sailors go around the world,' one of his courtiers – a soldier – observed, 'but they never seem to get into it.' Because of the closeness of life on board

Plate 7.1 Prince George as a Naval Cadet © By courtesy of the National
Portrait Gallery, London

ship naval officers tend to develop standardised patterns of comraderie that stress an easygoing, even charming, friendliness over deep, lasting friendships. His eldest son, later Edward VIII, once complained that George used to treat him like some mischievous matelot brought before a captain's mast.[3] The navy made George more dedicated, and inflexible. During his public duties as king he could appear cross and bored. 'We sailors never smile when on duty,' he explained.[4] Service at sea, where engineers were safely kept out of sight below decks, bolstered his distrust of the flamboyant and intelligent. He would have agreed with Daisy, Lady Warwick (one of his father's mistresses), that 'As a class, we don't like brains.'[5] Proudly sporting a naval beard, George V was obsessed with trivia. He had his civilian trousers creased the naval left to right, not the normal back to front, and would savagely reprimand anyone, his sons included, who appeared before him improperly dressed. Most important of all, the king's service as a naval officer convinced him that the conduct of war should be left to the professionals and not meddling politicians.

This would not have been significant had George not been king in 1914 when the First World War broke out on 4 August. 'It is a terrible catastrophe, but it is not our fault,' the king wrote in his diary that evening. Anxious for his second son, also a naval officer, he continued, 'Pray God that it will soon be over & that He will protect dear Bertie'.[6]

While George V firmly believed he had a constitutional right to be consulted, advise and warn his ministers, at first the intrigues between them and the military horrified him. On learning that Lord Kitchener, the minister for war, had told General Sir Douglas Haig to write to him informally evaluating his superior officers, the king was enraged. 'If anyone acted like that and told tales out of school, he would at school be called a sneak,' he told Herbert Kitchener, who retorted that they were no longer schoolboys.[7]

During a visit to the Western Front in October 1915 George V had dinner with General Haig, an old family friend, who told him that General Sir John French, the Commander in Chief, Western Front, who had been responsible for the recent débâcle at Loos, had lost the confidence of the army. The king passed this message on to Prime Minister Herbert Asquith who dismissed French, appointing Haig in his place. In a letter of congratulations the king assured Haig, 'Remember that it will always be a pleasure to me to help you in any way I can . . . I hope that you will from time to time write to me quite freely.'

In January 1917 the British army was placed under the operational command of the French general Robert Nivelle. Haig was quite understandably upset, and wrote the king long letters in which he discussed resignation. George begged him not to do so since this would be 'disastrous to his army'. So Haig stayed on, to see Nivelle dismissed after his plans for a knock-out blow to win the war failed abysmally at Chemin des Dames. The king continued to back incompetent generals – although to be fair he had very few competent ones – objecting to the dismissal of Sir William Robertson as Chief of the Imperial General Staff. When Prime Minister David Lloyd George threatened to resign and call an election, the king backed down. When the king opposed the dismissal of Sir Charles Trenchard, founder of the RAF, and Lord Bertie, the British Ambassador to France, Lloyd George accused him of 'encouraging mutiny'.

There is no doubt that the king and Lloyd George did not like each other. For one thing the prime minister was a Welsh firebrand, who threatened the establishment by reforming the House of Lords and taxing the wealthy. Lloyd George wanted the poor to inherit the earth, particularly the earth of rich English landlords. In June 1915 it was reported that the king opposed his appointment as minister for war and 'went into a most violent diatribe against Lloyd George'.[8]

Lloyd George disliked the king's confidant, General Haig, whom he once described as 'being brilliant to the top of his army boots'.[9] Haig was an old friend of the royal family. The duke of Cambridge had nominated him to a staff college position, and he stayed at Sandringham in 1898 before leaving to fight in the Sudan. He was an *aide de camp* to Edward VII and friends with Queen Alexandra, marrying Dorothy Vivian, one of her maids of honour, the wedding taking place in Buckingham Palace.

Although Haig had friends at court, in the long run it made little difference for the crown had hardly any real influence over the conduct of the war. To be sure in December 1916 Lloyd George bowed to the king's insistence that Sir Edward Carson and not Lord Milner (a far better administrator), be appointed First Sea Lord. Yet Lloyd George accepted the king's advice on only one other occasion. During the Russian revolution George persuaded the government to deny the Czar's request for political asylum for himself and his family because it would be 'awkward for our Royal Family'. As a result the Bolsheviks murdered the king's cousins.

Politicians listened to the king, sometimes with deference, more often irritation, and then did what they wanted to do. After the Battle of Loos General John French was finished: so the king's efforts to sack him were superfluous. After General Nivelle's appointment as commander-in-chief over the British Army the king wrote to Haig getting him to accept the decision of the politicians. No one, not even Nivelle, could have survived the disaster of Chemin des Dames, which did far more to enhance Haig's stock than, as Lady Haig claimed, the king's support. The king might encourage. 'The Anglo-Saxon race must save civilisation,' George told the American General Jack Pershing and his staff when he received them at Buckingham Palace. But when two months later he told Pershing that the American expeditionary force must fight under British command, the general wrote in his diary. 'I should have liked to have argued with the king and set him right, but seeing he is the king and that what he thinks will have very little influence on the situation, I let it go.'[10]

The king did all he could to support the war. He closed Balmoral, stopped going to the theatre, cut back on consumption of food, and at Lloyd George's behest gave up alcohol which the prime minister, in an excess of that hyperbole for which the Welsh temperance movement is famous, alleged had done more damage to the war effort 'than all the German submarines put together'. King George once told his troops (few of whom agreed with their prime minister's views on drink), 'I cannot share your hardships, but my heart is with you every hour of the day.' From the estate workers at Sandringham, he raised a company of the Norfolk Regiment (which was annihilated at Gallipoli). During the war the king visited hospitals 300 times, went to shipyards and factories as frequently, personally conferred some 50,000 medals, and made 450 visits to the servicemen, several of them to the Western Front. While inspecting the Royal Flying Corps in France in October 1916, their cheers frightened his horse which threw the king, fracturing his pelvis. During the next three days 'I suffered great pain and hardly slept at all.' George was evacuated by hospital train, where from his bed he presented Lance-Sergeant Oliver Brooks with a VC. His war wound troubled him for the rest of his life, adding to his innate irascibility.[11]

Some soldiers were not impressed by their monarch's inspections, which involved hours of spit and polish and days of drill. 'The king came to see us this morning,' Raymond Asquith, an officer in the Grenadiers wrote to his father, the prime minister, 'looking as glum and dyspeptic as ever.' Another junior officer thought that the visiting sovereign looked 'like a big rather worn nanny'.[12] But most of his subjects came to like the man. According to John Gore, the royal physician, 'His presence had an electrifying effect on the troops who saw him.' A photograph of the king talking to a young shipyard worker in Sunderland in 1918 shows a trustworthy, ordinary man, sincerely interested in what the young boy was doing. He was, as Harold Nicholson noticed, 'devoid of all pretensions, artifice and pose'.[13]

After the end of the war the king's reputation continued to grow. In November 1918 he and Queen Mary greeted some 30–35,000 wounded service men in Hyde Park. 'They broke through and came round me to shake hands. I was nearly pulled off my horse.' At the end of the month he inspected soldiers in France and Belgium where he was wildly cheered in spite of the cold, wet rain.[14]

Lloyd George had the grace to acknowledge the king's contribution. 'There can be no question,' he wrote, 'that one outstanding reason for the high level of loyalty and patriotic effort which the people of this country maintained was the attitude and conduct of King George.'[15] It was in some ways typical of the man that George never fully fathomed his popularity, which peaked during the silver jubilee of 1935. 'I am sure I cannot understand it,' he confessed, 'After all I am a very ordinary man.'[16] But it was this ordinariness during an age of people's wars which enhanced the reputation of George V (as well as that of his second son, George VI). Extraordinariness was to be the downfall of his eldest son, Edward VIII (January–December 1936).

Many things contributed to Edward VIII's abdication on 11 December 1936, which was the most severe crisis the monarchy faced between Victoria's withdrawal from public life after Albert's death in 1861 and the *annus horribilis* of 1992. The king's love for Mrs Simpson was overpowering and pathological, having its roots in his unhappy childhood and poor relations with his father, whom he saw as a naval martinet, the fierce ship's captain he could never please. In his simple, even humdrum life, George V was as ordinary a man as a king-emperor could be. With his hedonism, selfishness and neurotic promiscuity Edward VIII was, in the worst sense of that word, extraordinary. He was, as Alistair Cooke observed, 'one of those Prince Charmings who are at their best when the going is good'.[17]

When the First World War broke out Edward, who was twenty, desperately wanted to go to France with his battalion of the Grenadier Guards [Plate 7.2]. He was ordered to stay at home. 'It was a terrible blow to my pride, the worst in my life,' he recalled.[18] If he got killed, the heir argued, it would not matter for his father had two more sons. Lord Kitchener, the minister for war, refused, saying that while he could take the risk of Edward being killed, he could not accept that of his being taken prisoner. The heir was allowed no closer than five miles from the enemy. Edward was deeply hurt – and relieved. During the Passchendaele offensive he wrote to Marion Cole, the first of his married mistresses, 'I do resent being kept back, tho' really loath going forward and am terrified far more than anyone else could be.' He continued, 'but I have the devil of a big conscience, that's the trouble, and I do feel such a soft rotter.' Edward refused to wear the Legion of Honour and the Military Cross, which he had been awarded, because he felt he was not entitled to them since they were normally granted for bravery in the field. The symbolic warrior refused to be recognised as a real one.

Plate 7.2   Prince Edward and the Grenadier Guards © 'Getty Images'

In May 1919, on receiving the Freedom of the City of London, Edward looked back on the war:[19]

> The part I played was, I fear, a very insignificant one, but from one point of view I shall never regret my periods of service overseas. In those four years I mixed with men. In those four years I found my manhood. When I think of the future, and the heavy responsibilities which may fall to my lot, I feel that the experience gained since 1914 will stand me in good stead.

Edward was – as usual – wrong.

After the war his military service, as well as his guilt at having dodged the fighting, helped Edward identify with the ordinary soldier. During state visits around the empire he would stop in some outback town or prairie village to chat with veterans he had last seen on the western front [Plate 7.3]. He shared their disenchantment that the war had been such a terrible waste. While he wanted to retain the ancient privileges of royalty, he wished to be rid of the old discredited order. The experience of war radicalised many ex-servicemen – British, French, German, Italian and Russian – to the right towards fascism which believed that authority should be used undemocratically, even illegally, to make things better. For a constitutional monarch, with all the symbols of authority but none of the reality, such beliefs were fatal. Edward VIII's attempts to exert power horrified politicians, such as Prime Minister Stanley Baldwin. When during a visit to the depressed Welsh mining valleys in 1936 the king exclaimed 'something must be done', he had gone beyond the constitutional pale. Thus when he wanted to marry Mrs Simpson the establishment refused to do anything to support him.

After the abdication Edward confirmed their worst suspicions by hob-nobbing with the Nazis, a movement that grew out of the disillusion-ment of war veterans which he shared. Edward and his wife travelled to Germany where they kowtowed to Hitler and the Nazis. On the outbreak of the Second World War, Edward was allowed to rejoin the British Army as a major general, serving as a liaison officer with the French forces. When the Germans attacked in 1940 General HRH the Duke of Windsor left his post without permission (a crime for which lance corporals have been shot), and, requisitioning army transport fled with his wife first to Spain and then Portugal. During this period the Germans tried to persuade Edward to serve as their puppet ruler following a successful invasion of England. How involved he was in their overtures is a matter of debate, although no one has suggested that he immediately rejected them with the 'foul scorn' that Elizabeth I showed another invasion in 1588. Instead he haggled with Churchill (who was pre-occupied with the Battle of Britain) over his appointment as governor

Plate 7.3 Edward Prince of Wales presenting colours to the St John Fusiliers, New Brunswick, August 1919 © Photo courtesy of Heritage Resources and New Brunswick Community College, St John

of the Bahamas, and over trifles, such as the release of his batman from the Scots Guards. It was not Edward's finest hour. Eventually he left for the Bahamas, and lived the rest of his life in vain and vacuous exile.

The life of his brother, the reluctant monarch, George VI, could not have been more different. He was born on 14 December 1895, an inauspicious date, since it was the anniversary of Prince Albert's death. His early years were unhappy. His nanny abused him by pinching him cruelly before presenting him just before bedtime to his parents, who would hastily return the bawling infant to her malign care. Having not been given a day off for three years the poor woman was on the verge of a nervous breakdown. She was sacked. The damage could not be dismissed so readily. For the rest of his life George was scared with a neurotic insecurity. Underneath a shy demeanour, he seethed with an anger that erupted at the least provocation. He had a bad stammer that made public speaking an ordeal, and became a compulsive smoker who died of lung cancer.

In 1908 George and Edward were dispatched to the Royal Naval College at Osborne, which had been Victoria's favourite house, on the Isle of Wight. George did badly there. Everything was done at the double. He had never played team games such as cricket or football, was painfully shy and stuttered badly. At the end of his first term James Watt, one of the masters, reported that he 'has gone a mucker'.[20] He was, as his father warned him, in grave danger of being expelled, but thanks to the help of Surgeon Lieutenant Louis Greg, a naval officer posted to Osborne, whom the cadets admired since he had played rugby for Scotland, George managed to pass out last in a class of 68.

In January 1911 he transferred to the Royal Naval College at Dartmouth, where he enjoyed riding, beagling and tennis. He was once caned for setting off fireworks on Guy Fawkes' night. His work remained indifferent: in his first year he improved his class standing by one place, although he did manage to graduate 61st out of 68. 'A nice honest, clean-minded and excellently mannered boy,' reported one of his preceptors. George had the makings of a solid, decent naval officer.

In January 1913 he joined HMS *Cumberland*, a 9,800-ton cruiser, as a naval cadet, and sailed to the Canary Islands and West Indies, where he was warmly welcomed as the king's son. After an enjoyable visit to Canada, *Cumberland* returned home in July 1913. Two months after, promoted midshipman, he was posted to HMS *Collingwood*, a 20,000-ton battleship, which in October sailed to the Mediterranean for manoeuvres, visiting Alexandria, Gibraltar, Athens, Malta and Toulon. After spending a rather homesick Christmas in Gibraltar, George arrived home in time for the New Year's celebrations.

For George 1914 brought little to celebrate. While he was excited about the prospect of seeing action after war broke out in August, he immediately fell ill with appendicitis. Bitterly disappointed, he was landed at Aberdeen for an operation, missing the Battle of Heligoland Bight. After a posting to the Admiralty he was recovered enough to return to his ship in February 1915. Based at Scapa Flow, HMS *Collingwood* went out for three-day patrols, and on one occasion sunk a U-Boat, whose torpedo just missed her. In May 1915 a German submarine sunk the passenger ship, the *Lusitania*, with the loss of 1,198 lives. 'It makes one angry to think,' he wrote to his father, 'that we cannot do anything in revenge.' He found doing nothing intolerable, telling the king, 'Here we are, absolutely ready the whole time, and still we have to wait.'[21]

George's stomach problems continued to trouble him. His excessive nervousness exacerbated his physical condition. So in the summer of 1915 he had to leave the *Collingwood* for a hospital ship, and then convalescence in the Highlands. He recovered sufficiently to spend the winter doing light duties at the Admiralty and touring the Western Front with his brother, Edward. After passing his exams for promotion to lieutenant he was well enough to return to the *Collingwood* on 15 May 1916.

He was in the sick bay on 30 May when HMS *Collingwood* sailed with the Grand Fleet to meet the German Navy which at last had left its ports to challenge the British in the decisive battle for which the Royal Navy had been yearning ever since Trafalgar. At the Battle of Jutland George served in the forward turret. He saw the *Defence* and *Black Prince* blow up, and came under attack from the *Derfflinger* which *Collingwood* managed to straddle with three salvos at a range of 8,000 yards, doing considerable damage.

'I was sitting at the top of A Turret and had a pretty good view of the proceedings,' he wrote to his parents, 'The hands behaved splendidly and all of them in the best of spirits as their heart's desire had at last been granted, which was to be in action against the Germans . . . It was certainly a great experience to have been through.' To his brother Edward he confided, 'when I was at the top of the turret I never felt any fear or anything else.' He was mentioned in dispatches for bravery, and after the battle during a surprise visit to the fleet George V announced, 'I am pleased with my son.'[22]

Initially combat improved the prince's health, but in August his stomach problems returned and he had to leave *Collingwood* for a naval hospital and then Windsor. After pestering the Admiralty for a posting, he was sent to HMS *Malaya*, a 27,550-ton battleship, at Scapa Flow in May 1917, being aboard when the nearby battleship HMS *Vanguard* suddenly blew up as a result of an explosion in her magazine. Three weeks later George was back in a naval hospital with his usual stomach problems, having come to the sad conclusion, he admitted to his father, that 'I am not fit for service at sea'.[23] So he transferred to the Royal Naval Air Service at Cranwell.

Before reporting to Cranwell the doctors eventually diagnosed his problem as a duodenal ulcer, and successfully operated, ending years of pain and doubt. His health restored, George thrived at his new job, commanding a boys' training squadron. He had his first flight in a plane (which he confessed to his mother that he did not enjoy), and lived with Louis Grieg in a small cottage close to the airfield. He learned to fly, being awarded his pilot's wings without the inconvenience of having to go solo – his life being considered more important than what most pilots would consider the key to learning to fly. On the creation of the RAF in 1918 he became a flight lieutenant. Finding the chaos and conflict that attended formation of a new service distasteful, he had himself transferred from Cranwell to command a boys' training squadron in St Leonards-on-Sea. In October George and Grieg flew to France to inspect allied air operations, and after the Armistice he got a staff job in France.

George had a much better war than his brother Edward. In spite of illness he had acquitted himself manfully in combat, earning his father's approval. In 1920 George V made him the duke of York. Dr Grieg, with whom the duke competed – rather badly – in the Wimbledon tennis doubles in 1926, had become an excellent friend and adviser. 'My principal contribution was to put steel in him,' Grieg acknowledged.[24] George's wartime service training boys in the RAF led to his work in the National Playing Fields Fund, the Industrial Welfare Society, and the Duke of York's Summer Camps. To the latter he invited working-class and public school boys to spend a couple of weeks together under canvas, where they could experience something of that comradeship between the classes that had existed during the war. While in retrospect there is something charmingly naive about George, sitting surrounded by young men all in shorts singing, 'under the spreading chestnut tree', there was nothing politically dangerous about this ex-serviceman's view that something must be done.

Edward VIII's abdication in 1936 came as a profound shock that divided the royal family for half a century. Queen Mary and Queen Elizabeth never forgave the Duke and Duchess of Windsor, while George VI always felt that he had been catapulted into a job which was beyond his capabilities, and certainly his self-confidence.

Like the majority of his subjects, George VI was a staunch supporter of Prime Minister Neville Chamberlain's policy of appeasing Hitler. On

16 September 1938 he wrote to Chamberlain telling him, 'how much I admire your courage & wisdom in going to see Hitler in person.' He offered to appeal personally to the Führer, 'as one ex-serviceman to another', urging a peaceful solution to the Czechoslovakian problem. After Chamberlain flew back from Munich on 30 September, with the promise that letting Hitler take over the German areas of Czechoslovakia would bring 'peace in our time', the king invited him to Buckingham Palace. They appeared on the balcony to acknowledge the cheers of an ecstatic and much relieved crowd.[25]

Once Hitler had annexed the whole of Czechoslovakia and it had become obvious that war was inevitable, the king did what he could to help. In May 1939 he sailed to Canada, arriving in Quebec where he was warmly welcomed. On 9 June he entered the United States, notwithstanding the Mayor of Chicago's promise to punch King George 'on the snout' if he ever sullied American soil. After travelling to Washington he and the queen visited New York City, where their welcome was so rapturous that they were late arriving at Hyde Park, the president's upstate country house. 'My mother,' said Franklin Delano Roosevelt, as he welcomed them to his home, 'thinks you should have a cup of tea: she doesn't approve of cocktails.'[26]

'Neither does mine,' the king replied, accepting the proffered cup and saucer. It was a fine start to a sincere friendship. The president and his wife found the king and queen a touching young couple: simple yet honest. After dinner they adjourned to the library to discuss world events. 'I feel exactly as though a father had given me his most careful and wise advice,' the king recorded. He not only liked FDR – an easy enough thing to do – but found in the head of state of another great nation an equal with whom he could – unlike his own subjects – be completely at ease. The king acknowledged that, 'he had never met a person with whom he felt freer in talking and whom he enjoyed more.'

It would be absurd to suggest that George VI created the Grand Alliance between the United States and the United Kingdom. This was the result of shared interests, a common heritage and the labours of Churchill and Roosevelt. But George facilitated it. His honest earnestness did much to dispel the American view that the British were condescending imperialists, who looked down upon their uncouth cousins from across the sea. Instead George and Elizabeth seemed regular folk, who enjoyed the president's hot dogs, and savoured 'Rupert's Beer', the local brew.

When war broke out the royal family (unlike many of the establishment), did not send the Princesses Elizabeth and Margaret Rose across the Atlantic to the safety of North America. 'The children won't leave

Plate 7.4   Bombed Buckingham Palace © Corbis

without me,' explained Queen Elizabeth, 'I won't leave without the king, and the king will never leave.'[27] After the French surrendered in June 1940 George was relieved. 'Personally, I feel happier that we have no allies to be polite to and pamper.'[28] Three months later, on 9 September, the first German bombs fell on Buckingham Palace, which during the blitz was hit on nine occasions [Plate 7.4]. A delayed action bomb exploded on 10 September. The next day a bomb went off within thirty yards of the king and queen. 'The whole thing happened in a matter of moments. We all wondered why we weren't dead,' George recalled. Although some tried to dismiss the close shave with expected stoicism, the police constable on duty remarking, 'A nice piece of bombing, Ma'am, if you'll pardon the expression,' the royal family was badly shocked. 'It was a ghastly experience,' thought the king, who still had the shakes a week later.[29]

During the war George VI worked assiduously. He bestowed some 40,000 medals, being briefed on the recipient of each. He made 300 morale-boosting trips around the United Kingdom and travelled some 40,000 miles overseas. In the summer of 1943 he inspected the Eighth Army in the Western Desert, being entertained by Montgomery, and met Eisenhower, whom he liked; he even liked De Gaulle – a far more difficult feat. On his way home on 20 June he sailed into Valetta Harbour, a dignified solitary figure aboard the cruiser HMS *Aurora* to present Malta with the George Cross, the medal he had just instituted to recognise civilian gallantry. 'I shall never forget the sight of entering the Grand Harbour at 8.30am on a lovely sunny morning, & seeing the people cheering from the vantage view points,' wrote the king, 'which brought a lump to my throat, knowing what they had suffered from sixteen months of constant bombing.'[30]

When Churchill proposed joining the Normandy invasion on D-day 1944, Eisenhower was understandably horrified at the thought of being responsible for the prime minister's safety on a hotly contested beach head. He mentioned his predicament to the king. By suggesting that they both visit the beaches on the same day – a proposition which even Churchill realised was far too dangerous – George VI helped persuade the prime minister to delay his visit until 16 June. The following month the king flew to Italy to encourage the troops, and in October visited Holland, where he stayed in the rather Spartan conditions of Montgomery's headquarters caravan.

Although George was a profoundly shy man, hampered by a bad stutter, his visits unquestionably raised morale. As Dr Johnson observed, 'It does a man good to be talked to by his sovereign.' But the men he was talking to – the citizen soldiers, sailors and airmen of a democracy who fought in what has been called 'The People's War' – were not quite certain how to react to the king-emperor. Stories – almost certainly apocryphal ones – tried to humanise him. One told how a love-lorn soldier rushing off the train to meet his girlfriend gave the king, who was wearing the uniform of an admiral of the fleet to inspect the bomb-damaged station, his ticket in the belief he was a collector! Another tale had Churchill tell George VI that he thought Montgomery, a general with a gargantuan ego, was after his job. 'Thank God,' the king told the prime minister, 'I thought he was after mine.'[31]

When they encountered the king most citizen-servicemen were not quite certain how to treat him. On being presented to an army officer in the Western Desert the king asked if they had met before. 'I don't recall doing so,' the diffident captain replied. 'Well you damn well should,' his sovereign retorted. Early one morning during the same visit he stepped out on to the veranda of his beach villa, below which some three thousand men were swimming, many stark naked. Noticing their sovereign the troops did not know what to do. Army regulations require the wearing of a hat rather than a birthday suit in order to salute. So spontaneously they started singing 'God Save the King'. The national anthem over,

George VI walked down amongst them, as the men broke out in a rendition of 'For he's a jolly good fellow'.[32]

The king got on well with the Americans, whom he liked. Their equipment and uniform, he believed (quite rightly), was much better than the British. He had much enjoyed his 1939 visit to America, and in return entertained Eleanor Roosevelt at Buckingham Palace, where she told her husband how she ate off gold plates the same meagre rations the king shared with his subjects. Eleanor went on to tell Franklin how the palace's baths were marked with a paint line to designate the three inches of hot water the wartime regulations permitted. The rather austere dowager Queen Mary used to give GIs rides in her Rolls Royce, finding their cheerful openness refreshing. 'A charming young American parachutist, most friendly,' she noted in her diary about one of her passengers.[33] Eisenhower, as did many American soldiers, liked George the Sixth, notwithstanding their prejudices against the Third. *Time* magazine reported that crowds of GIs on furloughs to London gathered outside Buckingham Palace in the hope of seeing the king and queen. In the widely seen documentary film *Memphis Belle* the king and queen were warmly received when they went to congratulate the crew of the Flying Fortress for having completed their tour of missions.

The film was, of course, propaganda. During the war the royal family's image was always carefully manipulated. Take the blitz – their finest hour as well as their people's. In truth not everyone did very well. In October 1940 a confidential intelligence report stated that 'the morale of Londoners has deteriorated'. A quarter of its inhabitants had fled the capital. In other towns hundreds of thousands of people were on the move. At nightfall they would leave for the countryside to escape the bombing, returning at dawn. Sometimes the authorities acted with bureaucratic stupidity. At first they refused to let people shelter in the Underground. So Londoners bought a ticket to the next station, and missing the last train, spent the night safe from the Luftwaffe sleeping on a platform.

Bureaucratic insensibility might explain a September entry in Harold Nicholson's diary. He wrote, 'everyone is worried about the morale in the East End, where there is much bitterness. It is said that even the King and Queen were booed yesterday when they visited the destroyed areas.' Their visit on 5 December to Southampton, which had just been badly bombed, was a fiasco: it was poorly arranged at the last minute, hardly anyone knew they were coming, the loudspeakers did not work. The few people who saw the royal party said they would have preferred more tangible help, such as clearing the rubble, warm food, and rehousing. Yet ten years later Bernard Knowles's *Southampton: the English Gateway* recorded that Their Majesties were greeted 'with such fervent demonstrations of love, loyalty and enthusiasm as in days gone by were reserved for an Elizabethan progress or the return to the throne of Charles II'.[34]

These were the exceptions. As Churchill, whose appointment George initially disliked because he had championed Edward VIII during the abdication, declared, 'the war has drawn the Throne and the people of England closer together than was ever before recorded.' The blitz gave the royal family a sense of purpose, of confidence, even exhilaration. In October 1940, a month after they had been reported being booed in the East End, the Queen wrote to her mother, 'I feel quite exhausted, after seeing and hearing so much sadness, heroism and magnificent spirit . . . The destruction is so awful and the people are so wonderful.'[35] Having come to the throne reluctantly as a result of the abdication, which left something of a cloud over the monarchy, George began his reign as 'an improbable king'. During the war he came into his own. He ended it, to quote Walter Bagehot, as a 'virtuous sovereign' in whom widely admired 'domestic virtues' could 'be found on the throne'.[36]

Nowhere was this more so than in the image of family the royals projected. The war was a time of dislocation, displacement and death. The king lost his own brother George, duke of Kent, in a flying accident in 1942. The tragedy shocked him deeply: he went to see the mountain in Scotland into which the Sunderland flying boat taking his brother, an Air Commodore, to Iceland to inspect RAF facilities, had crashed in the fog.

Military service separated husbands from wives, fathers from children; evacuation severed children from parents and homes. This longing to be reunited – as the hugely popular singer Vera Lynn promised, 'to meet again somewhere, someday' – was an overriding emotion in the Second World War, to which the royal family gave expression. Fifty years later, on the anniversary of VE-Day, she sang the same song on a stage built outside Buckingham Palace to the Queen, Queen Mother and Princes Margaret on the balcony, as an audience of a hundred thousand outside wildly cheered.

During the war the Ministry of Information helped propagate two images of the royal children, Elizabeth and Margaret Rose. First, that they were enduring the hardships faced by all children in some unnamed location. Second, that they were healthy confident children, symbols of the better future that must follow Britain's inevitable victory. These two images came together in a widely heard and much remembered broadcast transmitted on 13 October 1940, one of the darkest days of the war. Appearing on the BBC radio programme *Childrens' Hour* with 'Uncle Mac', Derek McCulloch, Princess Elizabeth told the world how 'we children at home are full of cheerfulness and courage. We are trying to do all that we can to help our gallant soldiers, sailors and airmen.' Then, with the touchy bossiness of an older sister, she told Margaret to say goodbye.

In 1945 after Princess Elizabeth came of age for military service, she persuaded her father to let her join the Auxiliary Territorial Service (ATS) as a second subaltern. It was a way of escaping her father's over-protectiveness, as well as doing her part in the war. She took a month's course on driving and motor maintenance. She did not spend the nights in the barracks with the other junior officers, but at home in Windsor Castle. 'I never worked so hard in my life,' she told a friend, 'but I enjoyed it very much.' Fifty years later, during the celebrations for VE-Day, the queen recalled how much self-confidence the ATS had given her[37] [Plate 7.5].

While military service may have enhanced Elizabeth's self-confidence, it contributed nothing to allied victory. The king refused to let her continue in the ATS, although he did allow her to wear her army uniform for the VE celebrations on 8 May. After appearing eight times on the balcony at Buckingham Palace, where the crowd cheered Churchill and the royal family, George permitted his two daughters, escorted by guards' subalterns, to mingle incognito with the people below. (It was alleged that a Dutch officer, too drunk or too used to a royal family which rides bicycles around the streets, made a pass at them.) 'It was one of the most memorable nights of my life,' Queen Elizabeth recalled. 'Poor darlings,' wrote the king at the end of the European war, 'they never had any fun yet.' After the Japanese surrendered in August and the war was really over, he wrote, 'We have only tried to do our duty during these five and a half years.'[38]

Duty and family values – these were what the royal family tried to epitomise during the war. Their legacy continued for a generation, largely because the people wanted these qualities from them. The king became respected rather than popular. He was one of many ordinary men who rose to greatness in the People's War. The restrictions and rationing fitted his simple style. He preferred a quiet evening at home listening to ITMA, Tommy Handley's immensely popular comedy show on the wireless, rather than romp with café society and the louche married women his brother Edward enjoyed.

After the war the royal family continued their military connections. In 1947 Princess Elizabeth married Philip Mountbatten, a naval officer. Even though he had served with distinction in the Mediterranean, North Sea and Far East, being mentioned in dispatches for his courage at the Battle of Cape Matapan, and his uncle and mentor was the immensely powerful Admiral Lord Louis Mountbatten, Philip ended the war as a

Plate 7.5   Princess Elizabeth receiving vehicle maintenance instruction © PA
Photos. Picture reproduced by permission of the Imperial War Museum

lieutenant, a far lower rank than most of his classmates from Dartmouth
achieved. Because the queen has dedicated her life, as she promised on
coming of age in 1947, to the service of the nation and commonwealth,
she has left the bringing up of their children to Prince Philip. Perhaps
the feeling that he had not done as well in the war as he might, and
certainly a sense of bitterness that when his wife became queen in 1952
he had to give up command at sea and like William IV and George V
prematurely end his naval career, have shaped the way in which he has
done so. The results have been, to say the least, disappointing. 'If this was
an ordinary family visited by the social services,' observed Bernard Levin
in *The Times,* that erstwhile mouthpiece of the establishment, 'the lot
of them would by now have been taken into care.'[39]

Philip seems to get on with his only daughter, even though Princess Anne's marriage to Mark Phillips, an army officer so thick that his brothers-in-law called him 'the fog,' failed. She has since remarried Tim Lawrence, a decent enough man, and significantly a commander in the Royal Navy. Because he has wanted them to grow up in his own military image, Philip's relations with his sons have been far more problematic. He pushed his youngest son, Edward, into the Royal Marines, where he failed spectacularly, as he has of late in the less martial field of television production and public relations. To be sure Philip's second son, Andrew, was a heroic royal warrior, who flew a helicopter during the Falklands war, acting as a decoy for exocet missiles. No one minded when on his return Andrew had a fling with Koo Stark, an adult film actress. They did mind a few years later when his wife, HRH The Duchess of York, was photographed topless with John Bryan, an American financial consultant, sucking her toes while Andrew was off serving at sea. Their marriage was clearly over. Andrew received the lack of sympathy that has always been the lot of cuckolds.

The extremely messy and public break-up of Prince Charles's marriage to Princess Diana was even more damaging, particularly when the heir to the throne was overheard expressing the wish on the phone to be reincarnated as his mistress's Tampax. Gallons of ink and thousands of miles of video has been expended trying to explain Prince Charles's problems. He blamed them on his parents, especially his father, who subjected him to the quasi-military discipline of Gordonstoun, a public school in the north of Scotland famous for excess of physical and lack of intellectual rigour. After university Charles became an action man, learning to fly jets, parachute, and even command a mine-sweeper. But he was ill suited for a military career, particularly one where the press watched every step.

In military affairs Charles has been both ridiculous and reactionary. When the prince was inspecting the First Battalion of the Royal Regiment of Wales in Germany in 1972 the squadies complained that it was hard meeting the local women [Plate 7.6]. So as their colonel-in-chief he wrote them an English–German phrase book entitled *A Guide to the Chatting Up of Girls*. The prince – as Princes Diana acidly pointed out in a television interview after their marriage had broken up – is less of an authority in other matters. He lobbied heavily against the cutting of army manpower, the amalgamation of regiments, and reduction of the number of military bands by half, with no effect, for as his friend and biographer Richard Dimbleby explained, 'the Prince's attitude towards the armed forces was not only traditional, but openly reactionary.'[40]

Plate 7.6   Prince Charles as Colonel in Chief of the Royal Regiment of Wales
by Aubrey Davidson, Houston 1988 © The Royal Regiment of Wales

Conclusion

As I write in the spring of 2003 the royal family faces many challenges, while the United Kingdom is fighting a war in Iraq. The origins of monarchy lie in war. Tribes elected as their chief the man best able to fight and lead them into battle. Kings such as William the Conqueror and Henry Tudor became kings because they won battles. Others such as Edward II, Richard III or James II lost their thrones because they failed in war. Once the monarchy gave up its political and military powers (for the two were intimately connected) it had to find new roles. In the last two centuries it has done so extremely well by becoming symbolic warriors, icons of the nation's military prowess and determination.

In doing so the monarchy has been able to draw on a long tradition of military service shared by a large number of its subjects. While many men – especially conscripts – may not have greatly enjoyed having to wear the sovereign's uniform, afterwards far many more recall doing so with great pride. Today, however, hardly any of Her Majesty's subjects have served in Her Armed Forces, and those who have are dying off. With each year the memory of the Second World War fades, its last great royal warrior, the Queen Mother, being buried in 2002. In 1918 the armed services had 8,500,000 members, in 1944 5,000,000, in 1951, 719,000, and ten years later, as National Service was being phased out, just over 500,000. In 1998 they numbered 210,100. Prime Minister Blair's cabinet is the first in British history in which no member has worn the sovereign's uniform.

A few Englishmen still accept old-fashioned patterns of loyalty. 'I have eaten his salt,' wrote Simon Raven, the novelist, about George VI, whom he served as a soldier, 'and I have eaten that of the present monarch, and the oath is quite irrevocable: I am the Queen's man, and there is an end to it.'[41] Like some endangered species such convictions are remarkable because of their rarity. Few of the British troops who fought in the Falklands or are fighting in Iraq did or are doing so for Queen and Country. Indeed after the Falklands war Margaret Thatcher, not Elizabeth II, presided over the victory celebrations. The explanation of a 'palace spokesman' that Her Majesty had not attended the parade because 'it was not a *royal* occasion' rings hollow.

There is something hollow about today's connections between the armed forces and the crown. An exhibition on 'Royalty and the Army' held at the National Army Museum in Chelsea to celebrate the Queen's Golden Jubilee in 2002 contained such exhibits as the uniforms of various royal colonels-in-chief, cap badges bearing the crown, and photographs of various members of the royal family with soldiers, sailors and airmen. But it did not explore significant links between crown and the military in any depth – perhaps because they no longer exist. To be sure in 1991 the queen was colonel-in-chief of 45 regiments or corps, the Queen Mother 17, Prince Philip 18, Prince Charles 13, Princess Anne 12, and Princess Margaret 7. The navy and the air force are royal, as are most regiments and corps – a rare exception being the Intelligence Corps.

Since 1945 the crown has tended to exert military influence over amalgamations and budget cuts. In 1946 Field Marshal Montgomery's plans to cut the Brigade of Guards in the same proportion as the rest of the army were thwarted by the brigade's major general who appealed directly to George VI. Ten years later by giving a speech praising the regimental system Elizabeth II signalled her opposition to consolidations.[42] But by and large such royal interventions have been less to prevent amalgamations than to protect the hierarchy of units by ensuring that the burden is borne by the less influential regiments whose officers tend not to be promoted to general rank. Prince Charles intervened to protect the Parachute Regiment, the Queen the Royal Army Chaplains Department. In contrast the Welch Regiment and the South Wales Borderers were amalgamated into the Royal Regiment of Wales (the 'Royal' being a consolation prize), while the more prestigious Royal Welsh Fusiliers was spared.

Such issues count only within the armed forces. Who gets axed matters less to the public than cutting defence spending. The values which the military treasure – loyalty, honesty, self-discipline, the acceptance of established authority – have less and less of an appeal today. Even Elizabeth II had to admit as much about the next generation of royals, acknowledging in the 1992 film *Elizabeth R*, 'I think that this is what the young members find difficult – the regimental side.'[43]

The change in the past century or so in attitudes to military values can be seen in the fortunes of the Royal Tournament. This martial display began in 1880, when empire and jingoism reigned as supreme as did Queen Victoria. It continued far longer than one might expect, being held for several weeks every summer in Earls Court, London. In the 1980s it was still a delightfully old-fashioned exercise of patriotic spectacle – bands, marching, RAF police dogs, drill teams, and a nineteenth-century field gun race. But in 1999 it suddenly closed. The public was no longer interested: the armed forces were too small to spare men and women to take part. In a wonderfully droll, although perhaps not fully appreciated piece of symbolism, Rowan Atkinson, dressed as Captain Blackadder, television's most persuasive military anti-hero, was asked to call down the final curtain.

If – and when – the final curtain ever comes down upon the royal family is impossible to say. They face problems that go well beyond those of personal behaviour. For half a millennium, at least, the monarchy has been a viable symbol of a national identity that the European Union currently challenges. The queen is head of a Church of England which is in a tailspin of decline. She is at the apex of a pyramid of hierarchical privilege, into whose coffin the abolition of the House of Lords may be the penultimate nail. But of one thing we can be sure. War is an institution as old as human history: without doubt it has a future. So if the monarchy has one too, if the king or queen can be saved, then they will continue to remain inexorably connected with war. Subjects will still want the monarch to somehow 'Scatter his enemies' and 'Frustrate their knavish tricks'. As the national anthem, which was first publicly sung in 1745 during a time of war and rebellion, puts it:

Send her victorious,
Happy and glorious,
Long to reign over us,
God save the queen.

Notes

1. T. Nairn, *The Enchanted Glass: Britain and its Monarchy* (London: Picador, 1990), 377.
2. K. Rose, *King George V* (London: Phoenix, 2000), 11–20.
3. Before he became king Edward was known as David, while George as Albert. To avoid confusion I have used their regnal names.
4. R. Fulford, *Hanover to Windsor* (London: Batsford, 1960), 176–7, 181.
5. H. Nicholson, *King George V: his Life and Times* (London: Constable, 1952), 32–3.
6. D. Judd, *The Life and Times of George V* (London: Weidenfeld and Nicolson, 1973), 119.
7. J. Terraine, *Douglas Haig: the Educated Soldier* (London: Hutchinson, 1963), 151.
8. D. Woodward, *Lloyd George and the Generals* (Newark: University of Delaware Press, 1983), 298.
9. E. K. G. Sixsmith, *Douglas Haig* (London: Weidenfeld and Nicolson, 1976), 186.
10. Judd, *op. cit.*, 148. D. Winter, *Haig's Command: A reassessment* (London: Viking, 1991), 277–8.
11. Judd, *op. cit.*, 138–9.
12. Rose, *op. cit.*, 167–80.
13. J. Halperin, *Eminent Georgians: the Lives of King George V, Elizabeth Bowen, St John Philby and Nancy Astor* (Basingstoke: Macmillan, 1995), 46, 66–7.
14. Judd, *op. cit.*, 152.
15. Halperin, *op. cit.*, 46.

16. D. Sinclair, *Two Georges: the Making of the Modern Monarchy* (London: Hodder and Stoughton, 1988), 1.
17. Alistair Cooke, *Six Men* (Harmondsworth: Penguin, 1987), 92.
18. Duke of Windsor, *A King's Story* (New York: Knopf, 1951), 110–12.
19. P. Ziegler, *King Edward VIII* (New York: Knopf, 1991), 77.
20. D. Judd, *King George VI, 1895–1952* (London: Michael Joseph, 1982), 21.
21. Judd, *op. cit.*, 32.
22. J. Wheeler Bennett, *King George VI: His Life and Reign* (London: Macmillan, 1958), 90ff.
23. Ibid., 100.
24. Ibid., 131.
25. Ibid., 348–50.
26. Ibid., 389.
27. E. Longford, *Elizabeth R: a Biography* (London, Weidenfeld and Nicolson, 1983), 36.
28. K. Middlemas, *The Life and Times of George VI* (London: Weidenfeld and Nicolson, 1974), 134.
29. Wheeler Bennett, *op. cit.*, 468.
30. S. Bradford, *The Reluctant King: the Life and Reign of George VI, 1895–1952* (New York: St Martins, 1990), 336.
31. T. Aaronson, *The Royal Family at War* (London: John Murray, 1993), 182–3.
32. Judd, *op. cit.*, 202.
33. J. Pope-Hennessy, *Queen Mary, 1867–1953* (London: Allen and Unwin, 1959), 608.
34. T. Harrison, *Living Through the Blitz* (Harmondsworth: Penguin, 1978), 162.
35. Aaronson, *op. cit.*, 45.
36. W. Bagehot, *The English Constitution* (London: World Classics, 1936), 37.
37. S. E. Bradford, *Elizabeth: a Biography of Her Majesty The Queen* (London: Mandarin, 1997), 108–10.
38. Middlemas, *op. cit.*, 150–51.
39. Anthony Holden, *The Tarnished Crown* (New York: Random House, 1993), 30.
40. R. Dimbleby, *The Prince of Wales* (London: Little, Brown, 1994), 523.
41. S. Raven, 'A Monarch for me,' in Jeremy Murray-Brown (ed.), *The Monarchy and Its Future* (London: Allen and Unwin, 1969), 203.
42. Hew Strachan, *The Politics of the British Army* (Oxford: Clarendon, 1997), 75, 215.
43. E. Longford, *Royal Throne: the Future of the Monarchy* (London: Hodder & Stoughton, 1993), 63.

INDEX

Acre, 40
Act of Union, 108
Addison, Joseph, 123
Adolphus Frederick, duke of Cambridge, 135, 145
Agincourt, 47–8, 58, 59–62
Agnew, Sir Andrew, 121–2
Albert, duke of Clarence, 150–1
Alcuin, 13
Alençon, Siege of, 23
Alfred the Great, 11–16
amalgamation of regiments, 170, 173
American War of Independence, 139, 140
Andrew, Prince, 4, 170
Andromeda, 142
Anglo-Saxon Chronicle, 15, 16
Anglo-Saxons, 3, 9–10, 13
Anne, Princess, 170
Anne, Queen, 115–16, 118–19
Armada, 81
armed forces
 army, 108, 111, 114–15, 135, 172
 mercenaries, 56
 navy, 4, 94, 112
 Royal Air Force, 162
Arnold, Benedict, 140
Arras, Siege of, 93, 101
Arsuf, 40
Arthur of Brittany, 50
Arthur, King, 9–11
artillery, 56, 111
Aschaffenburg, 106
Ashdown, 13
Ashley, Maurice, 32
Asquith, Raymond, 155
Asser, Bishop, 13, 16
Athelney Marches, 11, 14
Athelston, 15
ATS (Auxiliary Territorial Service), 168
Aurora, 165
Austrian Succession, War of, 106, 120
Avalon, Isle of, 10

Bacchante, 151
Badby, John, 62
Bagehot, Walter, 167
Bagehot, William, 3
Bai Jhansi, 8
Baldwin de Redver, 36
Baldwin, Stanley, 158
Balfour, Arthur, 147
Bampfield, Colonel Joseph, 92
Bank of England, 110
Bannockburn, 53–5
Barnet, 65
Battle of the Dunes, 94
Battle of the Spurs, 76
bayonets, 111
Beacon Hill, 86
Beauclerk, Augustus, 140
Beechey, William, 135
Benfleet, 14
Beowulf, 15
Berengaria, 40, 42
Berkeley, Charles, 95
Bertrand du Bon, 56
Bertrand de Gurdon, 42
Bigod, Hugh, 36
Black Death, 63, 68
Black Prince, 161
Black Prince, 58
Black Week, 147
Blenheim, 110, 117
Blitz, 166
Blondel, 41
Boadicea, 5–9
Bochum, 113
Boer War, 147
Boleyn, Anne, 73
Bolsheviks, 154
Bosworth Field, 63, 69–70
Bouchain, 117
Boulogne, 77
Bouvignes, 51
Boyle, Richard, 95
Boyne, 99, 114

Bradmoor, John, 58
Brandon, William, 70
Breda, 96
Bridgenorth, 15
Britannia, 151
British state, 108
Brook, Christopher, 13
Brooks, Oliver, 155
Brounker, Henry, 95–6
Brown, Trooper, 122
Brundage, J. A., 43
Buckingham, duke of, 84–5
Buckingham Palace bombing, 164
Budé, General J., 139, 141
budget cuts, 173
Burnet, Gilbert, 102
Bury St Edmunds, 53
Buttington, 15

Cadiz, 84
Caen, 62
Calais, 33, 76, 79
Camlann, 10
Canada, 151
Cannon, John, 3
cannons, 56, 111
Cape St Vincent, 140
Cardwell, Edward, 148
Carlisle, 131
Carlyle, Thomas, 32, 48
Caroline, Queen, 120
Carson, Sir Edward, 154
Castledan, Rodney, 10
Caxton, William, 11
Cerialis, Petilius, 7
Chalus Castle, 42
Chamberlain, Neville, 162–3
Charity, 95
Charles I, 84–90, 91, 92
Charles II, 90, 91, 102
Charles, Prince of Wales, 170
Charles, the Young Pretender (Bonnie
    Prince Charlie), 130–4
Chatham, 96, 146
Chaucer, Thomas, 56
Chemin des Dames, 154
chevauchée, 57, 59
Chippenham, 14
chivalry, 57
Chrétien de Tours, 56
Chrétien de Troyes, 10

Churchill, John, duke of Marlborough, 48,
    99, 116–19
Churchill, Winston, 48, 165, 167
Civil War, 85–90
Clarence *see* William IV (formerly duke of
    Clarence)
Clontribet, 81
Coke, Sir Edward, 49
Colchester, 7
Cole, Marion, 156
Colet, John, 76
Collingwood, 160, 161
Commines, Robert, 29
Comnenus, Isaac, 40
Cooke, Alistair, 156
Cope, Sir John, 130
Corbeil, 92–3
Cornbury, Henry, 98–9
Cornwallis, Lord Charles, 137, 140
Cranwell, 162
Crécy, 57, 58
Crimean War, 146, 147
Cromwell, Oliver, 90, 91, 108, 109, 111
Cromwell, Thomas, 77
Cropredy, 86–7, 88
Crotch, William, 138
Crusades, 39–40
Culloden, 132–3
Cumberland, 160
Cumberland
    Ernest August, duke of Cumberland, 135,
        144–5
    William, duke of Cumberland, 127–33
Cyprus, 40, 43

Danes, 11–16
Davenport, Richard, 106
David, King, 37
Decianus, Catus, 5, 7
Declaration of Indulgence, 97–8
Defence, 161
Derfflinger, 161
Dettingen, 106, 121–3, 129
Diana, Princess, 170
Digby, Rear Admiral Robert, 139
Dimbleby, Richard, 170
Dio, Cassius, 5
Doutelle, 130
Drake, Sir Francis, 79
Drogheda, 109
Dudley, Edmund, 76

Dunbar, 54, 108
Dunes, battle of, 94
Dunkirk, 94, 137
Duppa, Brian, 91
Dutch Wars, 95–7, 108
Dutch-French wars, 112–13
Dyer, Gwynne, 1, 3

Earle, Peter, 101
Edgehill, 85, 86, 87, 90–1
Edington, 14
Edith Swan-necked, 28
Edmund, King, 13
Edward the Black Prince, 58
Edward the Confessor, 19, 24
Edward, duke of Kent, 135, 144, 145
Edward the Elder, 15
Edward I, 53
Edward II, 49, 52–5
Edward III, 55, 58, 75
Edward IV, 64–6, 67
Edward, Prince, 170
Edward, Prince of Wales (son of Henry VI),
    65, 66
Edward, Prince of Wales (son of Richard
    III), 68
Edward V, 67
Edward VI, 79
Edward VII, 127, 151
Edward VIII, 127, 153, 156–60, 162
Egbert, King, 13
Elizabeth, 130
Elizabeth I, 79–83
Elizabeth II, 1, 3, 4, 163, 167–9, 173
Elizabeth, Queen Mother, 150, 164
Elizabeth of York, 63
Empire, 108
Empson, Richard, 76
Eric the Wild, 29
Ernest August, duke of Cumberland, 135,
    144–5
Etaples, 93
Ethelred, King of Wessex, 13
Ethelred the Unready, 15
Ethelwulf, King of Wessex, 13
Evelyn, John, 96
Exeter Castle, 38

Fairfax, General, 91
Falaise, 21, 62
Falkirk, 131

Falklands war, 170, 172
Falstaff, Jack, 46, 57
Farnham, 14
Fastolf, Sir John, 57–8
feudal system, 33–4, 38, 55
First World War, 153–8, 161
Flodden, 77
Fontenoy, 129
Forkbeard, Sweyn, 15
Formigny, 63
Fortescue, Sir John, 137, 138
Four Days Fight, 96
Frederick, duke of York, 135, 137–9
Frederick the Great of Prussia, 121, 137
French, Charlotte, 139
French, General Sir John, 153, 154
Froissart, Jean, 5, 55
Fuller, J. F. C., 55
fyrd, 14, 15, 18

Gaeta, 130
Gaillard Castle, 41–2, 50, 52
Gallipoli, 155
Gate Fulford, 20
Gaveston, Piers, 53
Geoffrey of Anjou, 22
Geoffrey of Monmouth, 10, 11
Geoffrey of Vinsauf, 42
George, duke of Cambridge, 147–8
George, duke of Kent, 167
George I, 119–20
George II, 106, 119, 120–3, 125
George III, 125, 135
George IV, 126–7, 135, 143
George V, 127, 150–6
George VI, 150, 160–7
Gerald of Wales, 52
Giraut de Borneil, 57
Glendower, Owen, 58
Glorious Revolution, 98–9, 102, 109,
    113
Godfrey, Michael, 110
Godmanchester, 7
Godwin, earl of Wessex, 24
Gore, John, 155
Grave, 113
Great Reform Bill, 125
Green, J. R., 51
Grieg, Louis, 160, 162
Gruffudd, Elis, 77
Guthrum, King, 14

Guy, Count of Burgundy, 22
Guy of Ponthieu, 24

Haesten, 14
Haig, General Sir Douglas, 153–4
Handley, Tommy, 168
Hardrada, Harold, 20–1
Harfleur, 35, 59, 62
Harold, King, 18, 19–21, 24–5, 31–2
   battle of Hastings, 18–19, 27–8, 32
Harry, Prince, 4
Harvey, Dr William, 90–1
Hastenbeck, 133
Hastings, 18–19, 27–8, 32
Hawkins, Sir Richard, 79
Hawley, General Henry, 131
Hebé, 141
Henry, Bishop of Winchester, 36–7
Henry de Bohun, 54
Henry de Pommeroy, 43
Henry I, 35–6
Henry I of France, 21, 22
Henry II, 11, 37, 39
Henry IV, 58
Henry V, 46–9, 58–63, 64
Henry V of Germany, 36
Henry VI, 62, 64, 65, 66
Henry VI of Germany, 41
Henry VII (Henry Tudor), 11, 63,
   68–70
Henry VIII, 48, 72–9
Hereward the Wake, 29
Herleve, 21, 23
Hibbert, Christopher, 62
Hill, Abigail, 118
Hinton, Sir John, 91
Hitler, Adolf, 158, 162–3
honour, 73–5
Hood, Admiral, 140–1
Hopton, Sir Ralph, 87
Hotham, Sir John, 90
housecarls, 18
Howard, Catherine, 77
Howard, Sir William, 91
Howe, Lord, 141
Hughes, Ted, 150
Huguenots, 84
Humphrey, duke of Gloucester, 56
Hundred Years War, 58
Hyde, Anne, 101
Hyde, Edward, 93

Iceni revolt, 5
Indian Mutiny, 8
infantry, 57, 111
Ingoldsby, Brigadier, 129
Ingram de Umfraville, 54
Inkerman, 147
investitures, 5
Ireland, 81, 99, 108–9, 114
Isabella of Angoulême, 50
Isabella, Queen, 52
Ivan the Boneless, 13

Jacobites, 130–4
Jaffa, 40–1
James I (VI of Scotland), 83–4
James II, 90–103, 109
   battle of the Boyne, 99, 114
   Civil War experiences, 90–2, 102
   conversion to Catholicism, 96, 101
   Declaration of Indulgence, 97–8
   and the Dutch Wars, 95–7
   inherits the throne, 97
   loses the throne, 98–9
   military service
      French Army, 92–3, 101
      Spanish Army, 93–4
James, the Old Pretender, 108, 130
Jennings, Sarah, Duchess of Marlborough,
   115–16, 118–19
Joan of Arc, 63
John, King, 41, 49–52
Jordan, Dorothy, 143
Jutland, 161

Katharine, Princess, 46–7, 62
Keyne, Sir John, 70
Kipling, Rudyard, 147
Kitchener, Lord, 153, 156
Kloster-Zeven convention, 133
knights, 33–4, 56–7
   of the Round Table, 10
Knowles, Bernard, 166

La Rochelle, 84
land distribution, 33
land tax, 110
Landen, 114
Latimer, Hugh, 75
Lauffeld, 133
Lavery, Sir John, 127
Lawrence, Sir Thomas, 127

Lawrence, Tim, 170
Layamon, 10
Le Goulet, 50
Le Morte D'Arthur (Malory), 11
legal systems, 16, 34
Lennox, Charles, 137
Leopold of Austria, 41
Levin, Bernard, 169
Lightning, 143
Limerick, Treaty of, 114
Lincoln, 36, 38
Lion, 127, 130
Lloyd George, David, 154, 155, 156
Lollardy, 62
Londinium, 7
London, 96
longbow, 55–6
Longchamp, William, 50
Longsword, William, 51
Loos, 153
Lostwithiel, 87, 88
Louis XIV, 109, 112, 113
Lowestoft, 95
Lowndes, William, 110
Lugard, Frederick, 147
Lusitania, 161
Luther, Martin, 72
Lympe, 14
Lyttleton, Richard, 129

Maastricht, 112
McCulloch, Derek, 167
Macdonald, Flora, 134
McFarland, K. B., 62
Magna Carta, 49, 51
Majendie, John, 139
Malaya, 161
Malcolm, King, 30
Malory, Sir Thomas, 11
Malplaquet, 117
Mancetter, 8
Mansfeld, Count Ernest von, 84
Mantes, 30
Margaret, Queen, 64–6
Margaret Rose, Princess, 163, 167
Marlborough
    Churchill, John, duke of Marlborough,
        48, 99, 116–19
    Sarah, duchess of Marlborough, 115–16,
        118–19
Marston Moor, 88

Mary of Modena, 98
Mary Tudor, 33, 79
Matilda of Flanders, 23
Matilda, Queen, 11, 36–7, 38
Matthews, Miles, 91
medals for courage, 5
Memphis Belle, 166
mercenaries, 56
Merrick, William, 141
Middleton, Lord Charles, 98–9
Miller, John, 101
Milner, Lord, 154
Milton, 14
Milton, John, 8
Mirebeau, 50, 52
Monmouth, duke of, 97
Mont Cassel, 113
Moore, Thomas, 75–6
Moores Creek, 134
More, Sir Thomas, 66
Morris, John, 10
Mortemer, 22
Mount Badon, 10
Mouzin, Siege of, 93
Murray, Anne, 92
Muskerry, Donough, 95
muskets, 111
Mutiny Act, 109

Naarden, 113
Namur, 110, 114
Napoleonic Wars, 135
Naseby, 86, 88
nation building, 108
National Debt, 110
navy, 4, 94, 112
Nazis, 158
Nelson, Horatio, 139, 141
Netherlands, 95–7, 108, 112–13,
    114
Neville, Richard, earl of Warwick, 65
New Model Army, 108
Newbury, 88
Nicholas, Richard, 94
Nicholson, Harold, 155, 166
Nightingale, Florence, 146
Nine Years War, 110, 114
Nissa, 20
Nivelle, General Robert, 153–4
Nore, 96
Normandy, 21–4, 62

oath of allegiance, 3, 4
Odo of Paris, Count, 13
officer corps, 110, 111–12, 114–15, 138
Ogden, Matthias, 140
Oglander, Sir John, 83
Old James, 95
O'Neil, Hugh, 81
Opdam, Admiral Jacob, 95
Orange, 95
Ordnance Office, 112
Osborne House, 160
Osney Abbey, 91
Oudenarde, 117, 120
Oxford, 91
Oxford University, 16

Panmure, Lord, 146, 147
Paris, Matthew, 50
Parker, Captain Robert, 117, 118
Parliament, 109
Paston, Sir John, 65
Paston, William, 63
Pastoral Care, 16
Peebles, John, 140
Pegasus, 141–2
Pelham, Henry, 130
Penn, William, 101
Percy, Algenon, 91–2
Pershing, General Jack, 155
Peterborough Chronicle, 39
Pevensey, 27
Philip Augustus, 39–40, 41, 50–1
Philip I of France, 22
Philip II of Spain, 80–1
Philip, Prince, 168–70
Phillips, Mark, 170
Pitt, William, 122
Plutarch, 55
Poitiers, 58
Pole, Reginald, 73
poll tax, 63
Prasutagus, King of the Iceni, 5
Preston, 90, 108
Prestonpans, 130
prime minister's office, 109
Prince, 96
Prince George, 139, 140
Prince Royal, 83
purchase system, 111–12, 114–15, 120,
        138
Pye, Henry, 140

Ragnar Leather-Breeches, 13
Ramillies, 117
Ranby, John, 129
Raven, Simon, 172
Ravenspur, 65
Ré, 84
regimental colours, 1, 3
Rex Pacificus, 83
Riccall, 20
Richard, duke of York, 64
Richard I (the Lionheart), 39–43, 50
Richard II, 58, 63
Richard III, 66–70
Robert, Archbishop of Rouen, 21
Robert the Bruce, 53–4
Robert, duke of Normandy (father of
        William the Conqueror), 21
Robert, duke of Normandy (son of William
        the Conqueror), 35
Robert, earl of Gloucester, 36–7
Roberts, Michael, 110
Robertson, Sir William, 154
Rochester Castle, 51
Romans, 5–8
Romney, 28
Roosevelt, Eleanor, 166
Roosevelt, Franklin Delano, 163, 166
Rous, John, 66
Rowse, A. L., 11
Royal Air Force, 162
The Royal Charles, 95, 96
The Royal James, 97
Royal Navy, 4, 94, 112
The Royal Sovereign, 143
Royal Tournament, 173
'Rule Britannia', 16
Rumersheim, 119
Rupert, Prince, 87, 88
Russell, Admiral Edward, 101
Russian Revolution, 154
Ryswick, Treaty of, 114

St Albans
    sacking by Boadicea, 7
    Wars of the Roses battles, 64
Saint George, 95
St Martin, 84
Saint Michael, 96
Saladin, 40, 41
Salic Law, 49, 58
Sandhurst, 138, 147

Sandys, Charles, 142
Santo Domingo, 140
Sarah, Duchess of Marlborough, 115–16, 118–19
scorched-earth policy, 57
Scotland, 108
  Bannockbuen, 53–5
  Jacobites, 130–4
Sea Beggars, 80
Second World War, 1, 150, 158, 163–8
Sedgemoor, 97
Seneffe, 113
serfs, 33
Serlo, Bishop of Séez, 35
Seven Years War, 133
Shales, Henry, 113
she-soldiers, 9
Sheriden, Thomas, 131
Shoeburyness, 15
Shrewsbury, 58
Shuckburgh, Richard, 85
Sigismund of Germany, 62
Slingsby, Sir Henry, 87
South Africa, 147
Southwark, 28
Southwold Bay, 95, 96–7
Spanish Succession, War of, 116
Spencer, Charles, 118
Spurs, battle of, 76
Stafford, earl of, 86
Stair, Lord, 106, 121, 122
Stamford Bridge, 20–1
standing armies, 108, 111, 114–15, 135, 172
Stanhope, George, 132
Stark, Koo, 170
Steenkirk, 114
Stephen, Count of Chartres, 36
Stephen, King, 11, 36–9
Stirling Castle, 53
Stubbs, William, 42, 48
Suetonius, Paulinus, 7, 8
Swanage, 14
Sweyn Estrithson of Norway, 29
Sweyn II of Denmark, 20

taxes, 110
  poll tax, 63
Test Act, 97
Tewkesbury, 66
Thackeray, William, 138

Thatcher, Margaret, 172
Thérouanne, 76
Thorneycroft, Peter, 8
Thrush, 151
Thunderer, 151
Tilbury speech, 81–2
Tilly, Charles, 111
Tinchebray, 35
Tintagel, 10
Tostig, earl, 19–21
Tourcoing, 137
Tournai, 76, 145
Towton, 65
transubstantiation, 62
Trenchard, Sir Charles, 154
Trevor, Robert, 130
Trinovantes, 5
trooping the colour, 1
Troyes, Treaty of, 62
Turenne, Henri de, 92–3

Ubba, 14
uniforms, 135

Val-és-Dunes, 22
Valenciennes, 137
Vanguard, 161–2
Vauban, Sébastien, 111
Verney, Henry, 87–8
Verney, Sir Ralph, 91
Victoria, Queen, 1, 125, 145–8, 151
Victory, 127
Vikings, 13
Vitalis, Ordericus, 32, 38

Wade, Field Marshal George, 130
Wales, 10, 108
Walker, Sir Edward, 88
Walkinshaw, Clementina, 133–4
Waller, Sir William, 88
Walpole, Horace, 129–30, 141
Walpole, Hugh, 120
Walpole, Sir Robert, 109, 120
Walter, Hubert, 43, 50
Wars of the Roses, 63–70
Warwick, 140
Warwick, Sir Philip, 87
Washington, George, 140
Watt, James, 160
Weldon, Sir Anthony, 83
Wentworth, Frances, 142

Wessex, 13
Wexford, 109
White Ship, 35–6
Whitelock, Bulstrode, 85
Wild Geese, 114
Wilkie, Sir David, 127
William the Atheling, 35
William le Breton, 52
William, duke of Cumberland,
   127–33
William I (the Conqueror), 21–32
  battles
    Alençon, 23
    Hastings, 18–19, 27–8, 32
    Mantes, 30
    Mortemer, 22
    Val-és-Dunes, 22
  birth, 22
  childhood, 23–4
  claim to the English throne, 24–5
  conquest of England, 28–9
  death, 30
  invasion of England, 25–7
  invasion of Scotland, 29–30

  marriage to Matilda, 23
  personality, 23–4, 30–1
William II (Rufus), 34–5
William III (William of Orange), 98–9, 109,
   112–15
William IV (formerly duke of Clarence),
   135, 139–43
William of Malmesbury, 34
William of Poitiers, 27, 28
Wilton, 14
Winchester Castle, 37
Winchester, Peace of, 37
Wing, 87
Winne, Sally, 142
Wolfe, James, 129
Wolvercote, 91
women soldiers, 9
Woodville, Elizabeth, 65, 67
Woolwich Academy, 138
Worcester, 108
Wycliffe, John, 62

Yellow Ford, 81
York *see* Frederick, duke of York